THE PARADOX
OF THE
MEXICAN STATE

THE PARADOX OF THE MEXICAN STATE

Rereading Sovereignty from Independence to NAFTA

Julie A. Erfani

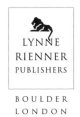

LYNNE
RIENNER
PUBLISHERS

BOULDER
LONDON

For
Anson Collins Murphy
and
Alice Christine Roat,
Gholam Reza Erfani,
Afsar Rezai

Toward transnational
cultural imagination
in the Americas

Published in the United States of America in 1995 by
Lynne Rienner Publishers, Inc.
1800 30th Street, Boulder, Colorado 80301

and in the United Kingdom by
Lynne Rienner Publishers, Inc.
3 Henrietta Street, Covent Garden, London WC2E 8LU

Library of Congress Cataloging-in-Publication Data
Erfani, Julie A.
    The paradox of the Mexican state : rereading sovereignty from
independence to NAFTA / Julie A. Erfani.
        p. cm.
    Includes bibliographical references and index.
    ISBN 1-55587-418-5 (acid-free paper)
    1. Mexico—Politics and government—19th century. 2. Mexico—
Politics and government—20th century. 3. Sovereignty. 4. Mexico—
Economic policy. I. Title.
JL1224.E74 1994
320.972—dc20   94-31535
                                                                    CIP

British Cataloguing in Publication Data
A Cataloguing in Publication record for this book
is available from the British Library.

Printed and bound in the United States of America

The paper used in this publication meets the requirements
of the American National Standard for Permanence of
Paper for Printed Library Materials Z39.48.

5 4 3 2 1

Contents

Tables and Figures

Tables

Figures

Acknowledgments

This book is the offspring of the interdisciplinary academic environment of a new university, Arizona State University West. The opportunity to build from scratch a university that would be less disciplinary, less hierarchical, and more democratic provided me with a lively intellectual environment in which to work. I attribute the completion of the book to all those colleagues who helped found and cultivate the climate of academic and cultural tolerance at ASU West.

A number of my colleagues in the Department of Social and Behavioral Sciences and in other interdisciplinary programs across campus made very specific contributions to the book. Suzanne Vaughan reminded me of the importance of the nineteenth century to understanding Mexican state sovereignty. Kristin Koptiuch, a founding co-architect of ASU West's transnational and global studies curricula, opened my eyes to broader linkages between the study of culture and political economy. Lupe Cárdenas gave me invaluable insights into Mexican national identity. Emily Cutrer, Carol Mueller, Patricia Spakes, and Kath Weston provided crucial moral support essential to the completion of a writing project of this magnitude. Lisa Kammerlocher, cybrarian par excellence, was an abiding source of electronic information and research support. Linda Stryker was a stellar example of sanity and goodwill. María Cardelle-Elawar and Linda Oviedo, my collaborators on a new global studies curriculum, exemplify to me the sort of transnational cultural imagination that I conclude in this book that NAFTA's architects lacked.

Over a number of years, many people contributed to the development of the book, though I alone am responsible for any errors. At the University of Minnesota, Raymond Duvall inspired graduate students interested in comparative politics to be equally interested in international relations. His perspectives on international political economy became the building blocks of many careers, including my own. Gary Wynia offered important insights into Mexican politics and the effects of the Mexican revolution on the Mexican political order. Jeffrey Edwards's perspectives on race, class, gender, sexuality, and the state have informed my thinking ever since we were graduate students. At Purdue University, I had the pleasure of working with colleague and political theorist Michael Weinstein and with many graduate

ix

students interested in connections between nation and state formation and international political economy. Nora Hamilton at the University of Southern California made valuable comments on earlier drafts of the book, and Lynne Rienner's insights and editorial comments were crucial. Dorothy Brandt did a marvelous job editing the book manuscript.

In Mexico, Rosario Green, then of El Colegio de México, encouraged me to interview Luis Echeverría. My various encounters with the former president helped set the tone of the book. Peter Cleaves, now of the University of Texas, encouraged me to interview Carlos Tello Macías, former secretary of programming and budget, who conversed with me at length about Mexico's economic troubles in the 1970s and 1980s and loaned me books in support of my research. I also owe a great debt to the many Mexican citizens, political activists, professors, policymakers, and business people who talked with me about Mexican political economy and culture. In preparation for my fieldwork in Mexico, Barbara and Flavel Shurtleff helped me with the ins and outs of getting around in the megalopolis known as Mexico City.

Hamid Erfani and the four people to whom this book is dedicated taught me both the utility and futility of national identities. As members of my transnational family spanning cultural and geographical boundaries from Herat to Peoria, they reread the meaning of sovereignty and national identity in their own lives.

Julie A. Erfani

1

(Dis)Integrating Mexico: Independence as an Invitation to Legal and Political Limbo

Mexico's Legal Sovereignty in Dispute, 1821–1924

Rereading Mexican State Sovereignty:
The Interplay of Legend and Law

Modern political mythology celebrates Mexican independence in the 1820s as Mexico's entrance upon the world stage as a nation-state as free as European nation-states. The transfer of legal sovereignty from the Spanish to the Mexican state supposedly liberated Mexicans from foreign domination.

Another mythology, that surrounding the Mexican revolution, claims that the revolution of 1910 permanently empowered the Mexican people by creating a "powerful" and revolutionary state. The "popular sovereignty" of the Mexican people supposedly guaranteed that the new state would and could use its presumed powers to protect the socioeconomic well-being of all Mexican citizens.

These two modern mythologies of independence and revolution helped Mexico's political elites consolidate a Mexican national identity and a national community. Contrary to revolutionary legend, however, Mexican state sovereignty still consists mainly of legalities rather than the power to achieve social justice. And despite modern legends about independence, the legal sovereignty of the Mexican state never did free Mexicans from foreign domination. On the contrary, the idea of national sovereignty was a legal concept originally invented by and for the conduct of European international relations.[1] Moreover, a European rather than an indigenous state first superimposed its legal sovereignty on the inhabitants of Mexico. Indeed, Mexico's indigenous populace was forcibly subjected to Spanish state sovereignty as a result of Spain's colonial conquest of the Americas.

1

As a European notion initially alien to Mexico's indigenous cultures, national sovereignty nevertheless became the battle cry of nineteenth-century insurgents who sought Mexico's political independence from Spain. The conservative Creole and Spanish elites who actually declared the independence of Mexico in 1821 and founded a Mexican empire in 1822 did so in order to secure colonial-era privileges for the military and the clergy, not to promote indigenous peoples' rights.[2] Agustín de Iturbide, Mexico's first independent ruler, wished to sever Mexico's colonial ties to Spain in order to preserve the colonial privileges earlier established for the military and clergy by the Spanish imperial state prior to Spain's adoption of a liberal constitution. After Mexican liberals replaced Iturbide's empire with a republic and the British government recognized Mexican independence, the new Mexican state was legally inducted into a European-centered system of international relations. In this system, the Mexican state's formal legal independence guaranteed neither Mexico's freedom from foreign domination nor its political or economic viability as a nation-state.

As a mere legal status backed up by a revolutionary myth about inflated state capabilities, Mexican state sovereignty in the twentieth century has ensured neither mass socioeconomic well-being nor freedom from foreign domination. Nevertheless, the myths and legalities associated with state sovereignty helped make the Mexican nation-state politically stable for most of the postrevolutionary era. This political stability was due, in part, to the modern state's rhetorical and symbolic links to Mexico's indigenous cultures. Since its legal creation in the 1820s, the Mexican nation-state has been mythologized to represent the crowning achievement of centuries of indigenous aspirations and struggles. Mexico's national myths associate preconquest stories of Aztec glories with modern narratives about republican presidents, such as Guadalupe Victoria, Benito Juárez, and Lázaro Cárdenas as architects of national sovereignty. In associating indigenous civilizations with the modern Mexican state, myths about state sovereignty became the cultural glue binding together the diverse inhabitants of the modern legal jurisdiction known as Mexico.

In fact, modern Mexican national identity rests on cultural notions that Mexico's legal independence and its constitutionalist, revolutionary state represent the triumph of Mexico's indigenous civilizations over foreign intruders. Three legal milestones gave rise to the legends that form the cultural foundations of a shared Mexican political identity. First, the legal creation in the 1820s of a new state juridically independent from Spain symbolizes the advent of indigenous freedom from foreign domination. Second, the legal formulation of the constitution of 1917 symbolizes a successful completion of an indigenous quest for national self-determination. Finally, the legal expropriation of foreign-owned oil companies in 1938 represents the ability of Mexican governments to enforce the revolutionary constitution without fear of losing the state's international legal recognition. In these three cultural milestones, legends intermingled with law to consolidate a Mexican nation-state and a shared national political identity.

One task of this book is to explore how legends about Mexican independence and about revolution added important mythological dimensions to the basic legal framework of Mexican state sovereignty. In conjunction with these myths, tangible elements of Mexico's sovereign statehood figure prominently in the discussion. In particular, twentieth-century Mexico's stable political regime and the country's territorial integrity are important attributes associated with legal sovereignty. However, this study finds these concrete components of Mexican statehood to be much less empowering of the Mexican nation or state than modern political legends claim.

Legends about state sovereignty pretend that Mexico's twentieth-century territorial integrity and stable national government are the attributes of a powerful state capable of ensuring "freedom," "national self-determination," and societywide well-being. In contrast, this study finds Mexico's twentieth-century territorial integrity and governmental stability to be the attributes of a state endowed with extensive legal authority but minimal power.[3] The state has had remarkable legal-political authority but negligible ability to fulfill the constitutional goals and promises of 1917—to be the provider of mass societal well-being.[4] Nevertheless, during much of the twentieth century the Mexican state has symbolized sovereign power to protect and benefit all of society. This book traces the story of how legends about Mexico's legal independence and its constitutionalist revolution succeeded and later failed to make a weak Mexican state the symbol of great domestic strength.

The interplay of legend and law led to the notion that Mexican independence gave birth to a state with a sovereign legal status equivalent to that of existing states in Europe and the United States, but historical evidence strongly suggests otherwise. International recognition of Mexico's independent statehood initially failed to endow the Mexican state with the same legal stature as Britain, France, or the United States. Instead, the United States and Britain initially invited Mexico to join the Eurocentric "Family of Nations" as a culturally inferior, racially mixed "nation" often regarded as an illegitimate offspring of Spaniards and Native American Indians. As a new state invited to subsist on the margins of European international relations, nineteenth-century Mexico acquired a tenuous legal sovereignty that became the object of frequent violations and even revocation.

In fact, the British, French, and Spanish governments all at one time or another considered Mexico's constitutional independence to be expendable, at least for a time. European and U.S. governments often violated rather than consistently respected Mexico's international legal entitlement as a sovereign state nominally equal in international law to European states. Indeed, U.S. and European governments repeatedly denied the Mexican state either governmental recognition, freedom from foreign intervention, or exclusive jurisdiction over Mexican territory. Saddled with an inferior cultural status in international relations, a weak military, and deep political divisions at home, nineteenth-century Mexico suffered invasion, occupation, vast territorial losses, and recurrent loss of international governmental recognition.

As a predominantly Native American Indian and mestizo "nation" mingling European-Caucasian and Native American Indian races, Mexico entered the world of nineteenth-century international relations as a nation and a people supposedly lacking some of the "civilized" cultural credentials more commonly ascribed to Europeans. Historically, European and U.S. governments often deemed the Mexican state less worthy of international legal rights and territory than the existing states of Western Europe. In addition, Mexico suffered from the fact that it often lacked the military might to defend its formal legal rights as a sovereign state. Throughout the nineteenth century, European and U.S. military forces periodically invaded and occupied Mexican territory.

However, even if the Mexican state had possessed military capabilities equal or superior to existing nineteenth-century states, that would not have altered the fact in international relations that Mexicans were considered racially and culturally inferior to peoples of strictly European heritage. With few exceptions, racial difference from Europeans virtually guaranteed an inferior cultural status in the Eurocentric world of nineteenth-century international relations.[5] This helps explain the immediate presumption of U.S. officials that newly independent Mexico did not deserve legal jurisdiction over the entire territory that had been New Spain.

In fact, as soon as Mexican independence was declared from Spain in 1821, U.S. government officials' first inclination was to recognize Mexico, with the goal of obtaining a new treaty of territorial limits.[6] The U.S. drive to acquire territory from Mexico seemed even to exceed U.S. interests in obtaining a favorable commercial treaty. Indeed, because U.S. officials persisted in demanding an unacceptable treaty of limits, Mexican officials did not approve a treaty of commerce until the 1830s.

Roughly the same cultural biases that motivated U.S. officials to assume that Native American Indians in the United States did not deserve legal title to very much territory also led them to analogous conclusions about the territorial scope of Mexico's legal sovereignty. In short, in spite of rapid U.S. recognition of the Mexican state in 1822, U.S. government officials refused to respect Mexican jurisdiction over all the territory formerly claimed by Spain as the European colonial master of Mexico. Consequently, the first thirty years of statehood witnessed Mexico's dismal struggle just to preserve the territory claimed from Spain when Mexicans declared independence. The fact is that Mexico had claimed Texas territory as part of its sovereign legal jurisdiction ever since independence. When the U.S. government decided to support the independence of Texas from the authoritarian government of Antonio López de Santa Anna in 1836, U.S. officials clearly contradicted earlier U.S. policy stances toward the new Mexican republic.

In the 1820s, U.S. officials proclaimed the U.S. government a believer in the ultimate viability of republican democracy in Mexico as well as in the Mexican state's legal sovereignty.[7] However, when President Santa Anna shifted to authoritarian and conservative policies, U.S. officials decided that Mexico was permanently unqualified to govern Texas. Then, as soon as settlers in Texas rejected Mexico's legal sovereignty over Texas, U.S. government officials quickly rejected it as well. Not only did U.S. officials support the permanent secession of Texas from Mexico by supporting Texas's independence as a state, but they eventually annexed Texas, thus placing it under the permanent sovereign authority of the United States.

U.S. officials' decisions to support Mexico's permanent loss of sovereignty over Texas signaled that U.S. officials judged Mexicans to be permanently unworthy of governing Texas—and culturally unfit, not just temporarily politically unqualified, to retain sovereign authority over the people and territory there. Indeed, by the conclusion of the U.S. war with Mexico in 1848, Mexico's loss of Texas represented more than a series of military defeats. It symbolized Mexico's inferior cultural-legal status in international relations.

Mexicans' nineteenth-century political identity as belonging to a militarily weak nation-state overshadowed by European culture and overrun by European and U.S. armies and investors was partly transformed in the twentieth century. A new legend grew up about the Mexican revolution's empowerment of the indigenous peoples of Mexico and of the Mexican state. Legend has it that the ouster of Porfirio Díaz and the revolution reinvented a state with the domestic power to defend Mexicans and Mexican "national interests" vis-à-vis the outside world. Although ensuing socioeconomic problems in the twentieth century demonstrated that the Mexican state lacked such powers, the revolution did culturally transform Mexican national identity. Postrevolutionary Mexican political identity embodied a new cultural confidence in *mestizaje* as the basis of a "cosmic race" and a great nation.[8] Mexicans' invigorated national identity of the 1920s and 1930s was reinforced internationally by the advent of new international norms proclaiming the virtue of small states and insisting upon respect for the juridical equality of all states, including those that were militarily weak.[9]

Indeed, by the 1920s, foreign violations and challenges of the Mexican state's legal jurisdiction had subsided as new international norms codifying the territorial integrity and political independence of militarily weak states emerged.[10] Less than one year after the new Mexican constitution was completed in February 1917, U.S. President Woodrow Wilson delivered his

Fourteen Points speech outlining a peace settlement after World War I. The fourteenth point led to the creation of the League of Nations, whose goal was to provide existing states with mutual guarantees of political independence and territorial integrity. The Paris Peace Conference, from 1919 to 1920, which led to the creation of the League of Nations, introduced "national self-determination" as an ideological principle justifying the sovereignty of states in Europe as well as of states, such as Mexico, that were spin-offs of European states in the Americas.[11]

The Wilsonian principle of national self-determination reinforced Mexico's international legal claims to territorial integrity and political independence regardless of the state's level of military capability and of Mexicans' particular racial makeup.[12] This is not to say that the League Covenant posited the racial equality of all peoples and nations: The Japanese proposed that statements about racial and national equality appear in the League's Covenant, but Great Britain and the United States rejected the proposals.[13] Moreover, the Wilsonian principle of "national self-determination" was not to be universally applied to all people: it was denied to all of the non-European peoples subjected to the League's Mandate tutelage in Africa, the Middle East, and Asia.[14] However, the international legal right to national political self determination and thus to greater *respect* for territorial integrity, did apply to Latin American countries that were already self-governing. For Latin America, however, the League Covenant contained a major caveat: Article 21 stated that the Covenant would not annul the Monroe Doctrine, thus leaving the League's Latin American member states legally vulnerable to U.S. military intervention.[15] In this respect, the Covenant contained a fundamental contradiction for Latin American member states: It conferred upon them the same legal rights and obligations of collective military security pertaining to European member states even while it failed to outlaw U.S. military intervention in Latin America. Although the League ultimately failed entirely as a mechanism for collective security, the League Covenant did formally codify the international *legal* rights of Latin American member states to territorial integrity in what was still a world militarily dominated by European states. Although the arbitrary use of military force by the United States in Latin America never ceased, U.S. and European use of military force and invasion to collect debt and to acquire Latin American territory did eventually wane in the twentieth century.

With the 1920s advent of new international norms condoning the sovereign legal rights of existing states to territorial integrity and nonintervention, Mexico began to move out of legal limbo as a tenuous territorial jurisdiction constantly subject to foreign military intervention. Although Mexico was not among the original eleven Latin American signatories to the League Covenant in 1920, it did become the League's most active Latin American member supporting the Covenant after being formally admitted in September 1931.[16] During the peak of the League's international influence, from approximately 1924 to 1929,[17] Mexico's postrevolutionary political regime was undergoing political consolidation. Aided by the League's new international norms, the early postrevolutionary Mexican state benefited legally from the League's emphasis on international respect for the legal sovereignty of existing states. Thus, during the Mexican state's most crucial years of domestic reconstruction, the League provided a new normative umbrella that reinforced Mexico's international rights to political independence and territorial integrity. This helped move Mexico out of its previous nineteenth-century legal limbo in international relations.

Domestic attacks on the Mexican state's legal right to govern also subsided within Mexico during the early postrevolutionary era. Domestic disputes of the state's legal authority had previously taken two major forms. First, nineteenth-century Mexican politics were characterized by an extreme polarization between conservatives and liberals, each group fundamentally disputing the state's authority whenever the other group was in power. Second, prerevolutionary Mexico was politically fragmented by regionalism, acutely so during the revolution, when regional and local armies led by competing *caudillos* fought for military hegemony over Mexico.

Both of these two types of domestic disputes of state authority dissipated after the revolution. The signing of the Mexican constitution of 1917, the formation of the League of Nations in 1920, Mexico's admission to the League in 1931, the U.S. adoption of the Good Neighbor policy of Franklin Roosevelt in 1933, and the Cárdenas government's enforcement of the new constitution to expropriate foreign-owned oil companies in 1938 all helped reinforce the Mexican state's legal sovereignty as the revolution came to an end. These events marked the advent of an international and domestic consensus in support of the sovereign rule of Mexican law within Mexican territory.

President Cárdenas's application of the Mexican state's legal right as a sovereign state to regulate private property, including foreign-owned property, within Mexican territory and to retain ownership of subsoil resources as specified by the 1917 constitution rallied unparalleled mass political support for the Mexican presidency. Furthermore, Cárdenas's successful demilitarization of Mexican society virtually eliminated the regional rebellions characteristic of the revolutionary decades after 1910.[18]

After 1940, the next thirty years of Mexican history consisted of an extended period of national political stability noted for the postrevolutionary regime's popularly recognized constitutionality and the state's internationally respected legal status. In short, by 1940 the international and domestic legal foundations of Mexican state sovereignty had never been more firm. The international legal bases of state sovereignty were further reinforced in 1945 with the formation of the United Nations, which extend-

ed the earlier Wilsonian principle of national self-determination to countries around the globe.[19]

Contrary to legend, however, the postrevolutionary consolidation of
the Mexican state's legal sovereignty provided no guarantee that the state
would be able to control the domestic economy for the benefit of mass
society. Enhanced respect for the Mexican state's legal jurisdiction over
territory, people, and property was not synonymous with state power to
accomplish the socioeconomic goals of the constitution of 1917.
Nevertheless, proponents as well as critics of Mexico's postrevolutionary
regime have often implicitly assumed that legal sovereignty somehow
empowered the postrevolutionary state to accomplish the mass societal
goals of the revolution. Political elites of the Institutional Revolutionary
Party (PRI) consistently made this claim for more than fifty years. Critics
of the PRI regime have often made similar assumptions when implying that
Mexico's most fundamental problems have stemmed from the corruption,
incompetence, or misguided policies of PRI governmental officials who
have mismanaged the alleged powers of the state.

The common thread and mystique implicit in both types of arguments
is the notion that revolution somehow created a state with the latent power
to protect the well-being of all citizens. According to this revolutionary
mystique, the exercise of state power after the revolution depended on the
quality of domestic government, especially the political will, commitment,
and knowledge of political leaders to wield state power effectively. Of
course, proponents of the PRI regime consider the ruling elite to have
always possessed these leadership qualities, whereas critics to the left and
the right of the PRI have insisted that a better set of political leaders could
employ state power properly if only given the chance to govern.[20] This
study indicates that the postrevolutionary state's failure to achieve the
goals of the constitution of 1917 is due to more than just leadership problems. Instead of assuming that the postrevolutionary state's legal sovereignty served as the foundation for a strong state, this study shows that
legal sovereignty ultimately proved to be a recipe for socioeconomic disaster in later twentieth-century Mexico.[21]

In spite of these socioeconomic failures, a cultural tradition about the
evolutionary development of a powerful state prevailed for approximately
fifty years after the revolution. Independence was considered the beginning
of Mexico's progression from political infancy as a new republic to the
maturity of a powerful state with the capacity to achieve the mass socioeconomic goals of the revolution. The origins of this misleading theory of evolution are best understood historically by recognizing the sharp contrast
between the dubious legal status of the state during the nineteenth century
and the preeminent legal stature of the postrevolutionary state.

First, the nineteenth-century state faced severe challenges to its legal
status for many decades, whereas the postrevolutionary state's legal sover-

eignty was soon accepted by foreign governments as well as by most Mexicans. Second, the cultural leitmotif of Mexico's first hundred years of independence was the legal and military vulnerability of a politically chaotic state constantly at the mercy of foreign governments, armies, and investors. In contrast, the ideological hallmark of the Mexican revolution and its aftermath celebrated the indigenous powers of the Mexican people to transform government and confront foreign intruders. Clearly, the revolution's new symbolism of people power as the basis of a strong state represented a major cultural departure from past themes of a legally embattled, invaded, and weak state during the previous century. Having gone from international and domestic legal limbo in the nineteenth century to constitutional supremacy at home and respected legal sovereignty abroad, the Mexican state of the postrevolutionary era did indeed appear to be empowered.

In contrast to that developmentalist thesis, this study adopts a nonevolutionary perspective on the changes in the Mexican state over the course of the nineteenth and twentieth centuries. Instead of evolving into a progressively more powerful state after independence, the Mexican state eventually collapsed under the weight of civil war and later a prolonged revolution. Moreover, the Mexican revolution was not the state's critical rite of passage to full maturity and potency. Instead, the advent of international legal norms reinforcing international respect for the territorial integrity and political independence of militarily weak states helped consolidate Mexico's international legal status. The advent of these new international norms coincided historically with the end of the Mexican revolution and the conclusion of Mexico's domestic constitutional battles after 1917. Thus, the League's extension of greater legal respectability in international relations to Mexico overlapped with and reinforced the domestic consolidation of the legitimacy of the new postrevolutionary state in the 1920s and 1930s.

Consequently, by the late 1930s the Mexican state *appeared* empowered because it no longer suffered from the legal and military vulnerabilities of the past. Unlike in the nineteenth century, fundamental constitutional crisis no longer prevailed within Mexico, and Mexican territory was no longer the object of land-grabbing annexations by the United States or of foreign invasions and occupations. Instead, the Mexican state's formal authority was respected abroad as well as at home throughout the various regions of Mexico. Finally, the constitutional legitimacy of the postrevolutionary regime was recognized by foreign governments and by most Mexican people. In fact, by 1938 the Cárdenas government's expropriation of foreign-owned oil companies rallied mass domestic support for the government's adherence to 1917 constitutional provisions regarding indigenous property rights to Mexico's subsoil resources. Although Mexico was still militarily weak in international relations, it did not suffer European or

U.S. invasion in retribution for the oil expropriation. British officials withdrew governmental recognition from Mexico for a few years, but the Roosevelt administration's decision to maintain U.S. diplomatic relations with Mexico inaugurated a new era of respect for the territorial integrity and constitutional legitimacy of the Mexican state.[22]

The state's newfound legal respectability at home and abroad made a new political culture of domestic state strength feasible within Mexico. Rather than a radical increase in the powers of the state after the revolution, this study sees a dramatic shift in the political culture of the Mexican state. Although not much more capable of controlling the economy than the nineteenth-century state, the postrevolutionary state was better equipped both legally and politically to invent a mythology about the state's powers over the domestic economy—for at least two basic reasons.

First, Mexico's lack of military might and Mexicans' lack of racial equivalence to Europeans were no longer obstacles to the state's legal respectability in international relations. Thus, although the Mexican state was not much more militarily capable than before, international respect for Mexico's territorial integrity and constitutional independence meant that foreign military invasion and territorial loss were much less likely than during the nineteenth century. Moreover, although most Mexicans could not claim strictly European descent, new international norms emphasized political "self-determination," "political independence," and territorial integrity for the world's existing states.

Second, at the same time that new norms about state sovereignty emerged internationally in the 1920s, the Mexican revolution ended domestically with the establishment of a new constitution and a new "revolutionary" state symbolizing the people power of mestizo Mexico.

The simultaneous demise of Mexico's international legal vulnerability and the formation of a constitutional, revolutionary regime paved the way for a new political mythology about the domestic powers of the state over the economy. This chapter examines Mexico's earlier legal and political troubles in the nineteenth century, when Mexican state sovereignty was little more than a disputed, violated, and even expendable legal status. The analysis indicates that nineteenth-century legends about independence as freedom from foreign domination ultimately proved insufficient to convince average Mexicans that the state was indeed sovereign. In fact, the state collapsed in the early twentieth century as many Mexicans assailed the weakness of the nineteenth-century state and demanded a state with the sovereign power to defy foreign governments and investors and to transform society. Thus, the historical analysis that follows provides the crucial, nineteenth-century background for understanding why the Mexican state *appeared* powerful at home once its legal battles subsided after the Mexican Revolution.

Independence as Legal and Political Limbo:
Nineteenth- and Early Twentieth-Century
State Sovereignty in Dispute

Mexico's nineteenth-century political leaders faced constant challenges to the state's new sovereign, legal status from foreigners and Mexicans alike. Unfortunately, Mexican leaders were in charge of a country caught in legal and political limbo. Internationally, Mexico had nominally emerged from the legal status of colony but hardly enjoyed the international legal respect or political consensus characterizing established members of the Eurocentric "Family of Nations."[23] Domestically, Mexico's two principal political groups fundamentally disagreed about the constitutional foundations of the new republic. In other words, in both domestic and international politics and law, nineteenth-century Mexico was trapped somewhere in between colonialism and Western European–style nation-statehood. In spite of its nominal independence, leaders at the helm of the Mexican state could not count on the legal respect, the political and legal consensus, or the political stability assumed to be the attributes of independent statehood. In fact, foreign governments and domestic opposition groups alike challenged the Mexican state's scope of authority over territory, people, and property; Mexican leaders' fundamental right to hold office; and the constitutionality of Mexican governments. At stake in these nineteenth-century disputes was not just the character of particular leaders or governments, but rather the validity of the Mexican state's legal authority within Mexican borders and vis-à-vis other states. In short, at stake were fundamental components of the legal sovereignty of the Mexican state.

Many of the political disputes of the nineteenth century stemmed from an overall lack of international or domestic political consensus concerning the new state's legal existence and scope of authority. In fact, on the domestic front, one major political battle of the nineteenth century stemmed from an irreconcilable disagreement over the purposes of Mexico's constitutional independence from Spain. On one side of the argument, Mexican liberals saw independence as an opportunity to establish indigenous, representative government in what had been a colony long governed by an absolutist monarchy.[24] On the opposite side, conservatives viewed independence as a mechanism for evading Spain's liberal constitution and thus protecting the privileged legal-political position of the church, the military, and conservatives in Mexico.[25] Consequently, conservatives implicitly considered independence secondary in importance or even expendable to the higher goal of protecting the privileges of those associated with the old monarchical-colonial order, especially the privileges of clergy and military officers. In fact, when the liberal army of Benito Juárez won Mexico's liberal-conservative civil war in the mid-nineteenth century, many Mexican conservatives threw their political support behind a foreign occupying army.[26] By renouncing the Mexican state's legal sovereignty in favor of French occupying forces and the installation of a foreign emperor in Mexico City, conservatives were able to undermine Mexican liberals' victory in the civil war.

Similarly, in the European-centered world of "great power" politics of nineteenth-century international relations, Mexico's legal sovereignty was subject to great dispute, frequent violation, and even revocation. When the Mexican state's internationally recognized legal sovereignty stood in the way of commercial, territorial-expansionist, or political interests of the British, U.S., French, or Spanish governments, all four governments intermittently withdrew recognition or simply invaded and/or occupied Mexican territory. Consequently, Mexican governments suffered from constant political instability, generated in part by repeated foreign violations of territorial integrity. These territorial violations were often triggered by or linked to relentless domestic infighting between liberals and conservatives holding polar opposite views as to the purpose of Mexico's constitutional independence from other states. As a result of the overall lack of consensus within Mexico and abroad about the Mexican state's legal validity, nineteenth-century leaders suffered from premature turnover in office, constant revolts, foreign invasions, and occupations.

The tenuous governmental authority of the emperors, presidents, and military *caudillos* who attempted to rule early Mexico was constantly undermined by foreign governments and domestic political factions alike. Both groups often violated or renounced the state's territorial integrity, constitutional independence, and sovereign right to exclusive jurisdiction over Mexican territory. When the legal sovereignty of the Mexican state stood in the way of higher goals, foreign governments and Mexican political elites alike were frequently willing to dispense with key elements of the state's legal sovereignty in pursuit of other objectives.

In the case of foreign governments, for instance, the diplomatic correspondence of the initial decade of Mexican independence in the 1820s suggests that the U.S. and British governments recognized Mexican independence with the confidence that a new, independent Mexican state would be militarily weak and therefore more vulnerable to their influence than a Spanish colony—a legal-military status that obstructed their commercial and political influence.[27] Both countries' officials favored the recognition of Mexico based on the assumption that Mexico's legal sovereignty could be easily violated when necessary. They reasoned that a new Mexican state would clearly lack the military capacity to defend legal sovereignty should they decide to violate it.

In the U.S. case, the correspondence and pronouncements of James Monroe and John Q. Adams, Henry Clay, and U.S. diplomat Joel Poinsett clearly indicate that the U.S. government saw in the rapid recognition of an independent Mexico the chance to achieve three major U.S. objectives.[28] First, U.S. government officials made no secret of the fact that they hoped to draw up a new treaty of limits and claim more territory for the United States. Second, U.S. officials hoped to gain commercial access to Mexico once Spain no longer claimed exclusive economic rights to its colony. Finally, the U.S. government had political ambitions to displace European political influence in the Americas by encouraging Spanish American independence and the formation of new, republican governments rather than conservative-monarchical regimes. Republican governments, after all, were considered more likely to look to the United States than to European states for political support and leadership in the region.[29]

Shortly after the United States recognized Mexican independence, James Monroe delivered his 1823 address to the U.S. Congress and first articulated what later became known as the Monroe Doctrine. The doctrine was dedicated to expanding U.S. political influence over the Americas and to safeguarding U.S. commercial access to the newly independent countries in the region.[30] The doctrine declared that the new countries of Spanish America would never again become the colonial domain of the states of Europe. In articulating this basic tenet, the U.S. government also rhetorically defended the political independence and legal sovereignty of the new American republics vis-à-vis hostile states on the European continent.[31] In spite of the rhetorical flourish, however, U.S. territorial and commercial interests in Spanish America soon overwhelmed U.S. respect for the legal sovereignty of the new states. U.S. officials were quick to dispute the Mexican state's legal jurisdiction over Mexican territory and to question the Mexican state's commitment to protecting foreign-owned property within Mexican territory. In fact, during the first four decades of Mexico's independence, Mexico lost half of all its territory to the United States and was charged with massive foreign debts due to an inability to protect the lives and private property of foreigners in Mexico.

In effect, U.S. and European property owners and investors in Mexico expected the Mexican state to protect foreign property more effectively than the property of Mexico's own citizenry.[32] The truth was that the new Mexican state could protect neither, but foreigners pushed their respective states to press their financial claims against the Mexican state.[33] Given these and a multitude of other difficulties with state authority, Mexico suffered from intense political instability often bordering on chaos. During the twenty-two years from May 1833 to August 1855, for example, there were thirty-six different presidential successions, with the average term lasting only seven and one-half months.[34]

Great Britain, like the United States, contributed in no small way to Mexico's international legal travails and to the political instability of Mexico's highest public office. Although the British government lacked the expansionist territorial designs of U.S. officials, British commercial interests in Mexico often outweighed British respect for the Mexican state's legal sovereignty. From the very inception of Mexican independence, British government officials made it clear that they preferred a conservative, centralist-monarchical government in Mexico to a republican government.[35] This was true for several reasons. First, during the 1820s, British Foreign Secretary George Canning was convinced that the U.S. government intended to restrict British commercial access to newly independent Mexico.[36] Canning feared that the intent of the Monroe Doctrine was not just to bar European colonization of the Americas but also to divide and separate the Old World and the New World in order to obstruct European commercial access to the newly independent American republics. Thus, he viewed U.S. recognition and support for liberal governments in Spanish America as an attempt to establish governments that would enter into exclusive commercial treaties with the United States.[37]

In a race to circumvent U.S. political and commercial influence over Emperor Iturbide's conservative government, Canning quickly dispatched a confidential British diplomatic agent to Mexico in December 1822, just nine days after the United States recognized Mexican independence and almost two years before any U.S. diplomat arrived.[38] Even though the British did not recognize Mexico until later in 1824, British agent Patrick Mackie managed to establish Britain as the dominant foreign governmental influence in Mexico in the early 1820s. Canning's explicit intent was to counteract the influence of the United States[39] and, if possible, to promote the establishment of a conservative-monarchical government in Mexico.[40]

First, the British government assumed that a monarchical government would look favorably on political and commercial ties with other monarchical governments in Europe, especially Britain. Second, a centralist, conservative government would reputedly be better able to protect British private property and maintain domestic order, thus facilitating British foreign investment.[41] Finally, a British-leaning monarchical government in Mexico would help establish an American state friendly to Britain in a vital Spanish American country sharing a border with the United States. Such a government could help check the U.S. drive for political influence and territorial expansion in Spanish America.[42] Conservative Mexican governments could also promote the expansion of British commercial influence throughout the region.

Contrary to British preference, however, a federal republic was founded in Mexico in October 1824 with the presidency of Guadalupe Victoria. The British government was quick to respond and in December 1824 recognized Mexican independence. British recognition of Mexico was thus more akin to an act of intense political and commercial competition with the United States than a bona fide affirmation of the British government's respect for Mexico's legal equality to European states. Ensuing events soon demonstrated that neither Britain nor the United States considered the recognition of Mexico as an invitation to join the Family of Nations as a state meriting the same legal respect as the states of Europe or the United States. A quote from George Canning captures the condescending and opportunistic spirit of the British invitation to independent statehood on the eve of England's recognition of Mexico in 1824:

> I believe we now have the opportunity (but it may not last long) of oppos-ing [erecting] a powerful barrier to the influence of the US by an amicable connection with Mexico, from which its position must be either sub-servient to or jealous of the US. In point of population and resources it is at least equal to all the rest of the Spanish colonies; and may naturally expect to take the lead in its connections with the powers of Europe. I by no means think it at present necessary to go beyond the relations of amity and commercial intercourse; but if we hesitate much longer, and especial-ly if our commercial treaty [July 23, 1824] with Buenos Ayres should not take effect, all the new states will be led to conclude that we regret their friendship upon principle, as of a dangerous and revolutionary character, and will be driven to throw themselves under the protection of the US, as the only means of security.[43]

For both the British and U.S. governments, the recognition of Mexico's legal sovereignty represented a new opportunity to dominate Mexico com-mercially and, in the U.S. case, militarily for the purpose of territorial expansion. Consequently, British and U.S. government respect for Mexico's legal sovereignty waxed and waned depending on whether respect for the Mexican state's legal authority served U.S. and British gov-ernmental and commercial interests.

Initially, from 1822 to 1824, the legal recognition of Mexico served both governments' interests in seeing Spain's political and commercial monopoly over Mexico formally come to an end. After initial recognition of Mexican statehood, however, British and U.S. disputes and violations of legal sovereignty proliferated. British-U.S. competition for commercial and political influence in Mexico mounted in the 1820s as U.S. and British diplomatic representatives vied for influence over the newly independent state. In the course of this competition, British and U.S. diplomats helped construct and exacerbate Mexico's key domestic political cleavage between liberals and conservatives.[44]

The U.S. representative, Joel Poinsett, allied himself with Mexican lib-erals associated with the York Rite Masons (*Yorkino*) lodges, known as the champions of republican, federal, and representative government in Mexico.[45] On the other extreme, British representatives Ward and later Packenham aided and supported the opposing conservative group of promonarchist champions of centralist government associated with the Scottish Rite Free Masons.[46] From 1825 until 1829, British and U.S. diplo-mats fought tooth and nail for political influence via these contending groups. One key objective of both foreign governments was to obtain the

most favorable commercial and navigational treaties possible with
Mexico's first two republican governments—those of Guadalupe Victoria
and Vicente Guerrero. In spite of the fact that both governments were
republican, the British obtained their treaty of commerce first in 1827. Due
to U.S. territorial ambitions and insistence that Mexico sign a new treaty of
boundary limits, the United States had to wait until 1832 for its commercial
treaty to be approved.[47]

One consequence, however, of the intense British-U.S. and liberal-conservative competition that fomented during Mexico's first decade of independence was that Mexico's first two republican presidents were both
plagued by conservative rebellions. Presidents Victoria and Guerrero both
faced revolts launched by their own conservative vice-presidents. Guerrero
was successfully overthrown and even executed by his former conservative
vice-president. Ultimately, British-U.S. commercial and political competition in Mexico contributed to the subsequent governance problems of succeeding Mexican presidents, who had to struggle to maintain the state's
legal authority over territory, people, and property throughout much of the
nineteenth century.

In aggravating political hostility between Mexican liberals and conservatives, British and U.S. diplomats played on a fundamental difference in
the two groups' interpretations of the meaning and purpose of Mexico's
constitutional independence from Spain. Beginning with Iturbide's conservative declaration of Mexican independence and the Plan de Iguala in 1821,
Mexican conservatives defined independence as a means of rescuing the
church, the military, and political centralism from the Spanish liberal constitution of 1812. In this respect, Iturbide's Plan de Iguala contained three
principal guarantees regarding Mexican independence: (1) the formation of
a constitutional monarchy for newly independent Mexico with the crown
offered to King Ferdinand or other appropriate European royalty; (2) the
recognition of Roman Catholicism as the monopoly religion with Mexico's
clergy retaining previous colonial privileges; and (3) the assurance of equal
treatment for *criollos* and peninsular-born peoples by the newly independent state.[48] On the opposite liberal side, independence represented a
chance to fulfill liberal aspirations for indigenous popular sovereignty and
universal male suffrage as embodied in the 1813 liberal Declaration of
Mexican Independence and the liberal constitution of Apatzingan.[49]

Thus, as a legal status, Mexico's sovereignty was the focal point of
incessant disputes between Mexican liberals and conservatives and their
respective foreign allies: the U.S. and British governments. The Mexican
combatants seemingly overlooked the fact that British and U.S. support for
opposing sides of the argument over the goals of Mexican independence
was motivated, in large measure, by a British-U.S. race to dominate
Mexico commercially. In this respect, Mexican conservatives and even lib-

erals were often more concerned with outmaneuvering each other politically than with safeguarding constitutional independence itself, the very object
of their political passions. For most of the nineteenth century, infighting
between liberals and conservatives proceeded full force with both groups
often oblivious to the fact that legal sovereignty was being violated and
even revoked through foreign invasion and occupation and vast losses of
Mexican territory. Although U.S.-British competition over Mexico eventually subsided by the late 1850s,[50] the liberal-conservative political cleavage
encouraged by the British and U.S. governments haunted Mexican politics
into the twentieth century.

The 1820s disputes between liberals and conservatives concerning
the goals of Mexico's constitutional independence grew in number and
intensity over ensuing decades, from the 1830s to the 1860s. As new
disputes emerged about the scope of the Mexican state's legal authority
over territory, people, and property, Mexico grew increasingly chaotic
politically. Over the first fifty-five years of independence, the presidency
changed hands seventy-five times.[51] Of the thirty-three different occu-
pants of Mexico's presidency in the first fifty-five years of republican
independence, López de Santa Anna and Benito Juárez were in office for
the longest time periods, a total of five and fourteen years, respectively.[52]

López de Santa Anna recorded the most terms in office of any Mexican
president, having assumed the office eleven different times. As Mexico's
two most influential leaders of mid-century, both men originally espoused
liberal political principles, although López de Santa Anna had quickly
abandoned liberalism in favor of conservative, centralist, and prochurch
stances by 1833. In fact, Santa Anna's rapid shift to conservatism helped
trigger the greatest defeat of his military and political career—the territorial
loss of Texas. Benito Juárez, on the other hand, fought a liberal-conservative civil war, which was quickly followed by a French invasion of Mexico
and the loss of the state's legal independence to a foreign emperor. In short,
for both Juárez and Santa Anna, early Mexico's ever present liberal-conservative struggle helped unleash devastating conflicts over the territorial and
political scope of the Mexican state's sovereign jurisdiction.

As general or president, López de Santa Anna intervened militarily in
repeated coups, revolts, foreign invasions, and occupations, all of which
were linked in some fashion to the conservative-liberal split in Mexico's
postindependence politics. In fact, López de Santa Anna's worst challenges
as president derived from Texan and U.S. government defiance of the
Mexican state's sovereign jurisdiction over the territory encompassing
Texas. Texans' decision to secede from Mexico was precipitated by Santa
Anna's swing to the right. His overthrow of the liberal government of
Valentín Gómez Fárias in 1833 and his subsequent annulment of the feder-

alist, liberal constitution of 1824 were proclaimed the last straw by the
Texans who could then declare independence because of a need to escape
the authoritarian government of Santa Anna.

For the United States, Santa Anna's assault on liberal government in
Mexico provided an excuse for the U.S. government to support Texans'
permanent secession from Mexico. Continued liberal-conservative infighting in Mexico and the ensuing instability of the Mexican presidency contributed to the Mexican government's failure to recover its territory during
the years of Texas independence from 1836 until 1845 and during the U.S.
war with Mexico from 1846 to 1848. In fact, a number of prominent
Mexican liberals, such as Lorenzo de Zavala, supported the independence
of the Lone Star Republic.[53] Later on, some Mexican liberals also supported Zachary Taylor's forces in the U.S. invasion of northern Mexico during
the U.S. war with Mexico. The intense political opposition of these liberals
to the centralist-conservative government of Santa Anna and his caretaker
presidents[54] mattered to them more than the massive territorial losses and
overall violations of legal sovereignty implied for Mexico.

Mexico's internal political divisions continued unabated throughout
the period of Texas independence and U.S. territorial expansion in the
1840s. Even when the United States annexed Texas in February 1845 and
Mexico prepared for war with an expansionist U.S. government, liberal-
conservative infighting continued to cripple the Mexican government. In
December 1845, the caretaker government of José Joaquín Herrera agreed
to receive U.S. envoy John Slidell, who proposed that Mexico formally
cede its legal sovereignty over Texas territory, which encompassed half of
New Mexico and Colorado, as payment to satisfy the monetary claims of
U.S. citizens who had suffered property damages in Mexico.[55] U.S. officials argued that since the Mexican government could not afford to satisfy
the claims with payments in currency, Mexico should pay its debts by forfeiting state sovereignty over territory.[56] If the Mexican government would
formally agree to forfeit the territory, the U.S. government promised to
assume responsibility for Mexico's debt to the United States. Mexico's
political factions did not pull together even after the Slidell mission to
Mexico made it clear that the United States wished to obtain California and
the rest of New Mexico as well as Mexico's formal recognition of U.S.
sovereignty over Texas.[57]

Instead of rallying together with the liberal Mexican government to
confront U.S. expansionism, Mexican conservatives rebelled. Less than one
month after the Slidell proposal, in January 1846, General Mariano Paredes
y Arrillaga overthrew Mexican President Herrera, who had just refused
Slidell's proposal for Mexico to cede thousands of square miles of Mexican
territory, claimed by the former Lone Star Republic, to the United States.[58]
Obviously, Mexico's precarious military position vis-à-vis the United
States did not, however, dissuade conservative General Paredes from top-
pling the besieged Herrera government.

With Mexico immersed in political upheaval and unwilling to relinquish the vast territories that Slidell had instructions to secure,[59] U.S. officials declared war on Mexico in May 1846. Approximately one year later,
liberal rebellions against Paredes occurred throughout Mexico, and his conservative government collapsed in August 1846. This new round of political instability and governmental collapse doomed the Mexican war effort to
preserve the country's territorial integrity. After Mexico lost the war with
the United States in 1848, the Treaty of Guadalupe Hidalgo and later the
Gadsden Purchase were both testimony to U.S. contentions that Mexico's
legal sovereignty over territory could simply be bought, whether Mexicans
wished to sell or not.

From a U.S. perspective, Mexico's territorial integrity was expendable
when it ran contrary to U.S. interests in territorial expansion. Thus, for the
sum of $15 million and U.S. government promises to assume responsibility
for $ 3.25 million in U.S. citizens' property damage claims against Mexico,
the U.S. government forcibly acquired half of Mexico's territory via the
Treaty of Guadalupe Hidalgo in 1848. This annexation included the vast
territories of Texas, California, and New Mexico. Five years later, the U.S.
purchased southern New Mexico and Arizona for another $10 million.[60]
President Santa Anna, whose government was strapped for cash after the
war with the United States, negotiated the Gadsden Purchase, which sold
Mexican territory to the United States. In an effort to justify the sale to his
political opponents, Santa Anna argued that if he had not sold the territory,
the United States would have taken it anyway.[61] These tremendous losses
of territory inflamed liberal opposition to Santa Anna and led to his permanent ouster from office.

Indeed, two years after the Gadsden Purchase, Mexican liberals seized
the presidency and launched a massive reform effort that soon culminated
in a full-scale civil war between liberals and conservatives. This three-year
civil conflict, in turn, opened the door to subsequent French occupation of
an internally chaotic Mexico that succumbed to rule by a French-installed
foreign emperor. At stake in the civil war of reform was once again the
scope of the Mexican state's legal authority. In particular, the dispute centered on the scope and substance of the state's legal authority vis-à-vis the
Catholic church and the military over the lives and private property of people in Mexico. Thus, whereas López de Santa Anna fought two wars trying
to preserve the state's legal jurisdiction over Mexican territory, liberal
reformer Benito Juárez fought two wars trying to consolidate the state's
legal authority in relation to two key institutions of the old monarchical-
colonial order: the military and the Catholic church.

Mexico's civil war of reform from 1858 to 1861 was sparked by the
new liberal constitution of 1857, which was instituted following the ouster
of López de Santa Anna. The new constitution provoked a strong conservative reaction because it codified the legal subordination of the Catholic
church and the Mexican military to the Mexican state. This liberal agenda

to separate church and state sought to divest the Catholic church of its
authority over education and the public registry of births, deaths, and mar-
riages in Mexico.[62] Liberals believed that such legal authority over people's lives should reside with the state. Furthermore, liberals sought to
eliminate legal privileges, or *fueros,* favoring the clergy and the military,
especially laws protecting the private property owned by the church and by
military officers.

These reforms, of course, struck at the heart of differences in conservative-liberal rationales for seeking the independence of Mexico from Spain
in the first place. Conservatives originally supported constitutional independence primarily to preserve the privileges of the church and the military
from Spain's liberal constitution. Mexican liberals had themselves instituted a constitution that did away with such privileges. Less than one year following the adoption of the reformist, liberal constitution of 1857, the
Mexican army rejected the reforms outright and declared conservative general Félix María Zuloaga as president in Mexico City. Zuloaga was, of
course, also backed by Mexico's clergy. In response, liberals proclaimed
Benito Juárez, in refuge from Zuloaga in Querétaro, as Mexico's legitimate
successor to outgoing, liberal president Ignacio Comonfort. With two rival
governments and two contending armies engaged in civil war, the domestic
constitutional foundations of Mexican state sovereignty had never been
more contested than during the War of the Reform.

Foreign governments, particularly those of the United States, France,
Britain, and Spain, added international complaints about legal state sovereignty to the powder keg of Mexico's domestic constitutional battles.
During the civil war and its aftermath, these governments grew concerned
that the Mexican state was not fulfilling its sovereign responsibility to
protect the lives and property of foreign citizens and investors in Mexico.
Related to these concerns about the protection of foreigners was an
apprehension that Mexico would not live up to its international financial
obligations. Foreign financial claims against the Mexican state had been
accumulating ever since independence as Mexican governments repeatedly
proved unable to protect private property while trying to cope with military
coups, foreign invasions, secessionist revolts, foreign war, and finally civil
war.

European and U.S. complaints about the Mexican state's failure to
meet its international legal and financial obligations as a sovereign state
derived from European and U.S. expectations that the Mexican state would
protect foreign citizens and foreign-owned property better than the state
was clearly able to protect Mexican citizenry and property.[63] During the
chaotic years from 1821 to 1860, massive damages to the lives and property of foreign nationals had occurred, thus constantly prompting foreign
governments to present financial claims against the Mexican state on behalf
of their respective citizenry. Given that Mexican governments during these

turbulent decades were as recurrently bankrupt as they were chaotic, foreign claims had accumulated into a sizable public foreign debt by the time
the civil war broke out.

The U.S. government differed from European governments in the manner in which it protested the failures of the Mexican state to protect foreign
lives and property. Unlike the British government's use of military shows
of force, U.S. officials followed a pattern of trying to settle U.S. citizens'
financial claims via the acquisition of Mexican territory. As mentioned earlier, U.S. officials considered Mexico's massive forfeiture of territory via
the Treaty of Guadalupe Hidalgo as a financial transaction, albeit a coerced
one, in settlement of the Mexican state's debts incurred against the lives
and property of U.S. citizens and investors. Moreover, unlike the British
and French governments, which anchored fleets in the port of Veracruz
demanding that Mexico abide by commercial conventions during the civil
war,[64] the U.S. government dangled a carrot of governmental recognition in
front of besieged liberal forces.[65] That is, U.S. officials bargained directly
over the question of diplomatic recognition with the Juárez government,
headquartered in Veracruz. As a result, in the midst of the Mexican civil
war in 1859, the U.S. government agreed to extend official recognition to
the besieged Juárez government in exchange for Juárez agreeing to settle
all U.S. citizens' claims against the Mexican state.

In addition, Juárez had to agree to protect U.S. lives and property in
the future, grant perfect trade reciprocity in U.S.-Mexican commerce, and
extend to U.S. ships perpetual navigational right of way over the Isthmus of
Tehuantepec.[66] The United States did recognize the Juárez government,
though Juárez ultimately could not keep his financial promises. After the
liberal army won the war, Juárez was elected president in March 1861 only
to find that no foreign debt obligations could be met with a bankrupt treasury.[67]

Once the civil war ended, the British, French, and Spanish governments collectively decided upon a military solution to Mexico's failure to
live up to its financial responsibilities as a legally sovereign state. Alarmed
by Juarez's suspension of payment on all foreign debt for two years, all
three European creditor governments agreed in October 1861 to occupy
jointly the customshouse at Veracruz. This obvious violation of the
Mexican state's international legal right to exclusive governance authority
within its own territory was ostensibly justified by the occupiers' contention that their seizure of Mexico's customs receipts was the only viable
means of collecting on Mexico's debts. In other words, Mexico's breach of
its international financial obligations as a sovereign state supposedly war-
ranted European incursion on the Mexican state's sovereign right to exclusive governance of Mexican territory.

After a brief tripartite occupation of Veracruz in early 1862, the three
European governments began to disagree about the final goals of the occu-

pation, especially about the future of Mexico's legal independence as a state. As a result, the British and Spanish governments reached their own separate debt accords with the Mexican government and withdrew their troops. Emperor Napoleon III, however, refused to withdraw French troops and set out instead to subvert Mexico's legal sovereignty as a constitutionally independent state. His ultimate wish was to reinvent the French empire in the Americas by conquering Mexico. Consequently, President Juárez, who had just emerged from civil war, was embroiled once again in another full-scale war by May 1862. This time it was war with the French army of occupation. Predictably, many of Juárez's conservative opponents in the Mexican civil war enthusiastically aided and supported the French army.

In May 1863, after a year of resistance, the Juárez army had to retreat from the capital city to San Luis Potosí, and the French army entered Mexico City. At this point, the Mexican state's international legal standing as a sovereign state had never been more tenuous. Although the U.S. government of Abraham Lincoln continued to recognize the Juárez government and later refused to recognize Mexico's new, French-imposed emperor, most of Europe, including Britain, did recognize the Second Mexican Empire of Maximilian von Hapsburg. Even the British government, an early champion of Mexican independence, sent an ambassador to occupied Mexico in November 1864. Since the United States was engaged in its own civil war, it could do little to help Juárez oust the French army from the capital and central Mexico.

The conquest of Mexico by Napoleon III was initially welcomed by Mexican monarchists and the clergy as a great conservative victory over the dreaded liberal government of Benito Juárez. With the same enthusiasm that Mexican conservatives greeted Iturbide's declaration of Mexican independence in 1821 as the salvation of the church and the military from Spain's liberal constitution, with equal acclaim they hailed the loss of Mexico's constitutional independence after the French invasion. They viewed the French occupation of Mexico as the salvation of Mexican conservatives from the liberal victors of Mexico's civil war of reform. In short, Mexican conservatives considered the Mexican state's legal sovereignty to be entirely expendable to the supreme goals of preserving centralist government and the clerical and military privileges of the old colonial order.

Thus, what began as a European dispute demanding that the Mexican state honor its sovereign duties to protect foreign people and property and pay its debts ended up as a European revocation of Mexico's legal sovereignty. This repeal of Mexico's legal sovereignty was supported by many Mexican conservatives. Unconcerned about the loss of Mexico's legal recognition as an independent American state, leading Mexican monarchists and church officials traveled to Europe in October 1863 to offer the crown of Mexico to Ferdinand Maximilian von Hapsburg, an Austrian archduke designated by Napoleon III to become the emperor of Mexico.[68]

The Second Mexican Empire was almost as short-lived as Iturbide's first. Both ended with the respective emperors in front of firing squads.[69] Unlike Iturbide, however, Maximilian espoused too many liberal principles to satisfy Mexican conservatives. Most important, he refused to return church properties confiscated by the Juárez government, thus alienating the clergy and other conservative Mexican backers.[70] When the U.S. Civil War ended, U.S. arms and former union soldiers poured in to reinforce the Juarista army of resistance.[71] As a result, Napoleon III began to withdraw Mexican troops in November 1866. Given Maximilian's refusal to return church lands, the pope in turn refused to persuade Napoleon to keep the French army in Mexico. In the end, Mexico's victorious republican army court-martialed and executed Maximilian for, among other crimes, usurping Mexico's legal sovereignty.[72] In liberal constitutional terms, however, Maximilian's refusal to return church properties actually upheld a key liberal tenet of the constitution of 1857. Ironically similar to Mexico's early liberal presidents, Maximilian discovered that his authority was at the mercy of another government's army and subject to the whims of disgruntled Mexican conservatives. Neither the French government nor Mexican conservatives would ultimately respect the Mexican emperor's independent decisions.

Beyond Legal Disputes of State Sovereignty: Revolution and the Search for a Powerful State

When the republic was restored in 1867, Mexico regained its previous constitutional autonomy from other states. However, the legal reinstatement of the liberal constitution of 1857 was no guarantee that Mexican governments would abide by or be able to implement restored laws. Inasmuch as the early-to-mid-nineteenth century was dominated by disputes regarding the purpose of Mexico's constitutional independence and the scope of the state's authority, the late nineteenth and early twentieth centuries were rocked by controversies surrounding the constitutional legitimacy of Mexican governments. At first these legitimacy debates centered on whether consecutive reelection of the same person to the presidency was in accord with the spirit of liberal constitutionalism.

Later, however, by the turn of the century, legitimacy debates mushroomed into deeper controversies about whether the government of Porfirio Díaz served foreign interests more than those of Mexico's citizenry. In this respect, legitimacy debates began to broach questions about the power and commitment of the state to protect mass social welfare. By the advent of the Mexican revolution in 1910, the previous century's juridical disputes surrounding the legal sovereignty of the Mexican state had grown into full-scale debates about whether a legally sovereign state also had to be strong.

In other words, questions arose as to whether the state's legal bases of international recognition, territorial integrity, and constitutional legitimacy were indeed sufficient for national sovereignty if the state lacked the power to accomplish societal goals.

Although the Mexican revolution began with Madero's legalistic demands for effective suffrage and no reelection, masses of peasants and workers soon expanded the demands and debates about state sovereignty beyond liberal constitutional issues. These average Mexicans demanded to know why the Porfirian state had failed to improve the socioeconomic welfare of most Mexicans. Their mass demands for social justice implied that for the state to be truly sovereign it had to have the power to ensure economic progress for all citizens. Thus, during the course of the revolution, expectations about state sovereignty increased dramatically to include not just recognized, legal authority but also state power to improve the socioeconomic welfare of mass society.

Although Francisco Madero's constitutionalist-legal demands for effective suffrage and no reelection precipitated the fall of Porfirio Díaz, peasant and worker cries for social justice for the poor mobilized a mass revolution. This mass participation culminated in a new constitution, which included three key articles indicative of a "powerful"-interventionist state charged with duties to defend the socioeconomic interests of the poor. Thus, the revolutionary constitution of 1917 redefined Mexican governmental discourse about state sovereignty. This concept was now defined as the state's legitimate, legal right to authority over territory, people, and property as well as the state's power and duty to exercise such authority to defend the economic well-being of the mass public. The Porfirian state had failed both tests of state sovereignty: that of constitutional legitimacy as well as that of power to defend the poor.

Porfirio Díaz rose to national prominence as a great defender of national sovereignty and then fell from national power as a great traitor to sovereignty and to the nation. He gained political prominence while fighting to uphold Mexico's legal sovereignty against Napoleon III's army of occupation. As the valiant brigadier general who engaged the invading French army at Puebla on *cinco de mayo* 1862, he rose to fame as a liberal champion of Mexico's political independence from the French and as a defender of the liberal constitution of 1857. He ended his career, however, known as the president who sold out Mexico to U.S. and British foreign investors and as the dictator who refused to relinquish power voluntarily after twenty-six consecutive years in the presidency.

Charged by Francisco Madero as a traitor to liberal constitutionalism and therefore to the entire nation,[73] Díaz finally resigned after rebel armies sprang up throughout Mexico. Ironically, like Madero, Díaz had originally sought the presidency as a staunchly anti-reelectionist candidate critical of his other liberal opponents, Benito Juárez and later Sebastián Lerdo de

Tejada, for seeking consecutive terms in office. Nevertheless, Díaz's pre-sumed devotion to the defense of Mexico's liberal constitution was soon replaced by his new concern to improve Mexico's political image in the world. Most especially, he wished to improve Mexico's political reputation in the eyes of the United States and of European governmental officials and foreign investors.

After Díaz was reelected in 1884, he abandoned all previous liberal commitments to the constitutional legitimacy of the Mexican presidency and made sure he was reelected for six consecutive terms. Díaz viewed his repeated reelection as the surest route to establishing the degree of political order necessary to convince foreign governments and investors to forget about Mexico's nineteenth-century image as a politically chaotic country unsafe for foreign investment. His dictum was that through political order would come foreign investment, which would finally bring economic progress to Mexico. It soon became clear, however, that the economic mod-ernization of the Porfiriato was only making a handful of elite families and foreign investors wealthier and the vast majority of Mexicans poorer. Nevertheless, Díaz sustained his push to impress Europe and the United States with Mexico's political stability and the state's ability to protect pri-vate property and provide incentives to foreign investors.

Díaz's plan to transform Mexico's political image abroad worked, and Mexico's international diplomatic relations blossomed. Within his first two years in office, most of Western Europe reopened diplomatic relations with Mexico; and eventually the previous occupying powers, England and France, signed new treaties of friendship, commerce, and navigation with Mexico.[74] At first, U.S. government officials were skeptical of the legiti-macy of Díaz's overthrow of Lerdo de Tejada, although this subsided once Díaz won an election.[75] More important to U.S. officials than issues about constitutional legitimacy, however, were their hopes that Mexico would sign a treaty granting the United States cross-border raiding rights prior to U.S. recognition of Díaz. In essence, the United States wanted the legal right to send troops across the Mexican border in pursuit of fleeing bandits.[76] Officially Díaz refused, arguing that cross-border raiding rights constituted an obvious violation of Mexico's legal sovereignty. However, Díaz complied by sending more troops to monitor the border to prevent Mexican bandits from taking stolen property into Mexico.

Prior to receiving U.S. recognition, the Díaz government also con-formed to U.S. demands that Mexico make annual payments on $4 million in U.S. claims. With Mexican agreement to repay debt and monitor cross-border banditry, the U.S. government recognized the government of Porfirio Díaz without interruption for nearly three decades.

Díaz fell in 1911, and a mass-supported revolution got under way as Mexicans rebelled against the constitutional illegitimacy of Díaz's constant reelection and against government policies that privileged foreigners over

Mexicans. Both his policies and Díaz's reelection undermined basic principles of legal sovereignty as articulated in the constitution of 1857. First, a diverse cross section of elites and members of the mass public were outraged with President Díaz's blatant electoral fraud and violations of the constitution of 1857. Second, Mexican peasants and workers rebelled against the impoverishing effects of the regime's "scientific" economic policies. In this respect, two distinct dimensions of state sovereignty were in dispute domestically.

First, Francisco Madero and his liberal followers questioned the fundamental constitutional legitimacy of the Díaz regime given the repeated reelection of Díaz to the presidency and the absence of clean and fair elections. Second, Zapatistas and other regional and local rebels questioned the sovereign "powers" of the central government vis-à-vis foreign governments and investors. These rebels resented the ill effects of Porfirian economic policies on people in particular regions and communities. Over the years of the Porfiriato, central government in Mexico City had become a hated symbol of damaging socioeconomic policies that privileged foreigners over Mexicans and resulted in the destruction of the basic livelihood of the inhabitants of many different Mexican communities.

As the sovereign legality and presumed powers of the Mexican state fell into fundamental dispute domestically and revolution commenced, the Mexican state's international legal status also deteriorated drastically. In fact, when freely elected President Francisco Madero was overthrown and assassinated, the U.S. government of Woodrow Wilson refused to recognize the new government that General Victoriano Huerta established via military coup in 1913. Although the British government recognized Huerta provisionally,[77] U.S. officials refused to recognize what President Wilson regarded as an illegitimate military dictatorship that had seized power unlawfully and murdered a constitutionally elected president, Francisco Madero.[78] In addition to U.S. charges that Huerta was an illegitimate usurper of the Madero government, the U.S. government soon charged that the Huerta government had offended U.S. "dignity" and violated international law.[79] More specifically, when Huerta's soldiers arrested a number of U.S. sailors in Tampico in early April 1914, Woodrow Wilson sent U.S. forces in to occupy Veracruz in late April. The U.S. government did not withdraw its forces until November 1914 after Huerta had resigned and Venustiano Carranza, the "First Chief" of the Constitutionalist Army, promised to protect the lives and property of U.S. citizens in Mexico.[80]

U.S. recognition pressures and U.S. foreign intervention in revolutionary Mexico did not end with the government of Victoriano Huerta and the U.S. occupation of Veracruz, however. In fact, the U.S. government repeatedly forced concessions on succeeding revolutionary governments in Mexico by threatening to withhold or withdraw recognition. U.S. officials also employed recognition as a means of tipping the balance in favor of particular revolutionary factions. In 1915, the Wilson administration attempted to shift the balance of revolutionary fighting against the Villistas in favor of Carranza's constitutionalist forces by granting de facto governmental recognition to Carranza, the leading constitutionalist general.[81] Even then, Carranza first had to promise to pay for damages claimed to have been suffered by foreigners during the period of upheaval. U.S. officials did not grant de jure recognition to Carranza until March 1917. In the meantime, before granting de jure recognition, Woodrow Wilson sent an army expedition into Mexico in 1916 as a punitive measure against Pancho Villa. Villista forces had raided a town in New Mexico, killing a number of Americans in retribution for U.S. government support of Carranza. As invading U.S. forces led by General John Pershing moved farther southward in Mexico in search of Villistas, Carranza decided to repel the U.S. invasion and ordered his troops to stop Pershing's forces.[82] Although the Pershing expedition failed to capture Pancho Villa, after U.S. troops were withdrawn in January 1917, the U.S. government's preferred Mexican revolutionary faction, the Carrancistas, formed the first recognized government of revolutionary Mexico.

Carranza convoked a constitutional convention, which in 1917 approved a constitution containing several provisions far more reformist than any sections of the draft Carranza originally sent to the delegates.[83] Three particularly reformist articles included in the constitution of 1917 immortalized the mass revolution as a search for social justice via a powerful state. These three articles exemplified average Mexicans' pursuit of a national state with the sovereign "power" to provide socioeconomic wellbeing for all citizens. In essence, the mass revolution became a search for sovereignty conceived as the state's power to employ national laws and public policies to protect and privilege all Mexican nationals, not just a handful of Mexican elites, and foreigners. For instance, Article 3 required that primary education in Mexico be secular, not religious, and that it be free and obligatory for all Mexicans. Article 27 was dedicated in part to relieving the plight of Mexican peasants deprived of land. It required the return of lands illegally confiscated from peasants during the Porfiriato, and it reserved for the national state the legal right to expropriate private property in the public interest should the private ownership of such property fail to employ the property in a useful manner.[84]

In addition to the return of peasant lands accumulated by Porfirian elites and foreign investors, Article 27 also contained another crucial provision symbolizing the revolution as a struggle for Mexican national sovereignty vis-à-vis foreigners. Article 27 reserved for Mexican nationals the exclusive legal right to own real estate or obtain rights to natural resources. Any foreigners desiring such rights were obligated to declare that they officially considered themselves Mexican nationals, thereby forfeiting any rights to seek protection from their governments.[85] More than any other section, this provision spelled out a Mexican law clearly privileging Mexican nationals over foreign nationals as part of a new revolutionary definition of national sovereignty.

Article 123 echoed this new definition of sovereignty in guaranteeing Mexican workers the right to organize, engage in collective bargaining, and strike against any owner, foreign or Mexican. Article 123 was especially significant in establishing the legal rights of Mexican workers vis-à-vis foreign employers. Historically, the modern Mexican labor movement began with a strike, which was repressed in part by foreign troops. In 1906, a dispute broke out between Mexican copper miners and the U.S. owner of the Cananea Consolidated Copper Company in Sonora. At the request of the owner of the mine, the governor of Sonora allowed Arizona rangers to cross the border into Mexico to put down the strike.[86] Consequently, for Mexican workers as well as peasants, the revolutionary constitution of 1917 reclaimed the national sovereignty ceded by Díaz by dedicating the national state to the protection of Mexicans more than of foreigners.

Carranza's presidential successor in 1920, General Alvaro Obregón, was immediately confronted by U.S. foreign investors and government officials, who perceived the new constitution to be a direct threat to U.S. property and interests in Mexico. Woodrow Wilson refused to recognize the Obregón government in spite of the fact that Obregón had been elected to the presidency in late 1920. U.S. officials insisted that the Obregón government sign a treaty guaranteeing the protection of the lives and property of U.S. citizens as a prerequisite for U.S. recognition.[87] Obregón contended that he could not sign such a treaty because it essentially extended greater security and protection to foreigners than to Mexican nationals.[88]

The U.S. position became even more entrenched when the probusiness, Republican administration of Warren G. Harding entered the White House in 1921. Several U.S. petroleum magnates who had backed Harding's presidential bid claimed that the Obregón government intended to use Article 27 to expropriate their oil interests in Mexico.[89] Backed by the Harding administration, the oil companies demanded that the Mexican government guarantee that the nationalization of land and subsoil natural resources proposed in Article 27 would not be retroactive. As a U.S. government prerequisite for recognition of the Mexican government, this demand placed Obregón in an impossible political situation. If he gave in to U.S. officials, he would be branded a traitor to the constitution, the revolution, and to national sovereignty. On the other hand, his government's failure to achieve U.S. recognition implied enormous political and financial setbacks for his government. Mexico's possible loss of oil revenues due to a U.S.-instigated embargo on the sale of Mexican oil implied enormous financial burdens that his government could hardly sustain. Both scenarios threatened the very foundations of the Obregón government.

In some respects, Obregón's recognition dilemma reflected a situation of legal limbo in which Mexico had been caught ever since the country's legal independence from Spain. Although newly independent Mexico formally shed the legal status of a colony, elected Mexican governments, such as Obregón's, were not automatically entitled to diplomatic recognition in international affairs. International recognition, of course, implied multiple privileges of a diplomatic, political, and financial nature. Instead, Mexican governments often had to demonstrate that they were worthy of the international legal status of European or U.S. governments. Often, as in the Obregón government's case, these worthiness tests required Mexican governments to forfeit some aspect of their domestic legal authority or sidestep some Mexican law or basic constitutional provision. Much of the nineteenth century was spent with Mexican governments giving up domestic authority over territory, people, or property as the cost exacted for Mexico's international legal status as an independent state.

Mexico's loss of Texas territory in the 1840s exemplified the Mexican state's forfeiture of legal authority over territory as the cost exacted for Mexico's international recognition. The Porfiriato of the 1880s to 1911 was essentially a prolonged period during which the Díaz government violated the spirit and letter of the constitution of 1857 as the price for the government's favorable international diplomatic relations and associated privileges. Although weak both militarily and financially, the nineteenth- and early twentieth-century state was expected to be strong enough to protect the lives and property of foreigners as a fundamental requirement of its international, sovereign legal status. Ironically, the international relations of Mexico's legal sovereignty obliged the Mexican state to privilege foreigners over Mexican nationals, precisely the opposite of what legal sovereignty and political independence were supposed to do.[90]

In other respects, the compromise that resolved Obregón's recognition dilemma in 1923 was symptomatic of a shift away from Mexico's nineteenth-century legal vulnerability. The Bucareli Agreements, which ended the recognition impasse in 1923, initiated a transition toward a more determinate legal status for the Mexican state both domestically and internationally. At the meetings with U.S. officials on Bucareli Street in 1923, the Obregón government agreed to honor concessions granted to U.S. oil companies prior to May 1917. The Mexican government would honor concessions of companies that had engaged in a "positive act," such as setting up equipment for the removal of oil, prior to the May date when the 1917 constitution went into effect.[91] In exchange, the Harding administration agreed to recognize the Obregón government. From a domestic constitutional perspective, the Bucareli Agreements were technically in accord with Mexican law. This was true because of a 1921 decision by the Mexican Supreme Court ruling that "positive acts" performed on oil lands prior to May 1, 1917, exempted those lands from public seizure as mandated by Article 27 of the Mexican constitution.[92]

However, the exemption of foreign-controlled oil lands from public seizure was clearly not the original intention of the authors of Article 27. Thus, at the Bucareli meetings, the Obregón government sidestepped the spirit of the 1917 constitution on property rights to subsoil resources without technically violating Mexican law. Although the Bucareli Agreements were obviously no great victory for Mexico's legal sovereignty, they suggested that the Mexican state's nineteenth-century legal limbo was coming to an end. Such transition was evident in the fact that Obregón seemingly decided that it would be political suicide to ignore Mexican law outright in exchange for U.S. recognition. Mass revolution had so raised Mexicans' expectations about the state's power to enforce the new constitution that "revolutionary" governments dared not blatantly ignore Mexican law.

The presidential succession in the following year, 1924, demonstrated further evidence of the increasing legal, if not political, respectability of Mexico's governments. The election of Plutarco Elías Calles transferred executive power in full accordance with constitutional provisions. This was a rather momentous event since power had not been peacefully and constitutionally transferred from one president to another more than three times in Mexico's entire history as an independent republic.[93] The legal status of the new Calles government was immediately confirmed internationally by the U.S. government, which recognized Calles without any delay or prior negotiations.

The international influence of the League of Nations during the mid- to late 1920s further buttressed Mexico's international legal claims to sovereignty, even though Mexico had not yet formally joined the League. As presidents in the tumultuous revolutionary years of the 1920s, both Obregón and Calles managed to complete their full presidential terms and transfer power constitutionally. This was rather extraordinary since neither one enjoyed a truly national, mass base of political support. Despite rhetorical flourish, presidents of the 1920s neither distributed much land to peasants nor consistently supported improvements in workers' wages, working conditions, or ability to organize independently.[94] Moreover, Obregón's agreements at Bucareli infuriated Mexican nationalists and gave average Mexicans little reason to trust national presidents to implement the constitution of 1917.

The Calles presidency was characterized by the same formal constitutionality but informal illegitimacy as the Obregón government. In effect, the constitution was nominally respected but, for all practical purposes, not enforced much. The increased political stability characterizing presidential successions in the 1920s certainly reflected change when compared with the unpredictability of successions during the early and mid-nineteenth century. However, the Great Depression soon disrupted Mexico's political landscape once again. The depression renewed popular revolutionary demands for a "sovereign" state with the power to implement the most reformist articles of the constitution. The satisfaction of these demands entailed reversing some halfhearted policies, such as the Bucareli Agreements, which bordered on being unconstitutional. Such reversals were the only way that Mexican presidents could convince average Mexicans that the revolution had achieved more than just an elaborate set of unenforced laws.

Conclusion: (Dis)Integrating Mexico

Although Mexico received a formal international invitation to legal sovereignty when the United States and major European countries recognized Mexican independence in the 1820s, foreign governments and investors repeatedly disputed or disrupted the Mexican state's legal sovereignty throughout most of its first century of independent existence. Mexican nationals also challenged the state's legal sovereignty intermittently from 1821 until the early 1930s. In fact, Mexico did not emerge from the legal and political limbo evident in Obregón's recognition dilemma and the Bucareli Agreements until the 1930s. Clearly, Mexico's formal independence in the 1820s had both integrating and disintegrating consequences for Mexico as an emergent nation-state. On one hand, Mexico's legal independence from Spain established a new nation and state, at least in name and in law. As such, independence set into motion a process of national integration, including the formation of a national state and economy and a national political identity and community. On the other hand, opposite forces undermining the integration of Mexico as a nation-state have been apparent ever since independence. Throughout much of the nineteenth century, for example, disputes about the scope and legitimacy of the state's legal authority constrained the development of a national political community and a stable, national political order.

The ongoing integration and disintegration of Mexico as a nation-state reflect a basic paradox characterizing the Mexican state since its creation. Independence paradoxically endowed the Mexican state with sovereign legal authority to benefit and protect Mexican citizens regardless of whether the state could wield sovereign power to benefit and protect Mexico's citizenry. Over time, the Mexican state acquired increasing legal sovereignty and constitutional duties but never much sovereign power to fulfill constitutional goals. This fundamental paradox in Mexican statehood produced the contradictory forces of national integration and disintegration evident in Mexico's history up to the present era.

Over the course of Mexico's history, these opposing sets of forces have varied in salience during particular time periods. During the nineteenth and early twentieth centuries, disintegrating tendencies were often more pronounced. On the other hand, during most of the postrevolutionary era of the twentieth century, processes of political-economic integration were more prevalent. During the final decades of the twentieth century, there are signs of increasing national disintegration evident in Mexico. This book traces the ebb and flow of these contradictory and omnipresent tendencies in Mexico's history as a nation-state. Chapter 2 focuses on the upswing in processes of national integration evident during the early postrevolutionary era, particularly during the presidency of Lázaro Cárdenas.

2

Beyond Legal Sovereignty: The Revolutionary Myth of a Strong Nation-State

Redefining Sovereignty as State Strength, 1924–1940

Reversing Bucareli: Popularizing Nationalism
by Implementing the Constitution of 1917

Early postrevolutionary governments faced two basic problems in generating mass-based, national support for the Mexican presidency. First, the signing of the new constitution in 1917 raised popular expectations about state support for land reform and improved workers' rights. However, the "revolutionary" presidents of the 1920s proved unwilling or unable to implement the reforms promised in the constitution. For example, presidential failures to adhere to the revolutionary spirit of the new constitution were evident in the Bucareli Agreements of 1923. To Mexican nationalists, these accords signified that Mexican presidents would compromise away key principles of the revolution and the constitution in exchange for continued international recognition for the government.

Second, postrevolutionary presidents were confronted by the fact that average Mexicans still clung to local political identities reinforced by regional and local political bosses and a plethora of military *caudillos*. The predominance of regionalism among average Mexicans and popular skepticism about national government shared a key common denominator: the weakness of mass nationalism in Mexico. With the Bucareli Agreements suggesting that Mexican presidents were obliged to sidestep basic tenets of the new constitution in order to maintain the government's recognized diplomatic status in international relations, there was little reason for average Mexicans to place much faith in the national government as a source of economic security or well-being. Moreover, regional political loyalties had intensified during the revolution as armed, local chieftains built and maintained local armies composed of often fiercely loyal followers. Early postrevolutionary presidents, such as Obregón and Calles, further compounded the fractionalization of Mexican society by exacerbating rivalries between various revolutionary factions. In short, from the mid-1920s until the Great Depression, regional political loyalties and popular cynicism about implementation of the constitution discouraged most Mexicans from relying on the national government for much economic security. The failure of revolutionary presidents throughout the 1920s to redistribute much land to peasants or improve the working conditions and wages of urban labor added to the lack of popular faith in the constitutional commitments of Mexico's national government.

The Great Depression, however, disrupted regional politics in Mexico and eventually helped reverse the 1920s legacy of popular cynicism about national government. When the Mexican export sector collapsed in 1929, the ensuing economic dislocations across Mexico overwhelmed the minimal economic patronage provided to people by regional and local political bosses. Popular political movements sprang up as dislocated workers sought to remedy their economic situation through mass political organizations independent of government manipulation or control. By the early 1930s, the demands of independent labor movements for improved wages and working conditions began to threaten the manipulative, personalist politics practiced in Mexico. Mexico's de facto president-behind-the-scenes, Plutarco Elías Calles, refused to accommodate workers' demands that the national government intervene to provide for greater economic security for working-class Mexicans. In 1933, however, presidential candidate Lázaro Cárdenas set out to wrest control of national politics from Calles by mobilizing independent labor movements in support of his presidency. Eventually, the political showdown that occurred between President Cárdenas and Calles in 1935 and 1936 left Cárdenas victorious as a popularly supported champion of independent labor.

Freed of Callista interference, Cárdenas sought to overcome the factionalism and regional politics of the 1920s and build a truly national base of mass support for the presidency. This entailed, in part, reorganizing regionally manipulated labor and peasant confederations along national lines and incorporating the new national confederations into the official party. Most important, it entailed convincing the public that the Mexican presidency would enforce important constitutional provisions protecting peasants and workers without fearing loss of international recognition of the government's legal sovereignty. In order to reverse 1920s cynicism about national government and the symbolism of the Bucareli Agreements, the president had to instill in the mass public a new confidence in the national government's willingness and ability to enforce 1917 constitutional provisions dedicated to popular economic security. In other words, the president was obliged to exercise the state's constitutionally specified legal sovereignty to popularize nationalist sentiments among Mexicans. The popularization of nationalism involved making national identity the primary political identity of average Mexicans, whose main trust or hope for economic security otherwise rested with regional or local elites.

The Cárdenas government's challenge of convincing average Mexicans to rely first and foremost on the national state for economic security was a daunting task. The revolution and its aftermath had fueled regional military rivalries and intense political factionalism. Moreover, people's regional identities were deeply rooted in Mexico's past. More than 300 years of Spanish colonial rule had accentuated differences between Mexican regions as part of the process of colonial economic exploitation. After independence, nineteenth-century Mexico was still characterized by a marked division between city and countryside. Although urban centers harbored an incipient nationalist intelligentsia, the overwhelming majority of the Mexican populace resided in remote rural areas where political allegiances were decidedly local or at most regional in character. Indeed, the vast majority of Mexicans of the nineteenth century and the mass participants in the revolution of the early twentieth century identified most intensely with local and regional political elites and causes.

The postrevolutionary northern presidents of the 1920s managed to establish the national government's military dominance over Mexico's various regional military *caudillos.* However, the Northern Dynasty of presidents governing from 1921 until 1933, including Presidents Obregón and Calles, failed to instill in the mass public much confidence in the national government's commitment and ability to enforce the constitution. When the Cárdenas government broke with Calles and the Northern Dynasty tradition, its challenge was to foment mass-embraced nationalism among a largely rural and antinational populace that had never relied heavily upon a central government for economic or military security. Although Cárdenas campaigned for the presidency with a vision of uniting revolutionary factions into one "nation," what he encountered when he entered office were the disparate "many Mexicos" that had characterized his homeland for centuries. This chapter explores how his government overcame revolutionary Mexico's cultural and political fragmentation.

"Many Mexicos" or One Nation?
Regionalism and Factionalism as
Obstacles to a Nationally Supported Presidency

Nationalist myths purport that the independence of Mexico was sparked by popular currents of mass-based nationalism. However, according to historians such as Brian Hamnett, regional political affinities rather than mass nationalism dominated Mexico's political landscape before as well as after independence. In fact, Hamnett argues that an intense regionalism was both a cause and an intensified consequence of Mexico's formal independence from Spain in 1821:

> The [preindependence] insurrection of 1810 magnified [Mexico's] . . . pre-existing local conflicts, which, understandably, continued to manifest themselves after the War of Independence proper had finished in 1821. In short, the achievement of political independence neither resolved nor eradicated these tensions—nor should one expect it to have done so. These local realities, rather than the superimposed nationalist rhetoric of the official leadership represented the essential *leitmotiv* of Mexican social and political history. We should regard, then, the complicated struggles of the 1810s and early 1820s as broader expressions of previous and subsequent tensions. Unless we strip the "Independence Period" of its nationalist framework, we shall not expose the continuing threads which run through both the colonial and early national experience of Mexico. We shall never . . . understand the Nineteenth Century, comprehension of which is, perhaps, the key to many contemporary mysteries.[1]

Hamnett's arguments imply that Mexican regionalism and rural localism were by no means eliminated by the Spanish crown, even though the Spanish absolutist state ruled Mexico for more than 300 years. Instead, colonial policy treated the various regions of Mexico differently for purposes of economic exploitation. By encouraging economic differences between Mexico's various regions, colonial administrators increased regional distinctions within Mexico.[2]

Second, colonialism further perpetuated regionalism by discouraging the rise of nationalism. After all, the most successful elements of the entrepreneurial class of merchant-investors in New Spain were of Spanish birth; thus, the most vital segment of the bourgeoisie was of foreign origin. New Spain therefore lacked a rising class of native-born entrepreneurs who could help engender an incipient national pride or identity. Finally, the crown's control often proved ineffective beyond urban centers, thus allowing New Spain's regions to remain introverted and isolated from the political center. Although Spanish colonial administrators aspired to control both the urban and rural areas of New Spain, colonial administration was primarily concentrated in the urban areas of the colony.[3] The administrative reach of the viceroy, the crown's representative, was problematic in remote, rural areas, especially given the lack of a national railway network.[4]

Mexico remained politically fragmented by region and by community from the period of its political independence from Spain until after the revolution of 1910. Regional and local political loyalties were not fully superseded by a Mexican national political identity until Lázaro Cárdenas consolidated a nationally popular presidency in the 1930s. The fact is that *precolonial* regional differences between various Indian populaces persisted up to and after Mexico's independence from Spain. Mexico's ethnic divisions were further compounded by the economic differences among regions carved out within New Spain by *colonial* administrators. All of these divisions were in fact *exacerbated* rather than eliminated by the regional insurgency that preceded formal independence from Spain. Regionalism persisted in the newly declared republic throughout the nineteenth century in tenuous coexistence with a rudimentary, incipient nationalism—one associated with the rejection of Spaniards and Spanish colonial control rather than with any popularly shared, positive national identity. These nationalist sentiments, inspired by the cult of the Virgen de Guadalupe, rallied a common resentment of Spanish rule but did not significantly disrupt regional political affinities.[5]

The importance of rural political authority and local political allegiances suggests that the prerevolutionary Mexican state failed to establish a unitary administrative reach over all of the territory it claimed. In other words, the political administration of Mexican territory was actually decentralized and dispersed among many regional and local authorities. The definitions and arguments of sociologist Anthony Giddens suggest that prerevolutionary Mexico was therefore not a *nation,* defined spatially and administratively as

> a collectivity existing within a clearly demarcated territory, which is subject to a unitary administration, reflexively monitored both by the internal state apparatus and those of other states. . . . A "nation" . . . only exists when a state has a unified administrative reach over the territory over which its sovereignty is claimed. (Emphasis added)[6]

The prerevolutionary Mexican state's lack of a unitary administrative reach over the territory over which the state claimed sovereignty was a deficiency the new republic inherited from the Bourbon monarchy and the colonial viceroy. Even the crown and the absolutist intendancy system had difficulty extending the colonial viceroy's administrative authority into remote rural areas.[7] Divisions between city and countryside characteristic of colonial Mexico remained intact throughout the nineteenth century and did not really diminish in political importance until after the revolution.[8]

Given the fact that there was no spatial nation in prerevolutionary Mexico in the sense defined by Giddens, it should be no surprise that there was no generalized nationalism or psychological national identity either. Again, Giddens's definition is instructive since he defines nationalism as "a phenomenon that is primarily psychological—the affiliation of individuals to a set of symbols and beliefs emphasizing the communality among the members of a political order."[9] Mass nationalism and a pervasive national identity and community associated with it were impeded by the local political allegiances of average Mexicans and by the state's lack of effective administrative control over the vast Mexican countryside where most

Mexicans lived. Hence, the state-societal conditions of prerevolutionary Mexico support Giddens's argument that "there can be no nationalism, in its modern form at least, without the formation of [spatial] nations."[10]

In the absence of both a nation and nationalism, the state in prerevolutionary Mexico could not be characterized as a national state.[11] In fact, relations between Mexico's central government in the urban, political center of Mexico City and local strongmen and residents in rural areas grew increasingly strained during the nineteenth and early twentieth centuries. As the federal executive in Mexico City encroached upon Mexico's localities, opposition to the central state grew, peaking at the end of the Porfiriato. Prerevolutionary governments faced considerable obstacles in attempting to impose central political authority on an atomistic, essentially antinational, rural society. Government in Mexico remained regionally mediated by local strongmen throughout the period of the Porfiriato (1884–1911), after which Mexico's central government collapsed into revolutionary upheaval.

As president and dictator, Porfirio Díaz relied on a network of regional political bosses whose imposition of central executive decisions on resentful local populace eventually helped ignite the revolution of 1910. The Mexican revolution consisted of many regional rebellions reflecting a Mexico that was more like a "mosaic" of regions, as Alan Knight writes, rather than a single nation sharing common national sentiments:

> To understand the Revolution, it is necessary to look beyond the capital.
> . . . For the Mexico of 1910 was . . . "many Mexicos," less a nation than a
> geographical expression, a mosaic of regions and communities, introverted and jealous, ethnically and physically fragmented, and lacking common national sentiments; these sentiments came after the Revolution and were . . . its offspring rather than its parents. The Porfiriato, it is true, saw trends working toward a more centralized state and national economy . . . ; nevertheless, Mexico on the eve of the Revolution still retained much of its nineteenth-century character as "a semifictitious political entity," a character which the Revolution revealed to an alarming extent.[12]

The various regional combatants, such as the Zapatistas, the Villistas, and the Carrancistas, represented, at least in their political inception, regional or local challenges to central authority and were motivated by specific regional grievances.[13] Furthermore, armed struggle during the revolution cultivated regional militarism and fostered the rise of *caudillos* or regional military strongmen who later threatened the early postrevolutionary consolidation of a national presidency. In fact, the most pressing problem of the early northern presidents of the 1920s was that of maintaining national authority in the face of the military threats posed by regional armies headed up by rebellious *caudillos*.[14]

In effect, the antinational social forces that led the protracted and unsuccessful insurgency for Mexican independence in the 1810s[15] paralleled the regional and local movements that fought the revolution in the 1910s. The imposing evidence recently amassed by historians concerning the significance of regionalism and localism throughout the nineteenth century reveals a set of centrifugal forces that had vexed centralist administrators from the Spanish monarchy until the Mexican revolution.[16] For example, in *The Mexican Revolution,* Alan Knight emphasizes the importance and independence of rural, atomistic opposition to the executive centralism of Porfirio Díaz.[17] Knight compiles extensive evidence of the autonomous, agrarian, and popular character of the revolution—a phenomenon he sees as driven largely by local resentments of central, executive intrusion on Mexico's localities. Knight provides overwhelming evidence of the autonomy and spontaneity of agrarian (e.g., Zapatista) and *serrano* (e.g., Villista, Oroquista) rebellion.[18] His work documents the particularistic, local character of revolutionary discontent and the importance of traditional, rural loyalties and charismatic linkages between revolutionary *caudillos* and their followings. During the revolution, the revolutionary generals from northern Mexico who served as presidents had to struggle to exercise presidential authority on the basis of the regional and local armies and political followings they had cultivated to fight the revolution.

Elites leading the postrevolutionary Mexican state did not begin to construct a unified administrative authority over Mexican territory until General Carranza and succeeding northern presidents, Obregón and Calles, gradually consolidated the military hegemony of a nationwide constitutionalist army. The broad military reach of the constitutionalist army helped form a *spatial* nation in Mexico by beginning to consolidate the state's administrative reach over the vast Mexican countryside. The constitutionalist army of Generals Carranza and Obregón reached into remote, rural corners of revolutionary Mexico and eventually established a military hegemony over all other revolutionary armies. Knight argues that the "intrusive, 'outsider'" character of the army and of Carrancismo in Mexico's regions allowed the constitutionalist army to establish apersonal, rational-legal authority on the heels of its intrusions into the Mexican countryside. He further argues that this apersonal authority helped the Carrancista coalition triumph over Villista forces in forming a "national coalition" in revolutionary Mexican society:

> The prime difference between the Carrancista and Villista coalitions. . . was that the former, frequently outsiders in hostile territory, at least comprised genuine Carrancistas, with a common political affiliation; while the "Villistas," more numerous, but also more uncertain and superficial in their allegiance, were often local, anti-Carrancista movements conveniently assuming a "Villista" label. The Carrancista national coalition was a reality; the Villista equivalent, because of the *loose, personal, antinational authority at its core,* was something of a sham.[19] (Emphasis added)

Through military hegemony, the northern generals (Carranza, Obregón, and Calles) consolidated a nation as a collectivity of people under a single administrative umbrella, but they did not consolidate mass-based political allegiance to the central government. The political construction of mass nationalism proved to be beyond the grasp of Carranza and the Northern Dynasty of presidents.[20]

Carranza, Obregón, and Calles failed to mobilize a mass base of political support for their presidencies. In consolidating the revolutionary state's monopoly of the means of violence through military triumph over regional chieftains, the constitutionalist army's military reach did extend the state's administrative control into remote, rural areas of Mexico.[21] However, securing the office of the presidency from regional military rebellion was not equivalent to establishing nationalist ideological linkages between the presidency and popular social forces. Mexico's northern presidents of the 1920s superimposed military linkages between state and society from above more deftly than they implemented 1917 constitutional reforms that would build truly nationalist ideological linkages from below.[22]

Throughout the 1920s, presidential authority depended largely on the political persona of Presidents Obregón and Calles rather than the institutionalized authority of the office itself. When Calles's presidential term ended in 1928, Obregón was reelected but was killed before assuming office. Following the assassination of president-elect Obregón, Calles manipulated the Mexican presidency behind the scenes for six years, from 1928 until 1934. During this time period, known as the Maximato, Calles's personal credentials as arbiter of all revolutionary interests and "supreme revolutionary chief" became the principal mainstay of governance at the federal level.

Although Calles did not personally occupy the office of the chief executive, he effectively governed as if he were president. During the Maximato, three different men assumed the presidency,[23] but Calles, "the strong-man of Mexican politics," proved to be the only figure with the political skills to manipulate Mexico's many revolutionary factions.[24] By helping sustain the presidency's national authority in the midst of revolutionary factions, Calles essentially served as de facto president behind the scenes.[25] The weight of his enormous personal authority sustained the alliance of disparate forces included within the new official political party he formed in 1929. In spite of the new party's attempt to unify revolutionary factions, by the early 1930s Mexican politics had deteriorated once again into factional infighting. The supreme chief's role as grand arbiter among revolutionary factions degenerated into a defense of Calles's own factional interests.

In the absence of mass support for the Mexican presidency, Calles relied on his personal ability to manipulate leaders of factions in order to sustain presidential authority.[26] Without mass political identification with the presidency, national governance was reduced to the problem of manipulating leaders of factions. The personal political prestige of Calles became increasingly ineffective in manipulating revolutionary factions once independent social movements of workers, peasants, and other economically affected groups began to form during the Great Depression.[27] These movements, such as the General Confederation of Workers and Peasants of Mexico (the CGOCM), quickly gained momentum even though they rejected organizational and political linkages with the state.[28] They did so with the explicit purpose of offering a true alternative to the state-manipulated, official popular sector organizations controlled by Calles. Given Calles's insistence on incorporating all "revolutionary" groups into his new official party, the National Revolutionary Party (PNR), he made it clear that he disapproved of independent popular movements. His animosity toward popular groups independent of the state eventually detracted from his personal political prestige as "protector of all revolutionary interests."

Calles's intolerance of independent mass movements was demonstrated by the 1932 resignation of President Ortiz Rubio, the second of three puppet presidents controlled by Calles during the Maximato. Ortiz Rubio was forced out of office after disagreeing with Calles, who refused to condone presidential support for striking labor unions.[29] Even more dramatic testimony to Calles's intractability toward independent mass movements was his own statement of June 12, 1935, condemning independent striking workers as "traitors to the national interest."[30] This statement directly challenged presidential candidate Lázaro Cárdenas, who had come out in favor of such movements in his presidential campaign and his proposed six-year plan. As a result of Calles's attack on striking workers, political lines were immediately drawn between those revolutionary groups firmly behind Calles, and those supporting independent popular organizations, such as Cárdenas.[31]

Unwilling to support the swelling popular social movements unleashed by the depression, Calles remained caught between his political origins as a *caudillo* and his national political aspirations to institutionalize the political authority of the Mexican presidency.[32] Ultimately, he was not successful in channeling the rising popular movements of the depression to support the emergent postrevolutionary state.[33] Although Calles formed a new official political party and with its formation announced Mexico's passage from a government of local *caudillos* to a regime of "institutions,"[34] he failed to seek popular political support for the presidency from a growing contingent of independent popular movements. Neither Calles nor his constitutionalist predecessors, Obregón and Carranza, had wholeheartedly implemented the 1917 constitution's specifications regarding agrarian reform.[35] And the Calles-controlled governments of the Maximato also ignored Article 27 of the constitution and thus also lacked political support from rural popular movements across Mexico's countryside.

At the same time, Mexico's independent labor movements continued to increase in strength in spite of Calles's disapproval. Independent labor movements of the 1930s called on the presidents of the Maximato to adhere to Article 123 of the constitution by supporting the rights of workers to improved wages and working conditions. In short, Calles and the puppet presidents of the Maximato generally ignored the demands of both workers and peasants, who now expected presidents to implement the revolution by enforcing the most reformist articles of the new Mexican constitution.[36]

Calles's animosity toward independent labor movements actually helped the Cárdenas government forge a new political alliance with labor. Calles's attacks on striking workers accelerated the political mobilization and unification of the independent labor movements, which Cárdenas used to break Calles's hold on the presidency.[37] Cárdenas responded to Calles's attack on striking workers with a strong declaration of support for the constitutionally designated rights of independent strikers to pursue wage increases and improved working conditions.[38] The cycle of broadening popular support for Cárdenas and mounting anti-Calles fervor eventually culminated in the formation of the independent national labor union, the CTM (Confederation of Mexican Workers), in February 1936, and the exile of Calles in April of the same year. The CTM specifically stated in its charter that it adhered to the tenets of the Cárdenas government.[39] Thus, Calles's confrontation with Cárdenas in 1935 and 1936 helped Cárdenas forge a strong political bond between the Mexican government and the independent labor movement.[40] That bond was institutionalized in 1938 when the Cárdenas government incorporated the new national labor confederation and a new national peasant confederation into Mexico's reorganized official party. The new party became the foundation of a new organizational and ideological linkage between the state and Mexican workers and peasants.

Various analysts disagree as to how to interpret the motives behind Cárdenas's progressive alliance with workers and peasants. Some scholars, such as Arnaldo Córdova and Arturo Anguiano, argue that by mobilizing and reorganizing Mexico's workers and peasants, Cárdenas reshaped Mexican society and politics in order to facilitate the continued development of private capitalism in Mexico.[41] This interpretation tends to view the independent social movements of the 1930s as pawns that Cárdenas used to facilitate his own political success. In this view, his ultimate intent was to incorporate national mass organizations into the official party in order to subject workers and peasants to long-term control by the state. In contrast, other analysts, such as Nora Hamilton, emphasize Cardenismo as an important departure from the politics of previous revolutionary presidencies in Mexico. Her work demonstrates the independent political significance of popular movements to the restructuring of Mexican society in the 1930s. In fact, her book *The Limits of State Autonomy* challenged the

Córdova and Anguiano interpretations of the Cárdenas *sexenio*. From Hamilton's perspective, Córdova and Anguiano

> suggest that even the more radical policies of the Cárdenas administration were oriented to the interest of capitalism, and that Cárdenas was simply continuing the orientation of his predecessors toward private capitalist development with considerably more foresight and vision. The agrarian reform brought social peace to the countryside. . . . Government support for the demands of workers and peasants, and state encouragement of labor and peasant organization, facilitated state control of these classes in the interests of capitalist production.[42]

In contrast, Hamilton argues that "the goals pursued by the Cárdenas administration were more complex."[43] She provides historical evidence of the importance of independent peasant and labor forces to the initial formulation of the goals of the progressive alliance, to the Cárdenas government's political victory over Calles, and to the Cárdenas government's ability to confront foreign and domestic capital. In short, she argues that popular forces were not merely pawns of a procapitalist political elite and even questions the presumably procapitalist orientations of Cárdenas himself by focusing on his government's experiments with new forms of ownership and control over the means of production.[44]

Both genres of interpretation of the progressive alliance provide important insights into the Cárdenas years. In some respects, Hamilton's emphasis on the autonomy and importance of independent popular movements in shaping the policies of the Cárdenas administration parallels historian Alan Knight's arguments and evidence of the importance of the autonomy and spontaneity of agrarian and *serrano* rebellions during the Mexican revolution.[45] Both analysts provide historical evidence undermining the thesis that popular social forces in revolutionary Mexico were merely pawns of national bourgeois leaders who simply molded popular groups into submission to "the needs" of an evolving capitalist state.

On the other hand, Mexico in 1940, by the end of the Cárdenas term, was no longer like Mexico in 1910. As Knight himself implies, the Mexican nation-state was no longer a "semifictitious political entity" by the end of the Cárdenas era. By that time, the culturally divergent "many Mexicos"[46] of 1910 had been eclipsed by the emergence of a single, national identity popularly embraced by Mexicans who had formerly identified primarily with regional and local leaders and causes. In short, the Cárdenas government ensured that a single nation triumphed culturally over the "mosaic of regions and communities"[47] that had previously divided and multiplied the political identities of average Mexicans in 1910. Most important, when the Cárdenas term ended, a single Mexican national identity persisted even though Mexican presidents stopped implementing reformist articles of the constitution.

In this respect, the arguments of Córdova and Anguiano shed more light on how and why nationalism and political stability prevailed even after revolution and Cardenista reformism ended. However politically autonomous and progressive peasant and labor movements may have been in the 1930s, the progressive alliance ultimately reinforced Mexican nationalism and the state rather than class-based, ethnic, or regional loyalties and organizations within Mexico. And Cárdenas's political frame of reference was ultimately more national in orientation than it was class-based, ethnic, or local in character.

It is not necessary to attribute to Cárdenas manipulative, social movement–silencing motives to conclude that his government's actions ultimately led to the manipulation and control of peasants and workers by the state. After Cárdenas left office, his cultural and political reconstruction of Mexico as a nation-state ultimately made the independent interests of peasants and workers subservient to a "national interest" defined by state elites. Inasmuch as Cárdenas viewed national sovereignty in both a legal and power-oriented sense as the key to solving social problems stemming from inequalities of class, race, or local community, the process of building the nation and state became his paramount concern. Thus, his inclusion of peasants and workers in the reorganized official party established a nationally supported presidency and a postrevolutionary political stability that was based in part on the official party's ability to manipulate peasants and workers.

One Mexico Emerges: Peasants and Workers Support and Depend on the National State

Nationalism was popularly embraced by Mexicans during the presidential administration of Lázaro Cárdenas from 1934 to 1940. Cárdenas reorganized the official party from a regional to a national configuration of social groups. Moreover, in the midst of the Great Depression, he founded a mass ethos about the official party presidency being the only secure defense of the revolutionary interests of peasants and workers. One of the cultural effects of the depression on Mexico was to help invoke mass nationalist sentiments that were introspective and internally defined rather than outwardly defined by British and French liberal philosophies prevalent at the time of Mexican independence in the 1820s.[48] The depression helped unleash a particularly popular national ethos quite distinct from the national ethos of the industrial bourgeoisies of Europe.[49] Whereas Western European nationalisms celebrated triumphant industrial bourgeoisies, Mexican nationalism of the 1930s celebrated a revolutionary peasantry symbolized by Zapatismo and rural *serrano* rebels of remote, autonomous communities led by such leaders as Villa and Orozco. In this respect,

Mexican national political identity was more profoundly popular in character than European national identities, but at the same time more politically centrifugal in its rural origins. Cárdenas became the political champion of Mexico's popular national ethos of rural and peasant origins and channeled the peasant and labor advocates of this ethos toward support for the national state.

Allied with peasants and workers in the progressive alliance, Cárdenas transformed a politically tenuous presidency manipulated by Calles into a nationally supported presidency as the key underpinning of a stable national political order.[50] A key impetus behind this transformation emanated from independent popular movements organizing to demand that the national state intervene to ameliorate the harsh economic conditions created by the depression. The collapse of Mexico's export sector in 1929 shattered any remaining faith some Mexicans had in Mexico's export economy earlier fostered by liberal free trade during the late nineteenth century. The economic failures of the export economy accelerated the formation of independent popular movements, which became the voices of a mass nationalism in search of a presidency committed to protecting the well-being of average Mexicans against international economic shocks.[51]

Determined to overcome the fractionalist tendencies in revolutionary Mexican society, Cárdenas embraced Mexico's independent popular movements as his government's political allies. Acting within the structural-conjunctural conditions of the time, Cárdenas redefined the political culture of the Mexican presidency. He convinced the mass public that the presidency had a revolutionary commitment to implementing the reformist principles of the constitution in pursuit of social justice and mass socioeconomic well-being.

Given General Cárdenas's swelling appeal to rising independent popular forces in 1933, Calles had little choice but to designate Cárdenas as presidential successor to President Abelardo Rodríguez in 1934.[52] When Cárdenas proposed his six-year plan in the Second National Convention of the PNR in 1933, it became clear that Calles would have to designate Cárdenas as the official party's presidential candidate regardless of Calles's own preferences.[53] In effect, Cárdenas's imminent political success in 1934 was not contingent upon Calles's official blessing or support because of Cárdenas's remarkable political appeal to social forces demanding a defense of native welfare vis-à-vis the vagaries of international capitalism. In order to actually seize presidential power from Calles and reorient its use to popular welfare purposes, Cárdenas revived a politics of the masses from its state of abandonment during the Maximato.[54] According to Arnaldo Córdova, Cárdenas's practice of mass politics differed from the politics of Obregón and Calles in that Cardenismo involved the mobilization of the popular sectors as political participants in state power.[55] Unlike Calles, who mobilized peasants and workers in order to manipulate mass movements, Cárdenas encouraged and drew support from politically autonomous popular organizations.[56] Córdova argues that, unlike Calles, Cárdenas believed that the state itself forfeited powerful political allies if such groups were made subservient through governmental manipulation.[57] Cárdenas opted to support the nationalist demands of independent peasantry and labor and invited the Mexican masses to play a central role in the process of national state formation.

Cárdenas was less fearful than Calles that mobilized peasants and workers would seize control of the state once they were formally included in the official party apparatus.[58] His most pressing concern was that the Mexican state was being weakened by resurgent, localist factionalism during the early 1930s.[59] Consequently, his prescription for state strength was to ally with nationalist social forces among independent peasants and workers and to associate or link such groups directly to the emergent national state, thus removing the tendency for the popular sectors to be used as political pawns by factional leaders. Cárdenas believed that if he could sever the manipulative political ties linking mass-based organizations to particular factions, then he would be able to convert the masses into "soldiers of the Revolution" once again, though this time in a political rather than a military sense.[60] In his estimation, the Mexican presidency, by allowing mass organizations to become partners in state power,[61] was capable of transforming the masses from political instruments controlled by particular personalities into active political agents supportive of institutionalized state structures. The presidential role would then be that of "leader of the masses" through the establishment of a convergence of interests between state and mass social groups. The emergent national state would be secure from attacks by lingering personalist politicians and "nonrevolutionaries" once the organized masses constituted an active social foundation for state power.[62]

Cárdenas's policies of active state support for independent labor and peasant organizations interlocked interests between the presidency and independent popular organizations.[63] When Cárdenas began to distribute land to peasants and to back strikes by independent labor unions,[64] popular political movements rejected Calles's leadership and actively supported the Cárdenas government. For the first time in Mexico, presidentialist governance linked itself to a psychological nation with wide-ranging mass social forces identifying presidential power with the defense of mass social welfare. Calles's personalist authority rapidly declined as Cárdenas used executive authority to promote popular economic recovery from the depression and to redress popular grievances against foreign enterprises.

If Cárdenas had failed to mobilize and reorganize the popular sectors into national groups replacing the regional peasant and labor organizations of Calles's PNR, political factionalism would most likely have escalated out of control. Arnaldo Córdova argues that Cárdenas's institutional consolidation of the national state presupposed that the masses be organized nationally before the state itself could be structured along national organizational lines. In fact, Córdova describes Cardenismo as a general political undertaking whereby the masses became organized in such a way as to precipitate a particular organization of the state.[65] Just as Calles had taken the first step toward a national presidency by uniting revolutionary factions through his personal influence and political prestige, Cárdenas completed the task by reorganizing mass organizations into national groups integrated into the state.[66] Ideologically and culturally speaking, this transformed the office of the presidency into a symbol of national popular consensus and national community.

In creating this symbolism, Cárdenas prevented the spontaneous mass movements of the 1930s from threatening Mexico's emergent, postrevolutionary government.[67] Mexico's popular sectors were highly disillusioned with the corrupt politics of the 1920s. This popular disillusionment was compounded by the economic chaos of the depression,[68] which renewed revolutionary demands for mass social welfare. Cárdenas was convinced that without a presidential appeal for support from mass movements, the postrevolutionary state would never survive the mounting political unrest.[69] His fears were not unfounded. In 1933, a disaffected segment of the leadership of the regional workers' union CROM[70] had formed an independent labor organization, CGOCM, which by 1934 claimed to have the largest membership of any popular organization in the country.[71] By encouraging independent strikes by organizations, such as the CGOCM, Cárdenas encouraged organization and unity among independent workers. Labor's unity and growing political vitality made it possible for Cárdenas to break free of Calles and then court even greater mass support for the national presidency.

Even though peasants organized in the Confederation of Mexican Peasants (CCM) were Cárdenas's first and most natural ally,[72] the rapid mobilization of independent labor at the outset of his administration was the crucial variable enabling the new president to confront Calles and conservative Monterrey business leaders. Since Cárdenas was originally politically associated with peasant groups,[73] his pursuit of the trust and political support of independent labor became a key priority during his early years as president.[74] He sought to allay the labor movement's distrust of his own agrarian leadership early in order to avoid a resurgence of the antagonism that characterized peasant-labor relations during much of the 1920s, especially after the assassination of president-elect Alvaro Obregón, a revolutionary figure identified with peasant interests. The economic chaos of the Great Depression was important in this respect, because it helped mobilize independent labor and helped convince Cárdenas of the labor movement's importance to the political defeat of Plutarco Elías Calles.[75]

In turn, Cárdenas's drive to demonstrate his sincerity toward independent labor greatly accelerated workers' political organization. As early as February 1936, a new national labor confederation, the CTM, formed and announced its explicit support for the Cárdenas government. Without workers' support organized in the CTM, Cárdenas would have been unable to transform fragmented, Callista personalist rule into stable national governance.[76] The Cárdenas administration's use of the independent labor movement as a battering ram against powerful Monterrey business leaders and other groups opposing reformism proved indispensable to the consolidation of a popularly supported presidency.[77]

Although Cárdenas gained the trust of independent workers and the CTM by 1936,[78] for much of his term he struggled with the problem of distrust between peasants and workers. The ongoing distrust between the two major independent social forces allied with the Cárdenas administration remained a problem for the government at least until the 1938 expropriation of oil and worker-peasant euphoria surrounding it. Prior to the petroleum controversy, however, conflict and violence between peasants and workers were commonplace during the 1930s. The progressive alliance that Cárdenas forged included both independent peasant and labor movements, even though these groups were often very distrustful of each other. This distrust dated at least as far back as the northern revolutionary generals' use of the Red Battalions of organized labor to defeat the armies of Villa and Zapata. In addition to the use of urban workers to defeat peasant armies during the Mexican revolution, numerous incidents throughout the 1920s and 1930s fanned peasant-labor hostilities. Those of the 1920s were generated in part by a lengthy political rivalry between Calles and Obregón. Calles allied himself with urban labor in the CROM while Obregón cultivated the support of peasants organized in the National Agrarianist Party (PNA). The assassination of president-elect Obregón in 1928 on the eve of assuming office for a second presidential term brought peasant-labor animosity to a peak.[79] This was because Obregón's peasant supporters accused Calles and urban labor of involvement in the murder.

By the time Cárdenas reached the presidency, peasants and workers were deeply divided, based on the decade of antagonism fostered by the political rivalries of Obregón and Calles in the 1920s. The leaders of peasant and labor movements were also deeply suspicious of each other based on the previous political manipulations of Calles and Obregón. As the leader of the progressive alliance, Cárdenas had to try to bridge these divisions and mediate between peasant and labor interests.[80] In particular, he had to cope with a barrage of problems associated with cooperative ventures between hostile peasants and workers. The CTM, which was the new labor confederation, antagonized peasants by insisting that the CTM alone control the sugar-processing plants in jointly owned peasant-labor sugar production ventures.[81] Nathaniel and Sylvia Weyl describe a particularly explosive confrontation over a sugar mill in Veracruz:

Sabotage began in the worker-operated factory. The sugar workers discovered that the ambitious local representative of the Bank of Ejidal Credit had incited the peasants to seize the mill and had maneuvered to have himself elected "factory manager" by the peasant assemblies. All cane deliveries were . . . stopped; the plant was blockaded, and angry *ejidatarios* flung barbed wire across the feeder roads. *The CTM high command in Mexico City retaliated by threatening a nation-wide general strike unless the peasants were ordered to keep hands off the cooperative.*[82] (Emphasis added)

Conflicts between peasants and workers over job control in cooperative sugar production continued until 1939.[83]

In addition to historical antagonisms and political disputes dividing peasant and labor leaders, the organized peasantry differed from organized labor in at least one fundamental organizational respect. Peasant organizations were considerably more dependent on the state than workers. Apart from the fact that the peasantry was more numerous but more geographically dispersed than urban workers, presidencies of the Maximato had crippled rural organizations by ignoring peasant demands for agrarian reform during the 1920s and early 1930s. This neglect of agricultural interests was partially due to reluctance of the presidents to disturb entrenched landed interests in the agricultural sector.[84] And Calles's political alliance with the CROM labor movement had served to diminish the strength of the peasantry organized by the PNA.[85] Even Alvaro Obregón's mobilization of peasant support in his second presidential campaign lacked the organizing impulse of extensive land redistribution.[86]

After Obregón's assassination, Calles and Pascual Ortiz Rubio made conscious attempts to eliminate agrarian reform[87] in the final years of the Maximato (1930–1932). This further debilitated peasant organizations. In fact, as part of a Calles-inspired plan, puppet president Ortiz Rubio attempted to unify all peasant organizations under the auspices of the PNR in February 1930. The result was that the National Peasant League suffered a very debilitating split into three factions. One was a highly independent, relatively radical, agrarian group concentrated in Veracruz and led by Adalberto Tejeda. A second faction was a group headed by Emilio Portes Gil and Graciano Sánchez that soon supported Cárdenas's presidency, and a third minor conservative group was tied to the PNR and was supportive of all official, Callista policy.[88] The Tejeda movement was destroyed in 1933 by government forces.

By the time Cárdenas announced his presidential candidacy, peasant movements were so fragmented that none could challenge state power.[89] The only politically viable organization was the pro-Cárdenas movement. Thus, from Cárdenas's perspective, the fragmented nature of the organized peasantry made it politically unwise for him to rely entirely on peasant support to defeat Calles and secure presidential power. At the same time, the

potential political clout of the independent labor movement was increasingly difficult to ignore, especially by 1933, the year of the presidential campaign. Recognizing the divisions existing between peasants and workers,
the Cárdenas administration endeavored to consolidate national political
consensus among factional groups. In particular, Cárdenas courted labor
support by condoning strikes while also reassuring peasant leaders that
organized peasants would not be situated next to labor within a single popular sector confederation.[90] By insisting on separate organizations for peasants and workers while also mobilizing both groups, the Cárdenas government built national political support for the presidency and prevented a
single popular sector confederation from entering and dominating the reorganized official party in 1938.[91] Two separate, less influential entities
would depend on the state rather than dominate public policy as a single,
united bloc.[92]

Added to this historical legacy of peasant-labor distrust, the organizational separation of peasants and workers within the party in 1938 can be
explained in part by the temporal sequence and manner by which the government helped mobilize and organize the two groups. This sequence
helped reinforce the isolation of the two movements.

Cárdenas began to mobilize the active political support of peasants
with his campaign promises of agrarian reform. Throughout most of his
presidential term, he sustained a high level of peasant support by redistrib-
uting land to peasants in a state-sponsored program. On the other hand, he
garnered the political support of independent labor organizations by supporting strikes by independent workers. While independent labor was transformed into an allied partner of the Cárdenas government, the organized
peasantry became very economically and politically dependent on the state.
In fact, constant state intervention at all stages of agricultural production on
the *ejido* (a collective, peasant landholding) was necessary in order for the
state to transform the rural economy.[93] Rural workers who received their
land from the state and whose productivity depended on access to public
agricultural credit became a social force financially dependent on the official party presidency.[94] Consequently, unlike the political partnership
between the Cárdenas government and independent labor, the chief executive became the economic lifeblood of the organized peasantry.

The mobilization and reorganization of peasants through land distribution was only one of several steps the government took to build mass support for the presidency. In implementing Article 27 of the constitution, the
Cárdenas government restructured rural society and economy and established the organized peasantry as a bedrock of political support for the
presidency. And by implementing Article 123, the government rallied the
support of labor by supporting strikes for improved wages and working
conditions as specified in the constitution.

However, a second crucial task involved eliminating regional and factional political manipulation of peasants and workers. This entailed replacing the regional organizational structures of peasants and workers with national organizational structures and then incorporating the new nationally organized groups into a reorganized official party.[95] Cárdenas wished to integrate two new national confederations into the official party as separate blocs associated with each other only indirectly through mutual ties to the presidency.[96] On the other hand, organized labor in the new CTM wished to form a single, overarching national confederation containing both peasants and workers. Thus, one of the government's key problems was to try to check the CTM labor leadership's desires to enter Mexico's countryside and organize Mexican peasants.

A number of countervailing forces pressured for and against the formation of one large confederation of workers and peasants. Agrarian distrust of the labor movement was strong, especially among national agrarian elites such as Portes Gil, who had bitter memories of past troubles dealing with organized labor in CROM[97] under the corrupt leadership of Luis Morones in the 1920s. But at the local, interpersonal level, a certain affinity between peasants and workers sometimes existed.[98] Locally, urban workers helped organize agricultural workers in several key states. In addition, urban workers often retained personal ties to the particular rural areas from which they migrated.[99] Consequently, when Cárdenas announced in July 1935 that the PNR would begin forming a separate, national peasant confederation,[100] the CTM objected vehemently. The Cárdenas government defended a separate peasant confederation by arguing that agricultural workers' needs were different from the needs of urban workers,[101] implying that organizations linking the peasantry to the state would have to be different.

Whatever the president's personal motivations for insisting on separate organizations,[102] peasant-labor disputes were frequent and appeared to bolster the government's position. In particular, conflicts associated with joint sugar production that began in 1936 continued through 1939 and seemed to reinforce Cárdenas's contention that peasant and labor interests were different.[103] Moreover, at the elite level an ongoing antagonism between Vicente Lombardo Toledano, who headed up the CTM (the labor confederation), and Emilio Portes Gil, a veteran agrarian leader and head of the PNR (the official party), seemed to corroborate the government's thesis that peasant and labor needs and interests were different. The government position was further reinforced by agrarian leader Graciano Sánchez, founder of the CCM in support of Cárdenas's presidential candidacy, who opposed the inclusion of peasants with workers in a single popular confederation.

In short, the opposition of key peasant leaders to joining up with labor, and ongoing antagonism between agrarian and labor leaders, seemed to reinforce the Cárdenas government's notion that separate confederations were needed for peasants and workers. In spite of this peasant support, however, the government did not form a new party with separate groups until the first euphoric weeks following the expropriation of the petroleum industry in March 1938.

The Cárdenas government employed the popular euphoria surrounding the oil expropriation to unite psychologically but separate organizationally the two key popular groups that made up the progressive alliance. Psychologically, both peasants and workers embraced nationalist sentiments regarding the expropriation as a victory for Mexican national sovereignty vis-à-vis foreign investors. Originating with a labor dispute between Mexican petroleum workers and foreign-owned oil companies, the petroleum controversy was a type of labor dispute in which the president could intercede as a legitimate arbiter and protector of Mexican "national interests" vis-à-vis foreign corporate interests. Even though peasants were not direct beneficiaries of the oil expropriation, Mexican peasants identified the expropriation as a sovereign victory against foreign investors. This perception stemmed from the fact that Mexico's peasants had benefited from the Cárdenas government's expropriations of foreign agricultural holdings, particularly in the sugar industry.

Moreover, even though the petroleum controversy originated as a labor-management dispute, the Cárdenas administration employed laws primarily associated with agrarian reform to resolve the controversy. Article 27, which was a set of laws symbolically identified with the expropriation and redistribution of land to peasants, provided the legal justification for the petroleum expropriation. Thus, when foreign oil companies ignored the Mexican Supreme Court's decision in favor of petroleum workers' right to strike for better wages and benefits, the Cárdenas government resorted to Article 27 rather than Article 123, containing Mexico's labor laws specifying the rights of workers to strike. Symbolically, the government's use of laws primarily associated with agrarian reform to protect the rights of Mexican petroleum workers impressed Mexican workers and peasants alike and rallied intense political support from a broad cross section of Mexican society.

The unification of nearly all peasant and labor groups in support of government-sponsored petroleum expropriation in March 1938 created an environment of national consensus that made it politically feasible for Cárdenas to reorganize the official party. Less than two weeks after the expropriation,[104] Cárdenas called a constitutional congress to form a new official party. The party's regional organizational configuration was replaced by a new organizational structure consisting of national peasant and labor confederations.

The new Party of the Mexican Revolution (PRM) contained a sectorally organized national labor confederation and, five months later, a similarly organized peasant confederation; these two groups were incorporated as separate entities into the official party. This reorganization of the party into national sectors reinforced the notion that average Mexicans belonged to a single Mexican nation and collectively possessed a national interest that the party and the presidency were dedicated to defend. Thus, the structure of the official party was altered to reflect the new political culture of one Mexican nation and the new national character of government. Governmental authority was no longer effectively dispersed across many local authorities and revolutionary factions but was centralized in the hands of the presidency and national party elite. This remarkable concentration of governmental authority became the hallmark of Mexican state sovereignty in the postrevolutionary era by consolidating a state paradoxically endowed with astonishing legal-political authority but negligible ability to achieve the societal goals specified in the constitution.

Laying Down the Law:
Sovereign Expropriation of Oil and the Legend of a Powerful Nation-State

The Cárdenas government employed the petroleum controversy to resolve several governance issues simultaneously. First, the government employed the oil controversy as an opportunity to get organized labor to consent to the inclusion of a peasant confederation separate from the worker confederation within the new party structure. Cárdenas began to reorganize the official party at approximately the same time that labor found itself engaged in the petroleum controversy. Moreover, the government's final steps toward the separate incorporation of labor and peasant organizations into the new official party occurred in 1938 in the midst of the popular groundswell of support that followed the government's formal expropriation of oil. The official party's new organizational makeup was politically feasible in part because of organized labor's euphoria over the oil expropriation. When the Cárdenas government decided to resolve Mexican petroleum workers' dispute with foreign-owned oil companies by expropriating the oil industry, all of organized labor in Mexico celebrated. Elated labor leaders who were otherwise opposed to the organizational separation of workers and peasants within the party permitted the formation of a separate peasant confederation.

Second, the Cárdenas government expanded the symbolism of the oil controversy beyond that of just a labor dispute. In fact, Mexican officials defended the expropriation in international circles, arguing that it was necessary to defend the vital interests of the entire nation. The Mexican government articulated this national interest rationale in a formal diplomatic reply to a British diplomatic note protesting the expropriation as illegal. The Mexican government reply read:

> Confronted by the refusal of His Majesty's Government to admit that
> expropriation was justifiable . . . my Government feel that they must
> explain . . . that the ground of public interest that directly led to the action
> taken was in this case established by the . . . Oil Companies in refusing to
> abide by a final and absolute judgment rendered by the Highest Court of
> the Republic. Said [refusal] . . . brought as a consequence a petition of the
> [oil] workers . . . based on constitutional provisions and the Federal Labor
> Law, praying that the contracts between said workers and the Oil
> Companies be declared canceled. Rescission of said contracts would . . .
> have resulted in total paralyzation of the Oil Industry, and this would in
> turn have fundamentally affected . . . the transport and processing indus-
> tries, to say nothing of the whole economic life and the vital interests of
> the Nation.[105]

By defining the oil expropriation as an act in defense of the entire
"Nation," the Cárdenas government popularized the idea of a Mexican
"national interest," which rallied people behind the presidency, the new
official party, and the party's new organizational configuration. Consequently, unlike Calles, who governed by manipulating political bosses,
Cárdenas invented a presidency and a party structure that the mass public
deemed indispensable to the defense of Mexico's national interest.

Third, the Cárdenas government's insistence that the entire nation's
interests were at stake proved just as helpful in justifying the oil expropriation to foreign governments as in rallying mass support for the Mexican
presidency. In fact, Mexican diplomatic officials very deftly employed the
notion of national interest to refute British charges that the Mexican government had violated international law. Since British investors in the
Mexican Eagle Oil Company were among those whose property was expropriated, British government officials argued that

> the expropriation was tantamount to confiscation carried out under a veil
> of legality formed by basing it upon labour issues; and that the conse-
> quences have been a denial of justice and a transgression . . . of interna-
> tional law [only] . . . remedied . . . by the restoration of . . . properties to
> the [Mexican Eagle Oil] company itself.[106]

Mexican diplomatic officials effectively countered these British charges by
maintaining that international law actually sanctioned the expropriation
because the oil companies had illegally ignored the Mexican Labor Board
and the Mexican Supreme Court and also endangered the national interest.
In other words, Mexican officials turned the British argument upside down,
implying that the oil companies violated Mexico's sovereignty and international law by refusing to abide by the supreme law of the land and by
demonstrating a total disregard for the Mexican national interest in continued oil production. Mexican officials essentially used British references to
the violation of international law to refute all British claims against Mexico
by maintaining that the oil companies violated international law:

It is a universally accepted principle of International Law that all sovereign and independent nations have the right to expropriate in the public interest on payment of adequate compensation; furthermore, said principle . . . admits that what constitutes the public interest is a matter to be left to the discretion of every State. . . . The [Mexican Labor Board] award and [Mexican Supreme Court] judgement were rendered in strict accordance with the laws of the Republic of Mexico. . . . The real motive of the Mexican government [for the expropriation] . . . was that of ensuring due respect for the Juridical Power of the Republic and to prevent . . . upsetting the internal balance between the social, economic, and political forces of the Nation . . . ; and therefore . . . there are no grounds for alleging either denial of justice or infringement of the principles of International Law; . . . the Mexican Eagle Oil Company—being a Mexican company—is legally disqualified to apply for the protection of an alien State in defense of its interests.[107]

The Cárdenas government's use of the principles of international law and of Article 27 of the Mexican constitution to justify the oil expropriation to foreign governments also served to mythologize the "powers" of the postrevolutionary nation-state. Legend surrounding the expropriation has it that the Mexican state used its sovereign legal authority to demonstrate its powers over foreign investors. And the Mexican "Nation" presumably demonstrated its financial powers vis-à-vis foreign investors by compensating the expropriated companies and thus upholding the Mexican state's international legal rights to engage in compensated expropriation for the public interest. Indeed, Mexican officials characterized the oil expropriation as proof of the nation-state's power to defend the state's exclusive, sovereign right and power to govern Mexican territory. In a note to the British government, Mexican officials proclaimed:

It has thus been shown that the main purpose of the resistance made by the [oil] Companies [to the Mexican Supreme Court] was that of placing obstacles . . . in the way of the Mexican Government.
    The good faith that has guided the acts of the Mexican Government . . . with the backing of the entire Nation—is proved by the nature of the measures adopted. The firm determination to pay for the property expropriated has been publicly manifested, before the whole world, and the Republic's capacity to pay is a real and assured fact.[108]

Thus, Mexico's myth of domestic state strength first gained widespread acceptance during the Cárdenas presidency. By 1938, the long-proven international weakness of the Mexican state appeared counterbalanced by a strong, revolutionary state that, at least at home, claimed to have the power to defy foreign investors in order to protect Mexican citizens. A marked increase in international respect for Mexico's legal sovereignty after the revolution made it easier for government officials to claim that the Mexican state was domestically strong. Franklin Roosevelt's Good Neighbor policy and the reduced likelihood of European intervention in

Mexico helped Mexico's new political elite appear to have control over a domestic sphere of affairs that the state claimed to have made impervious to a hostile, outside world.

When Cárdenas expropriated foreign-owned oil, he faced neither a foreign invasion nor domestic political upheaval, both of which would have been likely in the nineteenth century. In effect, he took Mexico's territorial integrity and his government's constitutional legitimacy as widely accepted givens when he announced the oil expropriation. In retrospect, his government obviously benefited from the Mexican state's newly accepted sovereign legal stature at home and abroad. Although Cárdenas and his successors did not claim to be able to control the world outside Mexico, they did claim that the new Mexican state could vastly improve the world inside Mexico's borders. Thus, although not denying that Mexico was still weak in international affairs, the new revolutionary mythology of domestic state strength claimed that the Mexican state was no longer weak at home.

Conclusion

Although Cárdenas's progressive policies were soon abandoned by his successors, Lázaro Cárdenas did envision and attempt to build a strong national state capable of controlling and employing Mexico's mixed economy for the benefit of the poor people who fought the Mexican revolution. Writing on July 9, 1933, Cárdenas maintained that

> if the state organizes production basing it on national consumption and necessary exportation, we will be able to see Mexico in a privileged position. Unplanned production that ignores the quantities we are able to consume will stagnate our economy. Urge . . . that the state intervene in determining what the country should produce and in organizing commercial distribution. This will undoubtedly bring enormous benefit to the country because in the state's very economic planning, the interests that private capital should perceive will be decided, as well as how the worker should participate and what contribution corresponds to the state itself.[109]

In the pursuit of this vision of a progressive and strong national state, Cárdenas set out to eliminate personalism and factionalism and to build a new national presidency founded on broad support from Mexican workers and peasants. In order to eliminate Plutarco Elías Calles's authoritarian manipulation of the Mexican presidency, Cárdenas rallied support from the independent labor movement and used independent workers' support to exile Calles from the country. In the countryside, Cárdenas organized mass peasant support for his presidency by distributing land to peasants. Finally, in a series of great culminating events in 1938, the Cárdenas government expropriated foreign-owned petroleum companies and then reorganized the official party less than two weeks later. The groundswell of broad popular support for the oil expropriation enabled the government to rebuild the party without major political opposition.

By implementing key reforms specified in the constitution of 1917 and by rebuilding the party, Cárdenas popularized the idea of a new national political community among Mexicans. The nation-state became an important symbol of socioeconomic protection for average Mexicans, who came to feel that they could rely on the new official party and the national presidency for socioeconomic support. As members of new national peasant and labor organizations incorporated into the new party structure, Mexican workers and peasants were linked through nationalist ideology, party organization, and patronage to the new national party and presidency. This process of incorporation significantly enhanced the party's "revolutionary" credentials. Moreover, since the formation of the new party occurred at nearly the same time as the petroleum expropriation, both the new party and the presidency became symbols of Mexican national sovereignty and state power. As the executor of the oil expropriation and founder of the reorganized party, the presidency acquired the political credentials of being permanently "revolutionary" and domestically "powerful." In effect, the presidency and the new official party became the symbols of "popular sovereignty" and sovereign power to achieve Mexico's constitutional goals. This symbolism later justified the perpetual election of official-party presidents by implying that such elections perpetuated the sovereign power of the revolutionary state.

In short, notions of national sovereignty, national identity, and national community captured the popular imagination simultaneously during the petroleum expropriation and official party reorganization. By 1938, sovereignty connoted much more to Mexicans than the state's internationally recognized legal rights to constitutional independence. It represented state strength to defy foreign investors in order to protect the socioeconomic well-being of Mexican citizens. Similarly, Mexican national political identity consisted of more than political loyalty to national as opposed to regional or local authorities. The political culture of "one Mexico" that Cárdenas popularized invented a national political community of citizens said to be permanently empowered and protected by a perpetually revolutionary state. Cardenista presidentialism thus established a myth claiming that official-party presidents personified the sovereignty of a perpetually strong state said to be dedicated to the protection of the poor. Although the Mexican state later demonstrated that it did not command such perpetual strength, Mexico's myth of presidential power persisted for more than forty years. During this time, PRI presidents claimed to have the power and will to protect the socioeconomic well-being of all Mexican citizens. Contrary to presidential claims, however, governmental authority was primarily employed by the presidents who succeeded Cárdenas to promote rapid industrialization rather than to attempt to protect the socioeconomic welfare of all the people.

In this respect, the cultural construction of the national presidency as the personification of the sovereign power of the state posed a basic governmental dilemma. In effect, from 1940 onward, when industrialization accelerated, the executive branch of government in Mexico was culturally and legally obligated, but not actually equipped, to control the economy in order to protect popular groups' socioeconomic interests. Given the inability of the national presidency to ensure an equitable distribution of wealth and well-being to all Mexican citizens, the political culture of the Cárdenas-constructed presidency of the 1930s set the stage for subsequent governance problems in the later twentieth century. In fact, during the forty years after Cárdenas left office, the main governance problems confronting Mexican presidents centered on the problem of sustaining the revolutionary myth that state sovereignty consisted of state power to fulfill the goals of the constitution. By the same token, during those forty years after Cárdenas, the state's legal sovereignty was rarely disputed either domestically or internationally. Instead, the legal foundations of Mexican state sovereignty remained essentially unshakable until after the myth of state strength shattered in the 1970s. Mexico did not enter a new period of legal and political limbo until the 1980s and 1990s when opponents of the Mexican state's extensive legal authority over the economy and over commerce predominated in both domestic and international affairs.

3

Sustaining the Myth of Sovereignty as State Strength

Industrialization Portrayed as "National Economic Planning," 1940–1970

In the midst of world war, Avila Camacho succeeded Lázaro Cárdenas in the presidency and altered the purpose of state interventions, from the Cardenista provision of social welfare to state promotion of private investment. Presidential support for workers and peasants had already begun to subside in the final two years of the Cárdenas administration as a result of international political-economic pressures imposed on Mexico after the petroleum expropriation.[1] The Avila Camacho government's push for import-substitution industrialization in 1940, however, marked the beginning of full-fledged presidential support for private investors, regardless of the negative side effects on mass social welfare. The Avila Camacho administration adopted a nationalist development strategy designed to stimulate private investment and support local industrialization. As presidential successor to Cárdenas, Avila Camacho manipulated popular nationalist sentiments to obtain worker and peasant acquiescence to the state's reduced provision of mass social welfare.[2]

The process of state-promoted industrialization initiated in 1940 proved incompatible with Cárdenas-style presidentialism as a political order founded on a myth about the presidency as a personification of a state strong enough to protect the poor. The most fundamental incongruence stemmed from the contrast between the myth's claim that a strong presidency would protect mass social welfare and the post-1940 presidential policy of postponing provision of popular welfare as financial constraints on local industrialization increased.[3] After 1940, the official party devised elaborate mechanisms to co-opt or repress people and social movements critical of the state and the presidential myth forged by Cárdenas in 1938.[4] On this basis, most conflicts between the PRI presidency and popular society were minimized from 1940 until the early 1970s, when conflict between state personnel brought the issue of deteriorating mass social welfare back to the forefront of national political discourse.

A second basic incompatibility between state-promoted industrialization and the political order stemmed from the fact that Mexico's myth of presidential power insisted that all governmental authority must reside with the president. This insistence on concentrated governmental authority was incompatible with state-promoted industrialization, which required the presidency to rely on technocratic experts and an ever expanding state apparatus dedicated to subsidizing private investment. Eventually, by the 1970s, the economic and administrative dilemmas of state-promoted industrialization undermined the presidency's ability to control economic technocrats and to sustain a coherent set of economic policies. As state involvement in promoting industrialization grew over the years from 1940, PRI presidents transferred authority for economic and social policymaking to conservative Treasury technocrats dedicated to promoting private investor incentives. Throughout the 1950s and 1960s, the presidency's reliance on the Treasury's orthodox economic formulas grew increasingly incompatible with the presidential image as supreme governmental protector of mass social welfare.

After 1940, PRI presidents' promotion of rapid industrialization involved the creation of parastatal enterprises and agencies as well as an expansion of the state's intervention in macroeconomic processes. Both of these forms of state economic intervention were designed to subsidize private investment and correct for private sector deficiencies restricting local industrial growth. Both forms of state intervention placed a premium on the Treasury's technocratic management of public spending, especially after World War II ended and the favorable international economic climate for Mexican exports disappeared in the late 1940s. Within the difficult financial straits of the 1950s, PRI presidents Miguel Alemán, Ruiz Cortines, and López Mateos were mainly worried about sustaining local industrial growth in the face of financial constraints and limited public revenues.[5] This meant that the technocratic expertise of the Finance secretariat/Treasury (*Secretaría de Hacienda y Crédito Público,* or SHCP) and of the Central Bank became vitally important to PRI presidents.

In fact, during the financially difficult postwar year 1954, Adolfo Ruiz Cortines adopted an orthodox economic development strategy called "stabilizing growth" or *desarrollo estabilizador,* which was devised by Treasury officials. This strategy's restrictive public spending and tax policies were designed to stimulate private savings and investment. As time passed, PRI presidents López Mateos and Díaz Ordaz came to rely ever more heavily on the Treasury to restrict public spending and to supervise the expanding parastatal sector according to stabilizing growth dictates. As industrialization became more difficult to sustain in the 1950s and 1960s, parastatal enterprises and agencies under Treasury supervision became the main mechanisms for subsidizing private investment and correcting for the private sector's inadequacies.

Given the stabilizing growth strategy's commitment to promoting private investors, the Treasury's logic of managing parastatal enterprises and agencies was intertwined with the wishes of the largest-scale private investors operating in Mexico.[6] In consonance with private investors' preferences, the Treasury's "planning" of parastatal activities was dedicated to decapitalizing the parastatal sector in order to subsidize the private sector. Such total commitment to private profitability stood in marked contrast to the economic and social reformism of an increasingly vocal group of technocrats involved with public enterprises and agencies under the shadow of Treasury's overarching control of parastatal spending.[7]

This growing reformist presence within the executive technocracy was symptomatic of an ongoing presidential dilemma concerning the Treasury's inordinate control of the parastatal sector and of public spending in general. On one hand, the state's deepening involvement in promoting industrialization led to the creation of growing numbers of state enterprises involved in actual industrial production. Under Treasury supervision, such enterprise was designed to invest in production in which the private sector was either unwilling or unable to invest. On the other hand, reformist technocrats associated with public enterprise activities through the secretariats of Presidencia and Patrimonio Nacional developed statist interests in planning parastatal investment for purposes other than subsidy and incentives to private investors. In consonance with the presidential myth of a strong state dedicated to the poor, many of these statist-reformist technocrats wished to break the Treasury's hold over the public sector in the interest of state promotion of economic and social reform.[8]

From 1958 until 1970, PRI presidents pushed forward a succession of laws claiming to disperse among several state agencies the Treasury's monopoly of financial control over parastatals and over public sector economic planning. Caught between the need to rely on the Treasury and the political imperatives of sustaining the Cardenista presidential image and myth, PRI presidents gradually constructed, between 1958 and 1970, the administrative skeleton of a goal-based national economic planning structure. However, the multiple laws passed to alter parastatal activity and promote national economic planning never actually diminished the Treasury's ultimate financial control over the public sector. Even though a new secretariat of the Presidencia was ostensibly created to "plan parastatal investment," it never did. And, although Patrimonio Nacional was nominally charged with controlling parastatal budgets, it never did. Instead, PRI presidents used these two secretariats to create a myth of "national economic planning" separate from the realities of the Treasury's absolute control over public sector spending and investment. This chapter is about the creation of that myth of national economic planning in conjunction with PRI presidents' promotion of rapid industrialization for the overwhelming benefit of large-scale private investors.[9]

Mexico After 1940:
Presidential Promotion of Rapid Industrialization

By the time Cárdenas left office in 1940, the process of import-substitution industrialization, phase one, was firmly under way in Mexico.[10] The industrial growth that had occurred in response to the Great Depression of 1929 (see Table 3.1) was further invigorated as war in Europe increased the demand for Mexican exports, including both raw materials and manufactured goods.[11] As an outside stimulus to the development of local industrialization in Mexico, the Second World War was important both in the economic sense of creating powerful incentives for local production by private entrepreneurs, and because the favorable, external economic circumstances created by the war prompted a proindustrialization stance on the part of the new president, Avila Camacho. The Avila Camacho government proclaimed that industrialization was to become the central concern of all national activity and redirected economic policy and state economic interventions to encourage private entrepreneurship.[12] The government contended that local industrialists should benefit as much as possible from the propitious international circumstances the war offered Mexican entrepreneurs. Workers' wage demands, largely ignored by the state by the end of the Cárdenas administration,[13] were now clearly relegated to second place as the goal of rapid industrialization became the Avila Camacho administration's number one priority. Table 3.2 illustrates this trend toward increasing federal expenditures on economic development and decreasing expenditures on social concerns, beginning with the Avila Camacho presidency and continuing through the administrations of Miguel Alemán and Ruiz Cortines up to López Mateos's term, when the trend was somewhat interrupted.

As presidential commitment to promoting rapid industrialization increased after 1940, contradictions between the presidentialist myth and industrialization became increasingly apparent as the administrative

Table 3.1   **Manufacturing Production, 1910–1945: Percentage Change in Index**

Years	Volume	Value
1920–1925	63.4	40.4
1925–1930	20.2	−1.7
1930–1935	16.0	24.1
1935–1940	35.5	86.5
1940–1945	34.8	128.9

Source: Sanford A. Mosk, *Industrial Revolution in Mexico.* Cited in James W. Wilkie, *The Mexican Revolution* (Berkeley: University of California Press, 1970), p. 264.

Table 3.2   Average Percent of Federal Budgetary Expenditures (by type of
emphasis and presidential term)

Period	President	Total	Economic	Social	Administrative
1900–1911	Díaz	100	16.0	6.6	77.4
1911–1912	Madero	100	17.6	9.9	72.5
1912–1913	Huerta	100	15.2	8.9	75.9
1917–1919	Carranza	100	16.3	2.0	81.7
1920	de la Huerta	100	17.2	2.3	80.5
1921–1924	Obregón	100	17.9	9.7	72.4
1925–1928	Calles	100	24.8	10.1	65.1
1929	Portes Gil	100	23.2	12.9	63.9
1930–1932	Ortiz Rubio	100	28.1	15.8	56.1
1933–1934	Rodríguez	100	21.7	15.4	62.9
1935–1940	Cárdenas	100	37.6	18.3	44.1
1941–1946	Avila Camacho	100	39.2	16.5	44.3
1947–1952	Alemán	100	51.9	13.3	34.8
1953–1958	Ruiz Cortines	100	52.7	14.4	32.9
1959–1963	López Mateos	100	39.0	19.2	41.8

Source: James W. Wilkie, *The Mexican Revolution* (Berkeley: University of California Press, 1970), p. 32.

complexities of state intervention in the economy multiplied. On the one hand, growing state economic intervention pushed the president to expand the organizational complexity of the state, thereby augmenting his reliance on a growing number of technically trained experts in the central secretariats and on state managers in the parastatal sector. In effect, increasing presidential reliance on technocrats was an unavoidable administrative outcome of the process of state-led industrialization. On the other hand, the president was also pressed to administer national economic growth in a manner consistent with the symbolism of defending the revolution inside Mexico. Consequently, presidents worried both about preserving the internal organization of governmental authority established in the 1930s[14] and about preserving the "revolutionary" credentials of the presidency. *Presidencialismo* represented the reconciliation of popular nationalism and centralist insulation of executive authority, and such a reconciliation depended on maintaining the concentrated, decisionmaking authority of the presidency. Therefore, presidents tended to resist the transfer of presidential prerogatives over key policy arenas to technocrats at the central executive level or to the parastatal sector.[15]

Even though technocratization and bureaucratization were unavoidable aspects of the presidency's own drive to promote rapid industrialization, Cárdenas-style *presidencialismo* contained a built-in tendency to retain as many prerogatives as possible over state promotion of industrialization.

The most fundamental incongruence, however, stemmed from the fact that the financial and structural difficulties of promoting local industrialization compelled presidents to postpone providing social welfare. This gradually divided presidential loyalties between commitment to industrialization and attention to the social needs of the popular foundation of presidential authority.

The negative effects of foreign economic relations on the Cardenista presidency's provision of popular welfare and support for progressive social policies became manifest as soon as the national state was politically consolidated. As Table 3.3 indicates, presidential resolutions reflected decreasing emphasis on the distribution of land to peasants as early as 1938. In fact, 1938 was also the year that Cárdenas's presidential support for striking workers began to diminish. Even earlier, in 1937, Cárdenas began to reverse his policy stance of wholehearted support for worker demands and labor union activities when he condemned various strikes.[16] By 1938, a number of strikes were canceled or postponed at the request of either the Cárdenas government or the newly founded, state-supportive labor union, the CTM.[17] As Table 3.4 indicates, the number of strikes dropped precipitously in 1938.

Table 3.3   The Agrarian Reform Under Cárdenas: Land and Peasants Affected by Presidential Resolutions, 1935–1940

Year	Amount of Land (Hectares)	Number of Beneficiaries
1935	1,923,457	110,286
1936	3,985,701	194,427
1937	5,811,893	199,347
1938	3,486,266	119,872
1939	2,223,733	96,480
1940	2,705,885	55,433

Source: Sergio Reyes Osorio, 1974, p. 50. Cited in Nora Hamilton, *The Limits of State Autonomy* (Princeton, Princeton University Press, 1982), p. 237.

This change does not necessarily imply that Cárdenas's diminished support of peasant and labor demands was the product of a conscious presidential shift toward commitment to rapid industrialization and postponement of social welfare. The explanation for Cárdenas's partial reversal of his support to labor and peasant demands lies mainly with international economic and financial pressures imposed on Mexico in retaliation for the Mexican government's expropriation of the foreign-owned petroleum industry.[18] Nora Hamilton argues that external economic pressures exerted

Table 3.4   Strikes, 1934–1940

Year	Strikes
1934	202
1935	642
1936	674
1937	576
1938	319
1939	303
1940	357

Source: Nora Hamilton, *The Limits of State Autonomy* (Princeton: Princeton University Press, 1982), p. 238.

by the petroleum companies and the U.S. government in conjunction with economic and political pressures from the Mexican private sector resulted in the Cárdenas government's "partial abdication of the struggle for labor benefits."[19] In general, the economic problems Mexico faced in the aftermath of the expropriation and the accompanying reductions in state revenues[20] left the Cárdenas government highly vulnerable to pressures directed against the progressive alliance.

Cárdenas did not necessarily undergo some sort of political transformation that led him to abandon his concerns for social justice. However, state commitment to social welfare and redistribution had clearly approached its limits by 1938. At that point, Cardenismo had established a governmentally preeminent presidency.[21] As the ideological and governmental center of the Mexican state, the Cárdenas-constructed presidency condensed governmental authority into the domain of a single actor. One peculiarity of this political formula lay in the fact that the institutional concentration and insulation of governmental authority in the hands of the president was achieved on the basis of mass popular support. The Cardenista presidency promised its popular supporters to protect the revolution from threats inside and outside Mexico. Paradoxically, the Cárdenas government's consolidation of a state that included peasant and labor sectors served as the ideological foundation for the restriction of popular access to presidential decisionmaking.

The contradictions between insulated, centralized presidential authority and the presidential role of protecting the popular revolution were not acutely evident until state-led industrialization began to place stringent expenditure requirements on the state. In its nascent stage in the late 1930s and early to mid-1940s, the first phase of import-substitution industrialization flowered in Mexico in the midst of a favorable international economic climate associated with the outbreak of the Second World War in Europe in 1938. The increased demand for Mexican exports of both primary commodities and manufactured goods breathed life into the process of local industrialization. Increased export earnings proportioned more foreign exchange for the importation of capital goods essential for industrialization[22] (see Table 3.5).

Table 3.5   Geographic Distribution of Mexican Imports (millions of pesos)

Year	Total	U.S.	U.S. as % of Total	Europe	Europe as % of Total
1935	406.1	265.3	65	127.1	31
1940	669.0	527.3	79	91.4	14

Source: Secretariat of Programming and Budget, General Bureau of Statistics (Nacional Financiera, 1977), p. 387. Cited in Nora Hamilton, *The Limits of State Autonomy* (Princeton: Princeton University Press, 1982), p. 201.

Furthermore, during this early phase of industrialization, Mexico's improved foreign exchange situation allowed the government to undertake extensive public investments in agricultural infrastructure, transportation, and communications. Seventy-five percent of these investments were financed through government revenues accruing from the export of goods and services.[23] Two-thirds of the remaining 25 percent of expenditures were covered through internal borrowing, so only a small fraction was financed through external borrowing.[24] Thus, even though all-out state support of labor and peasant demands had significantly diminished by 1938, when Avila Camacho became president in 1940, he encountered few financial or political obstacles to his commitment to rapid, state-led industrialization.

Avila Camacho's turn toward rapid industrialization and away from Cárdenas's emphasis on agrarian reform and workers' rights, facilitated by the call for national unity during the recent petroleum expropriation, encountered few governmental expenditure difficulties. As such, in terms of the increasing presidential ambivalence surrounding Avila Camacho's decision to pursue rapid industrialization, the contradictions between insulated, centralist presidential authority and the president's commitments to the defense of the interests of the masses were less salient from the perspective of public policymaking. The difficult choices as to where and how to obtain governmental revenues to sustain industrialization did not exist in the crisislike circumstances of subsequent years. Furthermore, Mexicans in the 1940s had yet to experience the unequal distributive effects of rapid industrialization. Therefore, popular sectors in Mexican society did not yet associate insulated presidential authority with the maldistributive effects of rapid industrialization.

Cardenista Social Welfare Replaced
by State Support for Private Investors

The Second World War entailed certain disruptions in the Mexican economy and thus stimulated limited planning initiatives by the Avila Camacho government. As early as 1942, Avila Camacho created a Federal Commission for Economic Planning, whose principal role was to provide technical support to the secretariat of the National Economy for coping with the economic and trade disruption caused by world war. According to Article 2 of the decree, the commission was to *analyze* "problems related to obtaining raw materials; the emergency production [of scarce consumer goods]; . . . the orientation of production for the post-war era; inter-American trade; [and] the economic coordination of public and private economic organisms."[25] Clearly, the concept of planning implicit in the creation of the commission was to strengthen private market forces through the technical analysis of the "concrete economic problems created by the war," as Article 1 of the presidential decree stated. The Emergency Economic Committee created one year later by yet another presidential decree was even more indicative of the executive's attempt to create an administrative mechanism charged with reacting to and correcting the effects of world war upon the Mexican economy.[26] Furthermore, although it soon became clear that postwar financial constraints were to have profound and negative effects on Mexican industry, a Commission for National Planning for Peace created in February 1944 was not endowed with any significant goal-based planning authority.[27] Instead, the commission was merely charged with "the study of Mexico's problems in the postwar era"[28] and was clearly conceived as a temporary mechanism whose date of dissolution, according to Article 8, the president would decide.[29]

Unlike his concept of planning, which was reactive to the emergency situations created by world war and transitory in nature, Avila Camacho's creation of state enterprises in heavy industrial sectors indicated a long-term commitment to state promotion of rapid industrialization. Clearly, the state enterprises created in heavy industry were symptomatic of the fact that the parastatal sector was to invest in areas where the private sector was unable or unwilling to invest due to high overhead costs and slow investment returns. This is evident in the following list of heavy industrial enterprises created during the Avila Camacho term:

- Altos Hornos de México, S.A. (steel)
- Fundiciones de Hierro y Acero, S.A. (iron and steel)
- Aceros Esmaltados, S.A. (enameled steel)
- Máquinas-Herramientas, S.A. (machine-tools)
- Productora Ferretera Mexicana, S.A. (iron)
- Industria Eléctrica Mexicana, S.A. (electricity)[30]

Other state enterprises created in the manufacturing and service sectors included:

* Sosa Texcoco, S.A. (sodium products)
* Compañía Nacional Distribuidora y Reguladora, S.A. (national distribution system)
* Cobre de México, S.A. (copper)
* Compañía Carbonífera Unida de Palúa, S.A. (coal)[31]

As Table 3.6 indicates, a total of fifty-one public enterprises and decentralized entities were created within a short six-year period, from 1940 through 1945, compared to a total of fifty-seven entities created over the previous twenty-three years, from 1917 to 1940. This rapid expansion of the parastatal sector reflected extensive state involvement in correcting for lapses in private sector initiative, especially in heavy industrial enterprise, yet the expansion occurred largely in the absence of goal-based planning mechanisms capable of controlling and planning parastatal activities. More formalized yet limited control over public enterprise was not established until 1947, when Miguel Alemán assumed the presidency.[32]

Table 3.6   Creation of Parastatal Entities and Public Enterprises by Period

Period	Enterprises with State Participation	Decentralized Entities	Total
1917–1921	2		2
1921–1930	8	2	10
1930–1933	6		6
1934–1940	29	10	39
1940–1945	37	14	51
1945–1950	30	20	50
1950–1959	65	36	101
1960–1970	105	27	132
Dec. 1970–May 1974	84	21	105
Total	366[a]	130[b]	496

Source: Alejandro Carrillo Castro, *La reforma administrativa en México* (Mexico City: Miguel Angel Porrúa, 1980), p. 215.
Notes: a. Includes 32 enterprises with state participation corresponding to the financial sector.
b. Includes 8 decentralized entities corresponding to the financial sector.

The explosion in the size of the parastatal sector that occurred during the Avila Camacho administration reflected increasing presidential ambivalence, which had not manifested itself to as large an extent during the

Cárdenas era. Whereas the principal changes in the state apparatus during Avila Camacho's presidency occurred in the expansion of parastatal enterprises for state promotion of industrialization, Cárdenas's principal changes in public administration were mainly confined to the creation of new departments in the central administrative sector to implement presidential redistributions of land to peasants. For example, the creation of the Agrarian Department in 1934 and the Office of Presidential Resolutions attached to it was representative of an expansion of the central administrative apparatus for the sole purpose of carrying out the president's directives on agrarian reform. José Fernández Santillán points out that Cárdenas created the Department of Public Health and other departments and secretariats in the area of social services.[33] These changes reflected administrative expansion for the implementation of Cárdenas's policies of support to independent peasant and labor movements and his consolidation of state authority through the inclusion of the popular sectors in the state.

In this respect, President Cárdenas's modest expansion of the central state apparatus in the 1930s had a reinforcing effect on the concentration of state authority in the presidency. New central secretariats were carefully linked directly to the president and were assigned restricted tasks related to presidential directives for distributing land and providing social welfare. In other words, central administrative changes were designed to coordinate the president's role in protecting and supporting agrarian reform and workers' rights. Such changes were obviously linked to the president's defense of the promises of the revolution.

In contrast to the rapid expansion of parastatal involvement in manufacturing and heavy industry by the Avila Camacho government, parastatal development during the Cárdenas years reflected presidential commitments to popular sector concerns. During the years 1934 through 1940, thirty-nine public enterprises and decentralized public entities were created, generally reinforcing the president's politics of the masses. Juan Felipe Leal documents that the following major entities were created: Petróleos de México (1935); Petróleos Mexicanos, S.A.–PEMEX (1937); the Board of Civilian Pensions and Retirement (1933); Federal Commission of Electricity, Inc. (1937); Mexican Export-Import Company, Inc.–CEIMSA (1937), today CONASUPO (Staple Products); National Railroads of Mexico, Inc. (1937); and Mexican Insurance, Inc. (1937).[34]

The creation of PEMEX, of course, was later linked to the petroleum expropriation, which followed in 1938, and was therefore part of the process of postrevolutionary nation-state consolidation. Most of the other parastatals that came into existence were either of the popular-subsidy type or represented attempts to gain greater national control over strategic industries such as electricity or transportation. In contrast, Avila Camacho's expansion of parastatals in heavy industry and in manufacturing in general were more clearly destined to foment rapid industrialization irrespective of the implications for state spending on popular welfare. This rather abrupt change in presidential orientation coincided with substantial reductions in governmental support for worker and peasant demands.

In terms of state support of the peasantry, for example, the Avila Camacho administration clearly favored policies that supported small and medium-sized private agricultural producers,[35] a shift from the previous Cárdenas norm of support to collective farms (*ejidos*) through distribution of land to peasants; increased credit facilities for the *ejido;* and emphasis on increasing the productivity of collective agriculture.[36] By the end of the 1940s, the average amount of capital invested per capita by the state on *ejido* agriculture had remained constant at 735 pesos, while state investment per capita on private agriculture had risen to an average of 1,164 pesos.[37] Furthermore, between 1940 and 1946, distribution of land to peasants diminished from the level of almost 20 million hectares distributed under Cárdenas to nearly 6 million hectares under Avila Camacho.[38] Finally, state-owned agricultural credit banks shifted emphasis toward funneling loans to support more profitable private agriculture rather than to increase the productivity of the *ejido.* As a consequence, collective farm production as a percentage of total national agricultural production decreased from 50 percent in 1940 to 37 percent by the end of the decade.[39]

The Avila Camacho government also abruptly shifted state orientations away from a prolabor to a proindustrialist stance. This shift did less damage to the popular ideology surrounding the Cárdenas presidency than might otherwise have been the case had World War II not provided the appropriate backdrop for the Avila Camacho government to adopt antilabor stances. The government sent out a call to both workers and employers for national unity against foreign intrusions and the external chaos associated with the war in Europe.[40] Furthermore, at President Avila Camacho's urging, central union organizers set out to subordinate the labor movement incorporated into the recently formed Confederation of Mexican Workers (CTM) to presidential political dominance.[41] According to Alejandro Carrillo Castro, the result of this effort was the emergence of an authoritarian type of corporatist relationship between the state and organized labor, which expressed itself most clearly in the Pact of Labor Unity (Pacto de Unidad Obrera) signed in 1942. In signing this pact, 90 percent of all organized workers agreed to the following:

1. To submit interunion disputes to the Secretary of Labor who was recognized as arbiter;
2. To suspend all strikes and accept arbitration in their place; and
3. To permit that a member of another union not having control of a determined shop or factory to work in said shop or factory upon having made arrangements with the union in control there.[42]

The Avila Camacho administration's ability to withdraw state support for workers' and peasants' demands and still retain the mass-based component of presidential authority is partly explainable in terms of the outside threat posed by world war and the character of the particular phase of industrialization that was undertaken in 1940. The horizontal import-substitution industrialization (ISI) that accelerated in Mexico in response to the increased demand for Mexican exports at the outset of World War II constituted the beginning of the first, easy phase of import substitution. Horizontal ISI involved the expansion of local production of previously imported nondurable consumer goods by local entrepreneurs.[43] Because investments in the nondurable consumer goods sector did not involve high start-up costs or technology that was beyond the capital limitations of local entrepreneurs, horizontal ISI set out to enhance the industrial strength of local producers.[44]

In this sense, ISI phase one constituted an economic nationalist industrialization project to increase local accumulation of industrial wealth. As such, it differed substantially from the foreign-controlled export economy and import dependence of the Porfiriato. Such economic nationalist industrialization helped reinforce the president's claim that his role was to protect the revolution inside Mexico by defending local producers from economic competition posed by foreign producers outside Mexico.[45] Although the industrialization project initiated by Avila Camacho clearly relegated social welfare to a secondary priority, the government's rejection of Mexico's export enclave status, which had characterized the Porfiriato, rallied nationalist, popular support from organized labor. To a certain extent, then, horizontal ISI shared some of the same symbolic attributes as the petroleum expropriation of 1938. Even though the president called on the popular sectors to sacrifice wage increases in order to reduce dependence on foreign producers, the president's objective of enhancing national control over local productive activities reinforced the popular consensus achieved during the Cárdenas era. That consensus relied in part on the presidency's claims to be a powerful, centralized governmental defense of prosperity and social equity inside Mexico vis-à-vis threats to such revolutionary goals from outside Mexico.[46]

Avila Camacho easily expanded state investment in manufacturing, extended public incentives to private investors, and withdrew state support for workers and peasants demands without disturbing the popular ethos and myth surrounding the presidency. This ease diminished, however, after the war ended in 1945. When Avila Camacho's successor, Miguel Alemán, became president in 1946, he did not inherit the same advantageous financial environment of the Avila Camacho years when increased Mexican exports provided foreign exchange for industrialization purposes. Instead, Alemán attempted to sustain horizontal import substitution in the face of declining demand for Mexico's exports after the war.[47] As a result of the continuing need to import machinery and raw materials for industrialization (see Table 3.7), both the rate of growth of gross national product and the value of the peso fluctuated, which interfered with the postwar adjustment process. In 1947, for example, GNP grew by only 1.2 percent,[48] and the value of the peso fluctuated in 1948 and 1949 until it was fixed at 8.65 pesos per dollar.[49]

Table 3.7 Balance of Trade (millions of pesos)

Year	Exports (1)	Imports (2)	Balance (1)–(2)
1940	960	669	291
1941	730	915	−185
1942	990	753	237
1943	1,130	910	220
1944	1,047	1,895	−848
1945	1,272	1,604	−332
1946	1,915	2,631	−716
1947	2,162	3,230	−1,068
1948	2,661	2,951	−290
1949	3,623	3,527	96
1950	4,339	4,403	−64
1951	5,447	6,773	−1,326
1952	5,126	6,394	−1,268
1953	4,836	6,985	−2,149
1954	6,936	8,926	−1,990
1955	9,484	11,046	−1,562
1956	10,671	13,395	−2,724
1957	8,729	14,439	−5,170
1958	8,846	14,107	−5,261
1959	9,007	12,583	−3,576
1960	9,247	14,831	−5,584

Source: Enrique Padilla Aragón, *México: Hacia el crecimiento con distribución del ingreso* (Mexico City: Siglo XII, 1981), pp. 14–15.

The financial difficulties of the postwar era took their toll on the presidency's defense of popular welfare while the executive attempted to sustain the rate of economic growth. Compared to the reductions in state support of peasant and worker demands by the Avila Camacho government, the Alemán administration's abandonment of mass social welfare was considerably greater. The total amount of land distributed to peasants, for example, dropped even further below that distributed under Avila Camacho (see Table 3.8), whereas the government's support to commercial agriculture

significantly increased.[50] The presidency's abandonment of a concerted
defense of peasant welfare meant that the popular support and consensus
achieved by Cárdenas was to be sustained on the basis of presidential
claims to be defending the national-territorial promotion of industrial
wealth, in spite of the possible maldistribution of such wealth.[51]

**Table 3.8   Ejidal and Communal Property: Signed and Published Presidential
Resolutions (1935–1978)**

President	Period	Number of Resolutions	Land Area	Beneficiaries
L. Cárdenas	1935–1940	11,334	20,145,910	764,888
M. Avila Camacho	1941–1946	3,074	5,970,398	122,941
M. Alemán	1947–1952	2,245	5,439,528	108,625
A. Ruiz Cortines	1953–1958	1,745	5,771,721	226,292
A. López Mateos	1959–1964	2,375	9,308,149	289,356
G. Díaz Ordaz	1965–1970	3,912	23,055,619	374,590
L. Echeverría	1971–1976	2,274	12,017,050	218,918
J. López Portillo	1977–1979	590	1,468,892	42,795

Source: Developed by the Dirección General de Análisis de Ramas Económicas, Secretaría de
Programación y Presupuesto, based on data from the Secretaría de la Reforma Agraria. Cited
in Gloria Brásdefer, "La empresa pública y el sector social de la economía," *Revista de la
Administración Pública,* nos. 59–60 (July–December 1984): 121.

President Alemán's commitment to labor was almost as tenuous as his
commitment to peasants, although more disguised via the state's corporatist
control over organized labor. According to José Fernández Santillán, the
secretariat of labor became the center of the resolution of all disputes
between workers and employers during Alemán's administration.[52]

Collective bargaining via the bureaucratic channels provided by the
state through the secretariat of Labor became the principal means of avoid-
ing strikes and of tempering labor demands.[53] Specific labor demands for
housing, health benefits, and social security were channeled through newly
created state organisms for the provision of such worker benefits. The
Mexican Institute for Social Security created in 1944 listed 631,000 persons as eligible for benefits at the beginning of the Alemán *sexenio* in
1946. That number had only increased to 1,155,000 persons by 1952, when
Avila Camacho left office.[54] This meant that slightly more than 4 percent
of the population was eligible for social security by 1952. As with other
sources of public provision of basic popular sector needs, however, the fact
that a state institution for social security existed at all was a symbol of hope
for future eligibility or obtainment of basic needs, such as housing.

In annual presidential addresses, Alemán went to great lengths to remind the general populace of his government's contributions to schools, hospitals, and other social services, even though such public provisions were minimal in terms of money actually spent. As Table 3.2 indicated, the percentage of total federal government expenditures on social welfare dipped to 13.3 percent, the lowest point since 1929, when the depression hit Mexico. Table 3.9 provides a clear indication of the Alemán government's diminished support for the creation of cooperative industry designed to alleviate unemployment and poverty.

Table 3.9   Cooperatives Registered by Presidential *Sexenio* **(1938–1982)**

President	Period	Registrations
L. Cárdenas	1938–1940[a]	1,527
M. Avila Camacho	1941–1946	1,326
M. Alemán	1947–1952	747
A. Ruiz Cortines	1953–1958	460
A. López Mateos	1959–1964	392
G. Díaz Ordaz	1965–1970	296
L. Echeverría	1971–1976	1,862
J. López Portillo	1977–1982[b]	3,642

Source: Developed by CENIET, based on the National Register of Cooperatives, Secretaría del Trabajo y Previsión Social. Cited in Gloria Brásdefer, "La empresa pública y el sector social de la economía," *Revista de la Administración Pública,* no. 59–60 (July–December 1984): 122.
Notes: a. Since the creation of the National Register of Cooperatives.
b. Data to July 31, 1982.

PRI Presidents Entrust State Intervention to the Treasury: The Myth of National Economic Planning and Policies of Public Subsidy to Private Investors

Beyond Miguel Alemán's attempt to *appear* committed to the provision of basic social needs, the presidency's creation and administration of the parastatal sector strongly indicated that the president's main objectives were to use insulated, presidential authority to support private industrial development. Alejandro Carrillo Castro notes that, from 1945 through 1959, fifty-one more public enterprises and decentralized public entities were created, especially in heavy industrial sectors, such as

• Industria Petroquímica Nacional, S.A., 1949 (petrochemicals)
• Diesel Nacional, S.A., 1951 (diesel trucks)
• Constructora Nacional de Carros de Ferrocarril, 1952 (train cars).[55]

As president, Miguel Alemán made a visible attempt to continue to create parastatal enterprises to sustain the momentum of industrial growth, even in the face of a declining export sector with resulting public revenue restrictions and balance-of-payment difficulties (see Table 3.7). The president's drive to promote sustained industrialization even in the face of financial difficulties led to the passage in 1947 of the first Law for the Control of Decentralized Organisms and Enterprises of Public Participation. This landmark administrative change entrusted control of the entire parastatal sector to the Finance secretariat. It was a direct result of presidential insistence on the need to sustain industrial growth in the face of external-structural obstacles. Hence, the origins of the Finance secretariat's immense control over the Mexican public sector lay with the political resolve of the presidency to sustain industrial growth in spite of increased international financial obstacles when the Second World War ended. The economic nationalist pursuit of local industrialization reflected Alemán's attempt to circumvent nationally the international constraints on Mexico's industrial development. Miguel Alemán's decision to entrust parastatal control to the Treasury reflected his own resolve to industrialize Mexico in spite of the obstacles stemming from the country's disadvantageous position in world financial and trade relations.

Article 5 of the control law specified that the Finance secretariat was to control and monitor the parastatal sector with the objective "of procuring its correct economic functioning" by means of permanent examination and verification of financial accounts and inspections. More specifically, Article 5 entrusted Finance with the following:

   I. Solicitation of financial reports;
  II. Revision, veto, or reform of annual budgets and plans of operation and investment
 III. The practice of all types of audits (pre- and postaudits); criticism of accounts and revision of balances
  IV. The verification of all receipts prior to disbursement [of funds]; . . . the authority to cancel any purchases not conforming to the budget, to the plan, to the agreements of directive committees or to applicable legislation; or [to cancel] purchases that might damage the economy
   V. The promotion of organizational and functional changes [in the parastatal sector]
  VI. The assumption of the responsibilities related to the management and operation of the goods of decentralized organisms and public enterprises
 VII. The authorization or the cancellation of credits to [parastatal] institutions[56]

Beyond these extensive financial and monitoring authorities, Article 8 authorized Finance to propose a general plan of operations for parastatals to be submitted to the Federal Executive for approval. Once approved, this plan was to govern all parastatal investment activity. Furthermore, Article

12 authorized the Finance secretariat to liquidate or reorganize parastatal entities that Finance officials deemed unnecessary for public purposes or duplicative of private activity. Article 16 established that each parastatal entity's annual expenditure budget be approved by Treasury, and Article 18 stated that any parastatal activity not authorized by Treasury was prohibited. In short, Treasury took on the role of revenue-based planning for virtually all parastatal activities in lieu of a de jure, goal-based planning secretariat.[57]

The control law also specified that Treasury be allowed to create the agency that would serve as the liaison between the Finance secretariat and the sixty-nine extant parastatals and implement the control law itself. On December 31, 1947, the liaison mechanism was decreed to be the National Commission of Investments. Formally, at least, this separate commission—created by and dependent on the Secretaría de Hacienda y Crédito Público—was charged with the control, monitoring, and coordination functions specified by the control law. The commission was to have twelve regular members: six from the Finance secretariat; two from the Bank of Mexico; two from Nacional Financiera, and two from Bienes Nacionales e Inspección Administrativa.[58] The secretary of the Treasury (Finance) was named president of the commission.[59] Finally, the Treasury had authority to veto any agreements reached by a plenum of five members of the commission.

Given these facts, it is clear that Miguel Alemán entrusted Hacienda with full control over the parastatal sector in 1947. The Treasury's enhanced responsibility for parastatals further reduced the presidency's ability to use the parastatal sector to promote social welfare. While attempting to cultivate the image of an administration committed to the provision of basic social needs, President Alemán placed Hacienda in control of the financial affairs of the very parastatal agencies that intervened in the economy and provided limited social welfare. The president's decision to rely on Hacienda for the financial and planning control of the public sector marked the formal incorporation and institutionalization of private investor interests as major components of the decisionmaking calculus on public spending.

When Alemán designated Hacienda as an extension of presidential control over the parastatal sector, he set up within the state apparatus a formal authority identified and compromised with the economic ideology and financial constraints of world capitalism. In concert with the ideology of economic liberalism and the financial restrictions of the global economy, the presidency relied on Hacienda to perform the role of financial policeman for the public sector. As the financial sheriff for the public sector, Treasury's enormous financial authority provoked the formation of a group of opposing state personnel critical of the all-encompassing, privatist-oriented financial vetoes exercised by Treasury.[60] Although the control law of

1947 did not immediately destroy the president's popular image of protecting the poor, the law did create antagonism within the state apparatus separating those state personnel associated with the coordination of parastatal investment from the financial sheriffs in Hacienda. Such antagonism was institutionalized by President López Mateos in 1958.[61]

When President Ruiz Cortines replaced Miguel Alemán in 1952, the presidency's reliance upon Treasury's control over the steadily expanding parastatal sector deepened as postwar inflationary pressures intensified and export opportunities diminished.[62] The resulting drop in foreign exchange reserves triggered a devaluation of the peso in 1954.[63] The internal and external borrowing[64] used to finance public extension of credit for the maintenance of rapid industrialization during the Alemán years eventually contributed to a form of inflationary growth, which faltered by 1954. Furthermore, the temporary increase in demand for Mexican exports spurred on by the Korean War ended, triggering a severe recession in Mexico after the war ended.[65] The resulting balance-of-payments pressures provoked a 50 percent devaluation of the peso in 1954, the year most scholars agree marked the end of the era of horizontal import-substitution industrialization. After that point, President Ruiz Cortines set his sights on alleviating recurrent balance-of-payments problems, inflationary pressures, and problems of public revenue scarcity by shifting to a strategy of heavier, vertical import-substitution industrialization.

This new strategy emphasized the local production of durable consumer goods and of capital and intermediate goods in order to reduce the balance-of-payments shortfalls produced by the importation of such producer goods.[66] Vertical ISI also involved imposing tariff barriers and quantitative restrictions on imports of manufactured items to protect local manufacturing industries.[67] Since the industries favored by ISI Phase Two were more technologically sophisticated and capital-intensive[68] than industries associated with horizontal ISI phase one, vertical ISI led to greater Mexican reliance on transnational corporations with the requisite capital and technology. Ruiz Cortines geared public policy to provide investor incentives designed to attract transnational corporate investment in manufacturing.[69] Vertical ISI was designed to reduce reliance on imported durable consumer goods and intermediate and capital goods. Such objectives were indicative of a revised, economic-nationalist strategy seeking to enhance local industrial production within the territorial confines of the national state.

However, the vertical phase implied greater reliance on foreign capitalist enterprise and therefore had an undeniably internationalist or foreign-oriented face. It was also divorced from the welfare interests of Mexico's poorest populace. Ruiz Cortines's general orientation toward the popular sectors was to avoid what were deemed inflationary wage increases and, instead, to rely on public sector enterprises and subsidies to provide a limited amount of basic welfare.[70] As is apparent in Table 3.2, the percentage of total government expenditures dedicated to social concerns increased only slightly from its all-time low point under the previous administration of Miguel Alemán.

This modest increase in emphasis on parastatal provision of social welfare was part of the new growth strategy called stabilizing growth (*desarrollo estabilizador*) formulated by the Treasury and the Bank of Mexico[71] and officially adopted by the government of Ruiz Cortines in 1954. Although the new strategy was not really fully under way until 1960, stabilizing growth increased the presidency's reliance on Treasury's financial control over public sector activities and prompted two fairly immediate, formal administrative changes. The first change was instituted by Ruiz Cortines on October 29, 1954—the same year that the new economic growth strategy was announced. An Investment Commission was created and linked directly to the Office of the President, who charged the commission with the following planning tasks for the parastatal sector:

    I.   The study of investment projects with the objective of evaluating . . . the particular importance of each project in *economic and social* terms [emphasis added]
   II.   The realization of necessary economic studies in order to establish— in a manner coordinated with the objectives of economic, fiscal, and social policy—the quantification and role that public investments are to play in the comprehensive development of the country
  III.   The presentation of a coordinated plan of public investments for consideration by the Federal Executive
  IV.   The suggestion, to the Executive, of changes that should be made in said plan, with attention to needs that occur as a consequence of the appearance of new economic facts[72]

Article 1 of the official "agreement" mandated a director and four members chosen by the director. According to Articles 4 and 5, all secretariats, departments, decentralized entities, and public enterprises were obligated to inform the commission of all past and projected investments. The commission was to submit its judgments concerning projected investments to the president, who was designated as the ultimate arbiter in the execution of each investment project. Perhaps the most significant specification, however, was Article 6, which stated:

> In order for the Secretariat of Hacienda to authorize disbursement [of funds] related to public investments, requests for authorization had to attach the Investment Commission's *opinion* [of the expenditure/project].[73] (Emphasis added)

The creation of the Investment Commission was the first major indication of an emergent presidential dilemma regarding control over the parastatal sector. Given the fact that the parastatal sector alone contained more than a hundred entities by 1954, the president's insistence on retaining ultimate decisionmaking authority over all public investments was administratively absurd. Not only were parastatal investments to be approved ultimately by the president, but so were the expenditure programs of all the secretariats and departments of state. By 1954, there were thirteen secretariats and three departments within the federal executive. To propose that all parastatal expenditure programs be approved by the presidency signified a centralization of decisionmaking authority that was, practically speaking, unworkable.

Given the presidency's inability to weigh each expenditure decision, the Treasury's authorization of fund disbursements became the de facto mechanism for controlling public expenditures. The fact that solicitations for funds merely had to include the commission's *opinion* did not imply that the commission or the president exercised consistent spending authority. In fact, given the administrative inadequacies of both the commission and the presidency, only the Finance secretariat contained sufficient technical personnel and expertise for monitoring all public expenditures.[74] Miguel Wionczek summarizes the four years of the functioning of the Investment Commission during the term of Ruiz Cortines as indicative of both presidential deference to Treasury and the persistent presidential attempt to retain a certain veto authority over parastatals:

> [The Investment Commission] . . . did not constitute a national office of planning . . . because the initiative for setting goals for all of the economy did not originate with it. Nor did it have powers to formulate a national plan of investment for the long run. The Commission was principally an intermediary between . . . Hacienda, the principal source of financial resources, and all the final recipients of funds, be they secretariats of State, or autonomous organisms and public enterprises. The Commission never attempted to become a supersecretariat with jurisdiction over other secretariats nor did it pretend to absorb from Hacienda the function of fixing the global level of income and public expenditure, or act as final custodian and distributor of public funds. It constituted a guardian of the public interest only in the sense that it enjoyed veto power over the global investment programs of parastatals.[75]

The president's halfhearted creation of a de jure planning capability in the form of an Investment Commission was indicative of a presidency torn between the drive to retain as much decisionmaking authority as possible and the opposite presidential motivation to defer to the technical-financial expertise of Treasury in order to sustain industrialization under difficult financial circumstances. The direct attachment of a commission to the presidency for the purpose of planning and monitoring public expenditures was an attempt to minimize technical advice on investment decisions while also channeling ultimate decisionmaking authority to the president. Wionczek describes the birth of the Investment Commission as the result of a presidency seeking to sustain an image or myth of absolute presidential authority while in reality deferring to the Treasury for the determination of public expenditures:

> The functioning of the Investment Committee [created in 1947 to monitor parastatal investment] under the control of multiple secretariats and federal agencies, [*but principally* under the control of] . . . Hacienda, created, on the one hand, political friction with the rest of the agencies [outside Hacienda] and, on the other hand, limited the freedom of action [in Treasury's capacity as supreme arbiter of public expenditure] of . . . Hacienda itself. As a consequence of these inconveniences, a proposal to transfer the Committee . . . to the presidential offices was made, based . . . upon the argument that planning . . . investments of the entire public sector was an affair of such transcendence that it went beyond the sphere of competence . . . of . . . Hacienda and . . . should be carried out at the highest level possible . . . : the presidency of the Republic. In this way, largely for political reasons, the Investment Commission was born.[76]

Presidential insistence on a minimalist skeleton of a planning infrastructure essentially left Treasury as the only secretariat administratively equipped to monitor public expenditure. Hence, Treasury became the de facto planner and controller of all public investment. Therefore, while the structural features of peripheral industrialization encouraged Treasury's technical sway over expenditure decisions, *the political-cultural myth of the all-powerful PRI presidency and the implicit political liabilities of Mexican presidents vis-à-vis popular sectors* motivated the construction of a skeletonlike, goal-based planning authority separate from the Treasury. The formal separation of a planning entity from the Treasury symbolized the popular-nationalist face of the presidency, which insisted on absolute authority for the chief executive and a popular, social welfare aura for economic decisionmaking.

Mounting Criticism of
"National Economic Planning"

The Investment Commission did not challenge the Treasury's control of parastatal enterprise and the Treasury's privatist pursuit of what was labeled "national economic planning" in the 1950s principally because President Ruiz Cortines fully accepted the Treasury's program of stabilizing growth. As long as the president agreed that the orthodox monetary and fiscal rules of the strategy were essential to the maintenance of industrial growth, the commission's nominal, goal-based planning function remained subordinate to Treasury's strict, revenue-based control over public spending. Nevertheless, the creation of the Investment Commission was a symptom of an emerging presidential dilemma: The Treasury's control over the parastatal sector contradicted the presidency's all-powerful, social welfare–oriented image. Increasing presidential reliance on Treasury's corps of financial experts, who advocated fiscal and economic policies favoring foreign investors and strict control over public spending on social welfare, directly contradicted the rhetoric of the revolutionary presidency.

The idea that presidential ambivalence had been mounting in an administrative sense over the years since industrialization commenced in 1940 became even more apparent in 1958. Before Ruiz Cortines left office at the end of 1958, increasing state repression of the labor movement resulted in a profound political crisis inherited by the succeeding administration of Adolfo López Mateos. To offset the negative political effects of Ruiz Cortines's violent repression of the independent railroad workers' strike, López Mateos claimed to govern "on the extreme left within the Constitution."[77] As Table 3.2 indicates, the percentage of total government expenditures destined for social functions increased from 14.4 percent under Ruiz Cortines to 19.2 percent under López Mateos. Expenditures on economic areas dropped, on the other hand, from 52.7 percent under Ruiz Cortines to 39 percent under López Mateos. More important politically than this modest increase in social expenditure, however, were the president's symbolic gestures toward labor and the verbal confrontations between the government and members of the private sector.[78] The revitalization of the presidency's popular image was critical during the López Mateos years (1958–1964), since these were the years when vertical import substitution was initiated on the basis of a burgeoning foreign corporate direct investment. An influx of new transnational corporations in the manufacturing sector occurred at the end of the López Mateos term after most of the state–private sector confrontations had subsided.[79]

Evidence indicating that López Mateos's gestures toward the popular sectors were more rhetorical than real is suggested by the fact that while in 1950, 50 percent of the population claimed 19.1 percent of national income, during 1963 and 1964, immediately before López Mateos left office, 50 percent of the population received 15.7 percent and 15 percent of national income, respectively.[80] Clearly, vertical import substitution concentrated wealth in the hands of fewer and fewer people during the years of López Mateos's symbolic restoration of the popular presidential image. In 1950, 20 percent of the Mexican populace with the highest incomes received 59.8 percent of the national income, whereas in 1963 that percentage had increased to 62.6 percent of national income.[81]

There were certain increments in the percentage of public investment dedicated to social concerns, as Table 3.10 indicates.

Table 3.10   Sectoral Distribution of Public Investment in Mexico: 1959–1963
(percentages)

Type of Public Investment	1959–1961	1962–1963
Basic development	80.0	71.3
Agriculture	9.0	9.5
Electric energy; petroleum	33.8	31.0
Transportation; communication	33.8	26.4
Others	3.4	4.4
Social investment	17.8	25.4
Administration/defense	2.2	3.3
Total	100.0	100.0

Source: Secretaría de la Presidencia, México, inversión pública federal, 1925–1963, Mexico
City, 1964.

The central administrative changes made by the Adolfo López Mateos
administration in 1958 evoked a presidency increasingly pressured to sustain a myth of presidential power and concern for popular social welfare as
a counterweight to the realities of the presidency's administrative reliance
on the Treasury, a secretariat whose social "scientific" recommendations
were derived from liberal economic principles tied to foreign investors'
economic ideology and interests. In the spirit of this presidential myth, on
December 24, 1958, López Mateos created a separate secretariat formally
entrusted with nominal authority to plan public investment and public
expenditure. The Law of Secretariats and Departments of State replaced the
previous Investment Commission with the new secretariat of the
Presidencia and changed the name of the secretariat of National Goods
(Bienes Nacionales) to that of Patrimonio Nacional (National Properties).
    Bienes Nacionales was originally created during the term of Miguel
Alemán in 1946 and entrusted with, among other tasks, "the coordination
of administrative improvement of [parastatal] dependencies; the study of
macro-organization; the suggestion to the Chief Executive of . . .
measures for the improvement of public administration; and consultation
[regarding parastatal activities] . . . with other governmental entities."[82]
The control law of 1947 that formalized Treasury's monopoly of control
over parastatal activity clearly relegated Bienes Nacionales to a secondary,
consultative role. José Fernández Santillán indicates that the change of
name in 1958 did little to alter the secretariat's relatively weak authority
over parastatal investment.[83] The creation of the new secretariat of the
Presidencia by the same law, however, involved the formal investiture of
planning authority over parastatal investment and public expenditure more

generally to the new secretariat. More specifically, Presidencia was charged with:

II. The collection of data for the elaboration of the general plan of public expenditures and investments
III. The planning of [public investment] projects . . . ; the projection of regional and local development as *indicated by the President* [emphasis added]
IV. Coordination of investment planning of all the diverse public entities
V. The planning and monitoring of public investment, [including] that of decentralized organisms and public enterprises[84]

The establishment of Presidencia as a planning secretariat separate from Hacienda marked the introduction into the state apparatus of an administrative skeleton of goal-based planning. Unlike the Investment Commission, Presidencia was not conceived as an intermediary between Hacienda and all the various secretariats and public entities receiving federal funds. The emergent administrative rivalry of Presidencia and Treasury became a clear indication of the incompatibilities of the political culture characterizing the presidency as opposed to the liberal economic influence of Treasury. The creation of a de jure, goal-based planning secretariat parallel to the revenue-based planning performed de facto by the Treasury snowballed into an administrative dilemma that was replicated and magnified through multiple administrative changes during the 1960s and 1970s.

Rhetorically, Presidencia had goal-based planning authority but in practice was not invested with sufficient public spending authority to actually plan public investment. The president's reluctance to entrust Presidencia with goal-based planning tasks was revealed in the design of the secretariat. The new secretariat's two main planning tasks were divided between two, separate subagencies contained within the secretariat. The old Investment Commission was incorporated into Presidencia and ostensibly charged with public investment planning, and a separate Directorate of Planning was presumably charged with planning public spending. The net effect of this division of labor was to deflate the spending authority of the new Directorate of Planning and consequently weaken Presidencia vis-à-vis the Treasury.

The Directorate of Planning, which clearly had the more all-encompassing task of planning expenditures, was *not* granted administrative superiority to the Investment Commission, but instead was given equal hierarchical standing.[85] In this way, the president's symbolic authority over economic and social policy was not threatened by a powerful Directorate of Planning, and Treasury's financial control over public spending was left intact. Presidencia was seemingly never invented or designed to challenge Treasury's revenue-based planning decisions, even though the rhetoric of goal-based planning nominally constituted the new secretariat's formal responsibilities.

From the standpoint of the president, deference to Treasury rather than Presidencia control over public expenditure and investment was the lesser of two evils, particularly during the 1960s, when Treasury's orthodox economic prescriptions appeared to be responsible for Mexico's high economic growth rates. In contrast to the 1960s, the financial difficulties of the early postwar era of the late 1940s and 1950s discouraged presidents from planning public spending according to social welfare goals rather than according to revenue restrictions. Miguel Alemán and Ruiz Cortines relied on Treasury as the financial sheriff for the public sector in order to promote industrialization and expand state enterprise during a period of financial crisis and economic stagnation. By the 1960s, however, economic growth rates reached "miracle" levels, and presidents were apparently more unwilling than unable to entrust a secretariat with de jure planning capabilities, as economic growth under Treasury tutelage reached the unprecedented levels shown in Table 3.11.

Overall, the sixties was a decade of increasing contradictions in the PRI presidency's orientations toward "national economic planning." The economic growth of the 1960s and the continuing expansion of the parastatal sector did increase the number of public enterprises over which Presidencia had nominal planning authority, but PRI presidents maintained Presidencia as an inoperative appendage of the office of the chief executive rather than an independent mechanism for meaningful goal-based planning of public investment. Treasury, of course remained de facto national planner throughout the decade even though formal increments in authority to Presidencia continued to occur.

From its inception in 1958, Presidencia was not given a separate secretarial budget allocation but was instead subsumed within the budget of the office of the chief executive until 1973, when President Luis Echeverría separated the accounts. Table 3.12 provides an indication of the differences in secretarial budgets within the state apparatus. Treasury's large budget expenditures are indicative of an older, more extensive administrative infrastructure in comparison to either Presidencia or Patrimonio Nacional. The maintenance of such a skeleton planning agency appended to the presidency and overwhelmingly dominated by Treasury's financial checks over public spending was, by the 1960s, a lesser evil sustained by a presidency intent on maintaining both rapid economic growth as well as the appearance of having ultimate decisionmaking authority and power, the latter being the hallmark of the Cardenista presidency.

Presidencia was essentially denied the authority to plan public expenditure because PRI presidents accepted orthodox, macroeconomic policies and administrative dependence on the Treasury. However, the existence of the administrative skeleton of a goal-based planning authority had the long-term impact of encouraging the presidency to attempt to reassert presidential leverage over Treasury by incrementally adding to the formal authority

Table 3.11   GDP, 1940–1970 (millions of pesos)

Year	Current Peso	1960 Peso
1940	7,774	46,693
1941	8,701	51,241
1942	10,066	54,116
1943	12,285	56,120
1944	17,719	60,701
1945	19,382	62,608
1946	26,322	66,722
1947	29,237	69,020
1948	31,196	71,864
1949	34,316	75,803
1950	39,736	83,304
1951	51,245	89,746
1952	57,482	93,315
1953	57,172	93,571
1954	69,680	102,924
1955	84,870	111,671
1956	96,996	119,306
1957	111,402	128,343
1958	123,815	135,169
1959	132,669	139,212
1960	150,511	150,511
1961	163,265	157,931
1962	176,030	165,310
1963	195,983	178,516
1964	231,370	199,390
1965	252,028	212,320
1966	280,090	227,037
1967	306,317	241,272
1968	339,145	260,901
1969	374,900	277,400
1970	418,700	296,600

Source: Nacional Financiera, S.A.

of goal-based planners. In a succession of laws altering the formal duties of Presidencia and Patrimonio Nacional, the presidency fueled the assertiveness and technical rivalry of what became a group of reformist technocrats bent on curbing the Treasury's control over public spending and investment as well as over macroeconomic policy orientations in general.

As the decade of the sixties progressed, Presidents López Mateos and Díaz Ordaz ascribed Presidencia and Patrimonio Nacional with increasing, nominal "powers" of planning and control over parastatal entities. These increases in nominal authority reflected a PRI presidency wrestling with the political fallout resulting from Treasury's immense economic decision-

**Table 3.12   Federal Budgetary Expenditures of *Hacienda y Crédito Público,*
Presidencia, and *Patrimonio Nacional* (in millions of pesos),
1958–1979**

Secretariat	1958	1959	1960	1961	1962
Hacienda	343	362	451	492	574
Presidencia[a]	29	67	189	83	118
Patrimonio N.	16	99	178	332	182
Secretariat	*1963*	*1964*	*1965*	*1966*	*1967*
Hacienda	689	733	735	855	960
Presidencia	165	183	139	166	175
Patrimonio N.	200	249	309	308	321
Secretariat	*1968*	*1969*	*1970*	*1971*	*1972*
Hacienda	1,827	2,211	2,418	2,943	4,072
Presidencia	225	280	374	311	177
Patrimonio N.	302	307	373	379	706
Secretariat	*1973*	*1974*[b]	*1975*	*1976*	*1977*
Hacienda	2,509	3,257	5,001	5,266	6,505
Presidencia/SPP[c]	300	323	590	711	2,460
Patrimonio N.	1,162	1,081	1,292	2,099	1,410
Secretariat	*1978*	*1979*			
Hacienda	8,106	9,439			
SPP	3,448	4,095			
Patrimonio N.	2,379	3,602			

Source: Based on data from Nacional Financiera.
Notes: a. From 1958 until 1973, Presidencia's budget was subsumed within the budget of the office of the chief executive. Hence, these are global figures for both.
b. This is the first year in which Presidencia had a budget separate from the office of the presidency.
c. Presidencia was reorganized into the Secretaría de Programación y Presupuesto (SPP) in 1977.

making authority. The presidency was committed to sustaining industrial growth under Treasury tutelage, but was also increasingly robbed of the legitimating popular-nationalist myth surrounding the chief executive. These contradictions gradually split the presidency's corps of economic advisers into rival camps. As the decade wore on, the presidency's political liabilities encouraged Adolfo López Mateos and Díaz Ordaz to ascribe even more formal planning authority to Presidencia and Patrimonio, thereby fostering among officials in these two secretariats a resentment of the Treasury for its control of public spending.

Evidence of growing hostility among technocrats appeared as early as 1962, when President Adolfo López Mateos felt compelled to create a new Intersecretarial Commission to attempt to coordinate and mediate between the functions of Presidencia and Hacienda in national planning and budgeting. The commission was composed of representatives of both secretariats and was formally charged with: "the formulation of national plans for the economic and social development of the country, in the short and long run."[86] The preamble of the agreement made it clear that the commission was established with the explicit purpose of fostering the coordination of planning and budgeting functions performed by Presidencia and Hacienda, respectively. More specifically, Article 3 stated:

> The commission will calculate . . . the amount, structure, and financing of expenditure and of national investment necessary such that the development of the country be realized according to a satisfactory rhythm and in a manner that will make possible the growing improvement of the standards of living of the popular sectors.[87]

In spite of the rhetoric of such lofty goals, the Intersecretarial Commission never convened a meeting.[88]

In the following year, yet another law for the control of the parastatal sector was passed, increasing Presidencia's *formal* control over parastatal investment planning and explicitly defining the functions of Presidencia and Hacienda once again. The revised functions ascribed to Presidencia included, among others:

(a) The intervention in the creation, fusion, and elimination of parastatal entities
(b) The authorization of the contribution of funds, materials, and federal resources for the constitution or increase in the capital or property of parastatals, attentive to the opinion of Patrimonio Nacional[89]

Hacienda, in contrast, was charged with:

(a) The dictation of the general rules governing parastatals in the negotiation and obtaining of credit within or outside the country; and the authorization of parastatals to negotiate and obtain foreign credits or *pagaderos* in foreign currency, and to issue titles or securities likely to be placed on the market
(b) The monitoring of national institutions of credit, insurance, and finance[90]

The Federal Law of Planning was passed in 1963, extolling the virtues of goal-based national planning, but Treasury's overwhelming control over public spending and investment remained unaltered.[91] By virtue of the fact that the Intersecretarial Commission of 1962 had never met, and planning remained within the domain of Treasury's control over credit, a group for the study of administrative reform was formed on April 9, 1965. This group was called the Commission of Public Administration (Comisión de

Administración Pública, or CAP) and was part of the secretariat of the Presidencia. CAP reflected the sentiments of mounting reformist-techno-cratic calls for administrative reform of central secretarial control over pub-lic investment and spending. One year prior to CAP's formation, an article entitled "Administrative Diagnosis of the Federal Government" appeared in the *Revista de Administración Pública* (Journal of Public Administration), deploring the absence of adequate planning mechanisms and maintaining that

> attempts at planning state action have been made; . . . the creation of the Investment Commission (1948), and then the secretariat of the Presidencia are examples of governmental planning initiatives. Nevertheless, . . . the Investment Commission as a consultative mecha-nism to the presidency . . . was formed to plan public investment expendi-tures while excluding current expenditures and the coordination of macro-economic policies; and regarding . . . Presidencia, in spite of having acquired investment duties and incorporated . . . a General Directorate of Planning, because Presidencia was conceded the same rank as the other Federal Dependencies, its planning efficacy was spoiled.[92]

In the same spirit of criticizing the ineffectiveness of "national economic planning" in Mexico, the National School of Economics at the National Autonomous University of Mexico (UNAM) organized a seminar on eco-nomic planning in Cuernavaca approximately two weeks after CAP was formed. The participants[93] consisted of economists and social scientists opposed to the orthodox, stabilizing growth strategy and to the financial control over public spending that such a strategy entailed for Hacienda. Horacio Flores de la Peña, a neo-Keynesian economist and a principal organizer of the seminar, who later became secretary of Patrimonio Nacional during the presidential term of Luis Echeverría, was particularly critical of the Plan of Immediate Action announced by Hacienda in October 1962 and covering the period 1962–1964. In his seminar, Flores de la Peña deplored the plan as having

> a sad history, both in its formulation by a commission [the Investment Commission] that did not operate and in its approval by international credit institutions. The result was that by 1964, a true plan did not yet exist.[94]

He claimed that, instead of an actual plan that adapts production to the necessities of society, Treasury's pseudoplan had as its *only* objective the public provision of incentives to private investors.[95] In other words, the Treasury's revenue-based version of "planning" for the sole purpose of maintaining private investor confidence was deemed pseudoplanning because of its inability to address social welfare needs. Flores de la Peña's concept of national economic planning, as he clearly indicates in his paper, was influenced in part by Paul Baran, Charles Bettelheim, and Oskar Lange, and advocated a major role for public enterprise in accelerating capital accumulation to overcome structural impediments to national wealth.[96]

Conclusion

Manuel Avila Camacho and the next four PRI presidents governing from 1940 until 1970 all sought to sustain the presidential myth created by Lázaro Cárdenas in the 1930s without spending generously on social welfare programs as Cárdenas had. PRI governments accomplished this in three general ways. First, in the midst of world war in 1940, the Avila Camacho administration cultivated the idea that the primary threats to the revolution were located beyond Mexico's borders. Unlike Cárdenas's progressive alliance of workers and peasants who banned together in the name of confronting and defeating enemies of the revolution both inside and outside Mexico, the Avila Camacho administration operated as if there were no political or socioeconomic differences dividing Mexicans and threatening the revolution from within. Based on this assumption of "Mexican homogeneity" and "perpetual revolution" at home, the administration ceased government support to striking workers and drastically reduced land distribution to peasants. The next four PRI administrations duplicated this pattern.

Second, the Avila Camacho administration and the next four PRI administrations adopted an economic nationalist development strategy in order to promote local industrialization. This strategy involved all-out government support for private investors via tax incentives, public subsidies, trade protectionism, and government restraints on wages. From 1940 until 1970, PRI governments justified this development strategy by arguing that rapid industrialization was in the Mexican "national interest" vis-à-vis an uncertain and competitive world economy that threatened to undermine the socioeconomic goals of the revolution. Thus, these PRI governments consistently spent public revenues on incentives to subsidize investors and expanded and employed public enterprise and agencies to do the same. Social welfare provision became a tertiary concern of these PRI governments because, it was argued, the national state's "strength" to promote Mexican industrial viability vis-à-vis an inhospitable world economy had first priority as the most important means of benefiting all Mexicans. By maintaining that state-promoted industrialization would benefit everyone, these administrations reasserted the presidential myth of a state whose strength was being employed for "revolutionary" goals in spite of the fact that public welfare provision dwindled and wealth was increasingly maldistributed.

Third, PRI governments rhetorically characterized their pro–private sector industrialization programs as "national economic planning." Between 1940 and 1970, PRI administrations created agencies and secretariats allegedly in charge of national economic planning, but PRI presidents consistently failed to entrust such entities with actual planning authority. This facade and administrative skeleton of national economic planning reproduced the myth of a strong, progressive state while the Treasury controlled all public spending and investment in the interest of private investors. Through its financial veto on public spending, the Treasury "planned" the budgets of all public enterprises and agencies such that essentially all state economic intervention was under the direction of the Treasury. Under the Treasury's pro–private investment directives, the public sector expanded considerably and gave the appearance of an increasingly strong state, and the state's inoperative national economic planning apparatus helped sustain the Cardenista myth.

All three of these PRI presidential strategies somewhat altered the Cardenista discourse of state sovereignty without disrupting the myth of the PRI presidency as the personification of a perpetually strong, progressive state. From 1940 to 1970, PRI presidents entirely exteriorized the enemies of the revolution and developed an economic nationalist development strategy and a "national planning capacity" ostensibly to confront the external threats posed by the world economy. Whereas Cárdenas's interpretation of sovereignty emphasized perpetual state strength manifested against enemies "inside" and "outside" Mexico, these post-Cárdenas presidents dropped the discourse about state strength vis-à-vis enemies of the revolution inside Mexico. Their assumption that there were no enemies within prevailed until the economic growth fueling industrialization began to fail in the late 1960s and early 1970s.

At the end of the sixties during the final two years of the Díaz Ordaz term (1964–1970), economists and administrative reformers critical of pseudonational economic planning in Mexico grew quite vocal. To a large extent, the inoperative planning secretariat, Presidencia, itself produced some of the principal critics of its own deficiencies. CAP, which consisted of the most vocal group of critics, was part of the Presidencia secretariat. The presidency's creation of Presidencia and failure to entrust it with actual planning clout triggered growing technocratic opposition to the Presidency-Treasury nexus committed to stabilizing growth. Thus, a fundamental schism began to emerge within the executive technocracy. The next chapter examines how this schism undermined the PRI presidency's ability to pursue a coherent strategy of economic development, thus shattering the presidentialist myth of a powerful, progressive state.

4

The State
Sovereignty Myth Shattered

The PRI President Personifies
a Weak State, 1970–1976

The long-accumulated weakness of the PRI presidency vis-à-vis private investors was exposed to public view in the early and mid-1970s. At that time, reformist technocrats temporarily employed the state apparatus to sustain economic growth, which was threatened by a recalcitrant private business community. Presidential weakness was partly a function of decades of prior PRI presidential support for private investors in the interest of promoting local industrialization. In spite of profound presidential weakness, however, reformist technocrats mustered a temporary organizational state strength based on the public sector's expanding share in national investment. Reformist technocrats critical of the Treasury's use of public enterprise for the exclusive promotion of private investment manufactured temporary organizational strength by pumping foreign borrowed funds into state enterprises.

The Patrimonio Nacional reformist technocrats who temporarily empowered the state apparatus contributed to a convulsive political and economic situation for Luis Echeverría by accelerating public spending and pushing economic reforms in defiance of private sector protest, capital flight, and investment strikes. A series of confrontations between the administration and the private sector ensued as Patrimonio technocrats pushed increased public spending and economic reform in defiance of private sector protest. These public-private sector confrontations ultimately exposed and accentuated the PRI presidency's persistent weakness with respect to large-scale private investors as President Echeverría backed down on nearly every administration attempt at economic reform. In the end, the Treasury's previous control over public spending temporarily collapsed, but the president was unable to replace past Treasury economic formulas with a coherent program of economic reform and economic development. This chapter explores how the Treasury's governance of economic affairs collapsed and why this collapse shattered the myth of the PRI presidency as the personification of perpetual state strength.[1]

These important events were triggered by the economic stagnation of 1971. The neo-Keynesian economists in Patrimonio Nacional persuaded the president that the stagnation in Mexican economic growth in 1971 was due to the Treasury's stabilizing growth development strategy. More specifically, reformist technocrats argued that the Treasury's restrictions on public spending and investment were creating an economic slowdown. President Echeverría's 1972 attempt to shift development strategy in response to these arguments revealed a presidency so weak that within the very next year Echeverría revived the Treasury's restrictive monetary policies. As the embodiment of the PRI presidency's weakness vis-à-vis private financiers, the Treasury's restrictive monetary policies reflected the internalization of large-scale, private investor interests within the state. Because the stabilizing growth strategy was so fully dedicated to nurturing private sector investment, it was a logic entirely responsive to large-scale, private profitability. When the stabilizing growth strategy failed to sustain economic growth in the early 1970s, neo-Keynesian reformers in Patrimonio gained sufficient credibility with the president to persuade him to liberate public expenditures and to attempt to initiate a series of economic and social reforms. Deficit spending and economic reform efforts provoked a series of private sector protests and a spate of contradictory economic policies.

When the administration restored restrictive monetary policies in 1973, the executive ceased to make coherent economic policy. Two factors contributed to this loss of policy coherence. First, the Treasury's prior control over public spending collapsed with the advent of neo-Keynesian deficit spending. Once public spending was liberated via foreign public borrowing, public investment in parastatal activities expanded without reference to Treasury's restrictive revenue considerations. Second, the president failed to entrust Presidencia with total authority over the budgetary process, thus preventing Presidencia from fully replacing the Treasury at the apex of public economic decisionmaking. Given the Treasury's loss of spending control and the Presidencia secretariat's lack of budgetary authority, coherent economic decisionmaking collapsed into the implementation of two rival economic strategies that in effect, counteracted each other.

This chapter shows that the demise of coherent economic policy was linked to a rupture in the societal foundations of the PRI presidency's ability to govern.[2] The contradictions in the Echeverría administration's economic policies were symptomatic of an emerging schism in Mexican society divided between large-scale private investors, who were the main beneficiaries of stabilizing growth, and the rest of Mexican society, who benefited least from three decades of state-promoted industrialization.

Businesspeople in Mexico had grown accustomed to a privileged position in the expenditure priorities of the Mexican state and vehemently objected to the proposed shifts in taxing, spending, and industrial policy attempted by the Echeverría administration. Unlike the 1930s, when independent labor and peasant movements allied with President Lázaro Cárdenas challenged Calles's authoritarian dominance of the state, the PRI presidency in the 1970s was primarily threatened by the private business community. The PRI presidency's profound weakness vis-à-vis the private sector revealed itself in the administration's backing down on every major reformist initiative the government attempted. The administration's tendency to waver on reform and its contradictory economic policies shattered the myth that the PRI presidency personified a state perpetually strong enough to defend popular interests.[3]

PRI Presidents Entrust Public Spending to Conservative Technocrats: The Treasury at the Apex of Economic Decisionmaking

The economic ideology of Treasury officials and PRI presidents increasingly coincided with the interests of private investors, particularly internationalized private investors, as the financial difficulties of state-promoted industrialization increased. This extended coincidence of interests was epitomized by the twelve-year tenure of Treasury Secretary Antonio Ortiz Mena, who authored and implemented the strategy of stabilizing growth from 1958 until 1970.[4] This strategy, advanced by orthodox technocrats in both Hacienda and its sister agency, the Bank of Mexico, sought stable, noninflationary economic growth on the basis of orthodox monetary policies. The technical proponents of *desarrollo estabilizador* in the Treasury argued that the Banco de Mexico's tight money policies would reduce inflation and encourage savings that could finance development.[5] In theory, orthodox monetary policy would supposedly increase private savings, which would be channeled through the private banking system. The Bank of Mexico, in turn, would capture a significant amount[6] of these newly available bank funds by setting high marginal reserve requirements for all other private banks.[7] New bank funds captured by the Bank of Mexico could then be transferred to the Treasury in order to finance public expenditures.

In practice, private savings did increase steadily throughout most of the 1960s, the golden age of the stabilizing growth strategy. The continuous expansion of the capital market financed domestic borrowing by both the public sector and private investors.[8] However, some analysts argue that factors other than orthodox monetary policies contributed to the successful functioning of this strategy. For instance, E.V.K. FitzGerald notes that retained corporate profits constituted the largest share of savings accumulated in the private banking system during this decade.[9]

According to FitzGerald, because savings were based on government-sanctioned wage constraints and reinvested corporate profits, it is inaccurate to assert that the lower rates of inflation during the 1960s *directly* stimulated either private investment or savings.[10] In fact, one plausible explanation asserts that the monetary orthodoxy of the Bank of Mexico and the fiscal conservatism of the Treasury inspired higher levels of investor confidence in both domestic and foreign capital.[11] Hence, high rates of saving by corporate investors could have been attributable to investors' confidence in governmental incentives rather than to low inflation rates.[12] Thus, according to Fitzgerald, the polity's capacity to contain wage demands and to safeguard corporate profits from tax increases provides a better explanation of savings and investment. In addition to politically inspired investor confidence, PRI presidents minimized public expenditures in order to match reduced public revenues.[13] In fact, government policies of restricted public spending reflected and reinforced Treasury technocrats' control of both parastatal investment and general public expenditures during the 1960s.

Mexican presidents clearly acquiesced to Treasury's spending controls: They approved of low tax revenues from corporate sources; they consented to minimized pricing policies for the products of state enterprises; and they resisted political temptations to borrow from foreign sources to finance public deficits. In short, PRI presidents approved the Treasury's minimization of three potential sources of increased public revenues: corporate taxes, prices for public sector goods, and public foreign borrowing. All three were minimized by monetary and fiscal authorities. Hacienda technocrats insisted that low tax revenues were necessary because a corporate tax hike would undermine investor confidence, reduce profit rates, and discourage both savings and investment.[14] From 1958 until 1972, PRI presidents consistently accepted the Treasury's orthodox economic arguments that economic growth would decline if corporate profits were heavily taxed and private investors' confidence fell.

The convergence of interest between Hacienda and the largest financial and investor interests in the private sector is unmistakable in the area of government fiscal policy during this period. For approximately two decades (1950–1970), PRI governments barely increased tax pressures in Mexico.[15] When Ruiz Cortines left the presidency in 1958, López Mateos attempted to implement a tax reform designed to raise federal tax pressure from 8 percent of GDP in 1960, to 12 percent in 1965, and then to 16 percent in 1970.[16] Part of the proposed reform included increasing direct taxation of property income by combining personal incomes from multiple sources into a single tax base.[17] In this way, aggregate personal incomes would be more progressively taxed because high incomes would shift into the upper reaches of existing tax schedules.[18]

The key to tax reform in the area of aggregate personal income was the proposed elimination of anonymous forms of holding wealth.[19] The proposed abolition of the *anonimato*,[20] which permitted anonymously held wealth, such as bearer bonds, was critical to the government's ability to increase tax pressures on citizens in the highest income brackets. As FitzGerald notes, however, the tax reform proposed by President López Mateos failed under pressure from private business interests:

> By 1962 business interests had managed to block the reform; in fact under the subsequent Díaz Ordaz regime (1964–70) the direct tax burden was shifted towards earned salaries, and the targets of the López Mateos reform were far from fulfilled—federal tax pressure had only risen to 9% in 1970.[21]

In short, the secretary of Hacienda, Ortiz Mena, persistently argued for maintaining lower tax rates to stimulate investment, and in the societal arena, private business interests succeeded in blocking the president's proposals for tax reform.

The Treasury's policies on corporate profits also converged with the economic interests of large-scale, private investors on the issue of maintaining high rates of corporate investor return. The Mexican profit-sharing decision, touted as López Mateos's personal gift to organized labor in the early 1960s, supports such a contention. The profit-sharing proposal was supposed to allow workers a mandatory share of the profits from the enterprises for which they worked. However, the president chose a Treasury expert on taxes, Hugo B. Margáin,[22] to head the National Profit-Sharing Commission, a tripartite committee of representatives from organized labor, the private sector, and the state. The commission was charged with the task of drawing up a commonly agreed upon profit-sharing arrangement.

Margáin had served as Treasury's director general of the Federal Income Tax Bureau[23] from 1952 to 1959, encompassing those years when *desarrollo estabilizador* was first promulgated. To fend off intense private sector opposition to tax reform proposals, López Mateos decided to pursue a profit-sharing scheme rather than a major tax reform that would redistribute income. With this intention, the president chose a tax technocrat from Hacienda to negotiate the arrangement. As a tax official with an extensive Treasury background, Margáin was relatively acceptable to large-scale investors and was able to minimize private sector protests against the profit-sharing scheme.

According to Susan Kaufman Purcell's study of the Mexican profit-sharing decision, López Mateos made only a symbolic gesture toward organized labor rather than implementing a substantial redistribution of wealth.[24] In fact, Margáin negotiated an arrangement with a net effect of shifting most of the profit-sharing burden to small firms. In accord with the fundamental views of Hacienda and Banco officials regarding the need to safeguard corporate incentives for savings and investments, "the main pre-occupation of the members . . . of the National Profit-Sharing Commission . . . was to elaborate a profit-sharing system . . . that would not prove detri-mental to the investment process."[25] Margáin did counter the private sec-tor's attempt to substitute other wage benefits for profit sharing,[26] but the final profit-sharing scheme was clearly *most* beneficial to Mexico's highly capitalized industries. These largest industries were required to share the bare minimum, a mere 2.8 percent of their profits.[27]

Predictably, the president selected private sector representatives for the commission from among the largest firms in Mexico. Furthermore, the president appointed state technocrats who proved to be most concerned about preserving the investment incentives for these largest enterprises. Composed of such interests, the commission guaranteed that the brunt of the new profit-sharing system fell upon smaller businesses, which compar-atively speaking had to share a much greater percentage of their profits.[28] Treasury's concern to safeguard high rates of profit for the largest firms in Mexico clearly dominated the thinking of the officials on the National Profit-Sharing Commission. Treasury Secretary Ortiz Mena's views on maintaining high levels of corporate profit to promote rapid economic growth severely limited the profit-sharing benefits finally adopted by the commission.

Beyond the defense and implementation of an economic ideology advocating low corporate taxation and high corporate profits, the Treasury profoundly influenced the character of PRI government *spending* in the late 1950s and 1960s. The Treasury employed its clout over fiscal policies and government revenue collection to acquire substantial control over the plan-ning of public expenditures. The convergence of economic ideologies espoused by Treasury officials and large-scale private investors helped the former gain disproportionate governmental influence over public invest-ment and spending.

However, private investors' political support alone was not sufficient to establish the Treasury as the key department controlling public spending. PRI presidents essentially empowered the Treasury to control spending by consenting to low levels of government spending and restrictive wage poli-cies. In other words, PRI presidents clearly sanctioned the overall financial equation whereby domestic banks financed small public sector deficits. Monies from domestic savings channeled from the Bank of Mexico and then to the Treasury were only sufficient to cover public sector borrowing needs because PRI presidents *allowed* the Treasury to minimize public sec-tor spending and deficits.

PRI presidents were governmentally responsible for permitting the

Treasury to minimize welfare expenditures and public investments in order to keep public borrowing needs low.[29] In fact, Miguel Wionczek argued that Hacienda officials and the heads of public agencies had an unspoken understanding about the levels and types of spending requests that the Treasury would tolerate:

> The projects destined to contribute directly to . . . [industrial] development have [long] enjoyed preference over social expenditures. . . .Three areas have always enjoyed . . . the highest priority: irrigation, energy [electricity and petroleum], and communications and transportation. Never in the last twenty years (1940–1960) have they accounted for less than three-quarters of public investment in Mexico. . . . Consequently, *all public entities that competed for federal funds knew, through past experience, what they could expect from . . . Hacienda,* and what request would be considered unreasonable by the Investment Commission and by Presidencia. In other words, in the annual process of presenting programs of investment to the commission, unspoken rules existed with respect to the portion of federal investment funds that could be assigned to each sector, entity, or enterprise. All this . . . limited the possibility that . . . entities . . . would present disproportionate investment programs lacking any chance of being approved.[30] (Emphasis added)

PRI presidents' acquiescence to low levels of public spending amounted to a blank check that permitted the Treasury to determine all public sector spending, including spending in the parastatal sector. In effect, PRI presidents granted the Treasury free hand to arrange the financing of the public sector's deficits in collaboration with the private banking sector. FitzGerald describes this accommodative fiscal relationship between Hacienda and private bankers as a "tacit agreement between the banks and the Treasury [allowing the banks] to finance a modest fiscal deficit in return for no tax reform."[31] As long as PRI presidents resisted all pressures to implement tax reform,[32] the Treasury was able to determine public expenditures and the size of fiscal deficit in collaboration with the twelve largest-scale Mexican bankers,[33] who controlled three-quarters[34] of the private credit in the country at that time. Private bankers accepted governmental requirements for higher reserve ratios and thus agreed to finance public spending through the mediation of the Treasury and the Central Bank as long as PRI presidents consented to low corporate tax revenues and minimal public spending. As a result, the private banking system helped set the parameters circumscribing government borrowing at the same time that the Treasury defined and restricted public sector spending projects.

Although PRI presidents demonstrated little autonomy from large-scale corporate actors, this is not to say that the state was simply the executive committee of monopoly capital, per an instrumental Marxist interpretation.[35] On the contrary, this chapter and the next argue that a major conflict between reformist state technocrats and Treasury officials pervaded the

Mexican state in the 1960s and burst out of control in the early 1970s.[36] From 1972 to 1976, these reformist technocrats tapped into the temporary organizational strength of the state by using public enterprise and parastatal agencies to sustain economic growth in the face of investment strikes and capital flight initiated by corporate investors.[37] Until this brief flourish of state organizational strength, however, the Treasury controlled the parastatal sector by defining and restricting public spending and investment. In theory, Mexico's state enterprises were *potential* generators of public revenues. In practice, under Treasury tutelage from 1940 until 1972, state enterprises were administered to subsidize private profitability and, therefore, drain rather than augment state revenues.

Two general criteria characterized state enterprises during the period of *desarrollo estabilizador*. Both criteria were linked to the stabilizing growth program's subsidy of private investment, maximization of private profitability, and minimization of inflation. First, to subsidize private profit, PRI governments minimized prices of parastatal products such as steel, power, petroleum, and transportation.[38] Second, parastatal economic intervention took on a last-resort character,[39] whereby the state expanded public enterprise only when private firms were going bankrupt, or when start-up costs for industries were too high and profitability too slow to attract private investors.[40] Parastatal enterprise specialized in revenue-draining activities, such as cheap finance, price supports, education, and research.[41] In this vein, FitzGerald has painted a pessimistic portrait of the financial liabilities of the parastatal sector by noting:

> In spite of the subsidies from the central government (which rose from 1.3 percent of GDP in 1950–1959 to 2.3 percent in 1960–1968 and 3.4 percent in 1973–1976), the parastatal sector was increasingly incapable of financing its own investment.[42]

PRI presidents permitted the parastatal sector to drain public revenues in large measure because the Treasury insisted upon using parastatal firms to subsidize high rates of private profit and maintain low levels of inflation. In order to avoid public sector encroachment on the private sector, Treasury officials refused to fund new, potentially productive parastatal investment activities.[43] Therefore, instead of striving for parastatal profitability, PRI presidents allowed Treasury officials to decapitalize public enterprise. This prevented any economic rationalization of the parastatal sector. Contrary to Treasury's economic ideology, rationalization to achieve parastatal profitability or at least parastatal self-financing presupposed extensive goal-based economic planning. De jure economic planning was also not appealing to PRI presidents, given the risks of private capital flight and the need to surrender public spending decisions to goal-based, technical planners. Consequently, for three decades, Treasury officials dominated and consistently decapitalized the parastatal sector with the approval of PRI presidents.

Instead of a de jure economic planning authority, a so-called administrative triangle of efficiency nominally governed parastatal investment behavior during most of the period of stabilizing growth. In reality, PRI presidents did not distribute administrative control evenly across the three central secretariats included in the triangle. The Treasury, of course, dominated the triangle. Patrimonio Nacional was charged with a vague form of administrative control over parastatals, including "vigilance, preservation, and administration of national properties."[44] On the other hand, authority to plan and budget parastatal spending officially resided with the secretariats of Presidencia and Hacienda. Nominally, Presidencia was charged with *planning* public spending; Treasury was charged with exercising *fiscal* control over public investments. As Figure 4.1 illustrates, in most categories of parastatal administration, Treasury's control over the parastatal sector far exceeded that of the other two agencies included in the triangle. As long as PRI presidents remained convinced that rapid economic growth and industrialization depended on maintaining the spending restrictions of *desarrollo estabilizador,* the Treasury's financial control over parastatal activities translated into de facto planning control as well.

Even though Presidencia and Patrimonio Nacional were granted offi-

Figure 4.1   Type of Control over Parastatals

Central State Agency	External	Internal	Generic	Specific	A priori	A posteriori	Permanent	Exceptional	Financial	Administrative	Legislative
Secretariat of the Presidency (Presidencia)	9	1	10	1	8	4	10	—	7	7	—
Hacienda	22	—	21	6	15	9	21	2	20	9	1
Secretariat of National Properties (Patrimonio Nacional)	15	—	13	3	9	9	14	1	10	12	—

Source: Secretariat of the Presidency Administrative Studies Division; cited by Alejandro Carrillo Castro *La reforma administrativa en México* (Mexico City: Miguel Angel Porrúa, 1980).

cial planning and administrative control over the parastatals, the Treasury dominated public enterprise financially and ensured that no new investments occurred without Treasury's approval and guidance. This financial grip was not broken until *desarrollo estabilizador* began to falter in 1970 and 1971 and the government launched a major program of foreign public borrowing. In response to accelerated public borrowing, reformist technocrats in Patrimonio Nacional used foreign borrowed funds to break Treasury protocol and inject large amounts of public monies into state enterprises and into small and medium-size firms to revive economic growth. For a brief four-year period, reformist technocrats were able to use the parastatal sector to sustain economic growth in the face of investment strikes by large-scale private investors. Although this cycle of borrowing, public spending, and rapid industrial growth was short-lived, the Mexican state's assertion of temporary organizational strength vis-à-vis large-scale capitalist interests had profound effects on Mexico's national political order. However, until this public borrowing and spending spree occurred in the mid-1970s, Hacienda controlled all public sector spending, and Presidencia's role of "national economic planning" consisted of little more than official rhetoric.

The Treasury's Fall from Grace:
Political-Economic Crisis and
Technocratic Struggles over Economic Policy

When López Mateos created the secretariat of the Presidencia and reorganized National Goods into National Patrimony (Patrimonio Nacional), he probably never imagined that this symbolic gesture would ever give rise to any serious attempt to curb Treasury's control of public spending. Throughout the 1960s, Presidencia and Patrimonio Nacional lacked the necessary financial clout to check the Treasury's grip on public spending. Nevertheless, during the decade of the sixties, these secretariats nurtured a new set of reformist economists who grew increasingly critical of Treasury's control of public spending. In fact, López Mateos's first secretary of Patrimonio Nacional founded a long line of mentors and protégés, who advocated economic reform throughout the sixties, seventies, and early eighties. López Mateos selected Eduardo Bustamante to head the new Patrimonio Nacional in 1958. Bustamante was mentor to Horacio Flores de la Peña,[45] Echeverría's secretary of Patrimonio Nacional in the early 1970s and the technocrat who spearheaded the expansionist public spending that upset Treasury's control of the public sector in 1972.[46] Flores de la Peña, in turn, mentored both Francisco Javier Alejo,[47] head of Patrimonio Nacional from 1975 to 1976, and José Andrés de Oteyza,[48] head of Patrimonio in

December 1976, during the change of administration. Finally, de Oteyza and Alejo, in collaboration with Carlos Tello and President José López Portillo, orchestrated the nationalization of the private banking system in 1982.[49]

During the tumultuous early seventies, Patrimonio Nacional housed the statist-reformist technocrats who undermined the stabilizing growth program implemented during the long tenure of Treasury Secretary Ortiz Mena. From 1970 to 1976, these reformist technocrats articulated and began to implement an alternative development strategy that circumvented the Treasury's control of public sector spending. In fact, Flores de la Peña's strategy of liberating public spending from dependence on private Mexican bank financing catapulted public economic decisionmaking into internal disarray in and after 1972.

Presidencia technocrats, on the other hand, did not necessarily advocate a rival development program. Instead, during the late 1960s, they concentrated on administrative reform and advocated major administrative overhaul of the central secretariats, including a new economic decisionmaking structure to replace the triangle of efficiency in charge of the parastatal sector. As mentioned earlier, within the triangle, Presidencia never acquired the actual planning clout over public enterprise nominally granted the secretariat by President López Mateos in 1958.

Instead, by the late sixties, the reformers in Presidencia concentrated primarily on the formulation of a comprehensive administrative reform of the federal executive. Thus, although Presidencia itself never supplanted Treasury's control over public sector spending, Presidencia became the breeding ground for the administrative reform that redistributed some of the Treasury's authority as leading economic secretariat. The administrative reform process was completed in 1977 when Presidencia was dissolved, and the Secretariat of Programming and Budget (Secretaría de Programación y Presupuesto, or SPP) took Treasury's place as the state's key economic decisionmaking agency.

As early as 1965, Presidencia initiated a formal campaign to check Treasury's enormous control over the public sector by creating the Commission for Public Administration (Comisión de Administración Pública, or CAP).[50] CAP was directed by long time advocate of administrative reform José López Portillo,[51] a founding professor of political science and public policy at UNAM. López Portillo was responsible for establishing the Ph.D. program in administrative science at UNAM.[52] From the mid-1960s onward, he acted as the intellectual forerunner and public mainstay behind the concept of administrative reform. Not only did López Portillo preside over CAP from its inception, but he continued to push CAP's recommendations in spite of the reservations of President Díaz Ordaz during the crisis-ridden period following the Tlatelolco massacre in 1968.[53] After that massacre of protesting students and bystanders,[54] a severe political crisis ensued and Díaz Ordaz refused to consider any CAP recommendations for administrative reform.

In a deliberate effort to counter the president's abandonment of reform, López Portillo published the CAP'S recommendations elaborated between 1965 and 1967 in a treatise entitled *Report on Public Administrative Reform*.[55] In this way, López Portillo kept the intrastatal impetus for administrative reform alive during the final, politically tumultuous years of the 1960s. Lacking Díaz Ordaz's support, López Portillo turned the Presidencia secretariat's sights toward preparation for the next *sexenio* when it became apparent that Luis Echeverría, López Portillo's boyhood friend,[56] would assume the presidency. With the change of presidential administration, the governmental momentum for administrative reform was sustained by new President Luis Echeverría's 1970 appointment of Hugo Cervantes del Río, a former student of López Portillo, as secretary of Presidencia.[57]

Luis Echeverría was selected as the official PRI candidate for the presidency in the midst of the intense political fallout resulting from the Tlatelolco massacre. He had no reputation for being a particularly radical or reformist member of the PRI,[58] as Appendix 4 indicates. Yet during his administration, the reformers he appointed to Patrimonio Nacional and Presidencia used their public posts to launch a major policy attack on the Treasury's preeminent, governmental position vis-à-vis other secretariats. Essentially, Luis Echeverría's presidency became a battleground between two rival central secretariats, Patrimonio and the Treasury. This battle was less a product of the president's own personal initiatives to reform the economy than of the initiatives of reformist technocrats who were spurred to action by economic and political crisis and eager to take advantage of crisis conditions to undercut the Treasury's inordinate governmental authority.[59] Crisis conditions were certainly ripe because Echeverría not only had to deal with political fallout from the government's violent repression of the student movement of 1968, but also had to cope with economic stagnation, which set in between 1970 and 1972.[60]

When Echeverría assumed office in December 1970, Hacienda was still firmly in command of public sector spending,[61] but rapid economic growth officially associated with the orthodox *desarrollo estabilizador* strategy was beginning to falter. The growth slowdown was aggravated by the foreign economic policies of U.S. President Richard Nixon. The 1971 economic recession in the United States, coupled with the Nixon administration's devaluation of the dollar and imposition of a 10 percent surcharge on all goods imported into the United States, immediately shocked the Mexican economy.[62]

Of even deeper consequence for the Mexican economy, however, were the negative socioeconomic effects of the stabilizing growth strategy itself.

By the mid-1960s, for example, Mexico's strong performance in agriculture began to decline as agrarian expansion fell below the rate of population growth.[63] Agricultural stagnation stemmed from declining public investment dedicated to rural areas.[64] Many years of PRI governmental decisions to cut public funds to agricultural development were the direct result of the public spending restrictions imposed by the stabilizing growth strategy. Agricultural stagnation had a negative impact on industrial growth as well, since agricultural exports were an important source of both foreign exchange and urban food supplies.[65] Larger import bills for agricultural products purchased abroad negatively affected Mexico's ability to acquire the capital goods necessary to sustain rapid industrialization.

By the late 1960s, growth in heavy industrial sectors also began to falter.[66] PRI governments' pursuit of vertical import-substitution industrialization to advance the local production of capital, intermediate, and durable consumer goods initially began in 1954 and 1955, when the *desarrollo estabilizador* strategy was devised.[67] For approximately a decade, vertical ISI and heavy industrial growth proceeded without major interruption. A complete exposition of the multiple explanations accounting for the stagnation of heavy industry in Mexico during the late 1960s[68] is beyond the scope of this work. One undeniable factor explaining industrial stagnation, however, was the unwillingness and/or inability of the private sector to invest in industries where overhead costs were high and profits not immediately forthcoming.[69] In spite of the fact that an entire state-subsidized growth strategy existed to maintain high rates of private profit and low corporate taxation, the private sector still preferred to invest in light manufacturing, where profits were generous, or in lucrative real estate speculation or tourism.[70]

By the late 1960s, the private sector's reluctance and/or inability to make the necessary investments to sustain vertical import-substitution industrialization created a need for massive public investments to inject scarce capital into heavy industry.[71] The desperate need for state capitalization of both agriculture and heavy industry powerfully reinforced the credibility of the economic arguments made by the reformist technocrats appointed to Patrimonio Nacional. The prospect of injecting massive doses of state capital into industry and agriculture not only presupposed the liberation of public spending from the restrictive rules of *desarrollo estabilizador* but also the reorganization of central economic decisionmaking structures. In short, the possibility of large-scale deficit spending by the government implied disruption of the Treasury's long-lived financial control of the entire state apparatus.

Presidencia officials advocating administrative reform were less dedicated to overall reform of the economy than the statist-economists in Patrimonio Nacional. Comparatively speaking, Flores de la Peña and his colleagues in Patrimonio Nacional constituted the most economically progressive voices among all the reformers within the state. Flores de la Peña argued for a major change in economic development strategy based on a neo-Keynesian expansion of public spending to revive demand and stimulate the economy through increased consumption.[72] In a major departure from past orthodox thought, Flores de la Peña argued for an expansionist revival of economic growth. His proposals sounded increasingly appealing to the president as the public spending restrictions mandated by the stabilizing growth program failed to overcome economic stagnation during 1971.[73]

In contrast, the administrative experts in Presidencia and their intellectual forerunner, José López Portillo, were more cautious than Patrimonio economists. In a minimal sense, Presidencia technocrats shared certain goals with Patrimonio economists, such as curbing Treasury's immense control over public investments and spending. However, historically, during the 1960s, administrative reformers had already demonstrated their willingness to proceed with administrative changes without alteration of the Treasury's economic development program. As the head of CAP in the 1960s, José López Portillo emphasized the need to establish a new centralized administrative capacity to pursue a coherent "global vision" of public sector activities.[74]

Soon after the creation of the commission, from 1965 to 1967, CAP members advocated combining administrative reform with a new national development program pursuant to progressive new development goals. However, when Díaz Ordaz failed to formulate a new national economic program, CAP members salvaged the idea of administrative reform[75] in the absence of an alternative development strategy indicating precisely which new economic policies the administrative reforms would seek to advance.

As the Echeverría term proceeded, it became increasingly clear that López Portillo differed fundamentally from Flores de la Peña and other reformers in Patrimonio in that López Portillo was willing to advocate administrative reform unattached to a statist-reformist economic program. López Portillo obviously shared some of Flores de la Peña's goals of reducing Treasury's influence over public sector spending and investment activities. For example, government rhetoric portrayed López Portillo as secretary of Hacienda (1973–1975), as Echeverria's personal envoy sent to transform the Treasury. What is more, as Treasury secretary, López Portillo's public rhetoric claimed that Hacienda had to be wholly restructured before the rest of the public sector could be adequately reformed.[76]

Nevertheless, López Portillo clearly demonstrated that he was *not* as dedicated to discrediting and replacing the *desarrollo estabilizador* economic program as was Flores de la Peña. In fact, as Treasury secretary, López Portillo revived restrictive monetary policies in July 1973, after the resignation of Hugo Margáin.[77] Such policies essentially counteracted the policy of expansionist public spending that the administration was pursuing in accord with interventionist public sector plans of Flores de la Peña in Patrimonio Nacional.

Throughout Echeverría's term, López Portillo's more "moderate" stance on development policy permeated the Presidencia secretariat. López Portillo's student, Hugo Cervantes del Río, served as secretary of Presidencia for most of the term, from 1970 to 1975.[78] The more economically reformist or "radical"[79] elements earlier associated with Presidencia were shifted out of Presidencia in 1970 or shortly thereafter. For example, Carlos Tello, who sought to connect the goal of administrative reform to an alternative, statist-reformist strategy of development,[80] was appointed as President Echeverría's subdirector general of credit in Hacienda from 1970 to 1975.[81] Instead of working on economic reform within Presidencia, Tello was busy redirecting the allocation of credit in the economy, using monies borrowed from foreign banks. Although such reallocation of public credit eventually resulted in the collapse of the Treasury's administrative-financial dominance over public spending, the lack of economic reformers, such as Tello in Presidencia, left technocrats with little passion for economic reform to plan the important administrative reform soon to be implemented in 1977.

Porfirio Muñoz Ledo was another reformer earlier associated with Presidencia, but he served in a different secretariat under Echeverría. As a member of CAP, Muñoz Ledo had always insisted that the most crucial part of the proposed administrative reform would be the execution of decisions that would transfer power from Hacienda to other parts of the administrative apparatus.[82] Muñoz Ledo, however, was transferred from the post of subsecretary of Presidencia to secretary of labor, from September 1972 to 1975. He served in Presidencia only during the first two years of the Echeverría presidency, at a time when public sector activities were still dominated by Hacienda and status quo elements.[83] Later, from 1976 to 1977, when López Portillo became president, economic reformer Carlos Tello[84] was brought back into Presidencia at the last minute to preside over the administrative transformation that replaced Presidencia with the Secretariat of Programación y Presupuesto (SPP). Tello, however, quickly lost his post due to policy disagreements with both President López Portillo and the Secretary of Hacienda, Julio Moctezuma Cid.[85]

As will be discussed shortly, the administrative reforms of López Portillo's presidency demonstrate that moderate administrative reformers prevailed over all other contending technocrats in 1976, when the Echeverría presidency ended. After all, moderate administrative reformer and new PRI president López Portillo, rather than vocal economic reformers, such as Flores de la Peña or Muñoz Ledo, finally controlled the creation of the secretariat of Programación y Presupuesto, the new locus of economic decisionmaking authority created in 1977.

Moderate administrative reformers lacking commitment to economic reform essentially dominated the administrative reform process, but the technocratization of PRI governance commencing with the 1977 creation of the SPP would not have happened if the more "radical" economists in Patrimonio Nacional had not temporarily seized the Treasury's prior control of public spending. Oddly enough, the fact that statist-reformers from Patrimonio temporarily governed public spending in the early seventies partly accounts for how antistatist technocrats eventually came to dominate the Mexican government.

In 1971, the continuation of orthodox monetary and fiscal policies led to growing stagnation of per capita income and increasing unemployment. As a result, Flores de la Peña's alternative development strategy became increasingly appealing to the president.[86] Following another incident of student protest on June 10, 1971, when various protesters were killed, Echeverría feared a revival of the political morass of 1968.[87] Faced with the possibility of increased governmental repression and simultaneous economic stagnation, Echeverría decided to replace some of the policies of *desarrollo estabilizador* and pursue a new public spending program, beginning in 1972. Even though he had announced a shift to a "shared development" strategy at the outset of his administration in 1970, the president did not abandon the public spending restrictions imposed by Hacienda until 1972.

The president's acceptance of the expansionist public spending policies advocated by Flores de la Peña and his colleagues[88] threw public economic policymaking into disarray. With the 1972 acceleration of public spending, Treasury lost its financial clout over public enterprises and agencies. However, some of Treasury's past influence was revived when private sector protest of economic reforms forced the reintroduction of restrictive monetary policies in 1973. Thus, the partial disruption of *desarrollo estabilizador* involved both the intense division of the state as an organization and the crippling of the state as a decisionmaker. Once Echeverría decided that increasing public expenditures to stimulate demand was more likely to revive economic growth than Treasury's policies of restricting public spending, the state's capacity for coherent public economic decisionmaking began to unravel.

During the previous thirty years of stabilizing growth strategy, Hacienda technocrats had acted for PRI presidents to determine the direction and level of public expenditures. The termination of the Treasury's financial control further alienated private investors, who effectively pressured the president to revive Treasury's orthodox monetary policies in 1973. Such restrictive monetary policies directly contradicted existing policies of expansionary public spending. In effect, the president proved incapable of enforcing a single, logically consistent set of economic policies as societal conflict about the distribution of wealth played itself out in struggles between economic technocrats within the state.

After June 14, 1972, when the Echeverría administration announced a program to reactivate the economy via a liberation of public expenditures, a stalemate developed almost immediately between two major technocratic groups aspiring to control economic governance.[89] The appropriate means of financing public expenditures, of course, was the key issue that polarized technocrats into two groups. Eventually, a deadlock emerged between the two groups over the question of how public spending should be financed. First, the president concluded that raising the prices of public sector goods was too politically destabilizing and too inflationary to serve as a viable, expanding source of public sector finance.[90] Consequently, the secretary of Hacienda, Hugo Margáin, announced a fiscal reform. His proposal included an attempt to devise an effective property tax of aggregated incomes based on an elimination of anonymous forms of wealth holding.

Margáin's proposal was essentially a resurrection of the López Mateos tax reform proposal.[91] When López Mateos came under pressure from private investors, he abandoned the idea of fiscal reform and relied instead on the political symbolism of a national profit-sharing arrangement. Margáin negotiated the profit-sharing agreement. In fact, in his earlier 1960s profit-sharing role, he arranged for the largest enterprises to share only the bare minimum of their profits.[92] Thus, for the 1972 fiscal reform, President Echeverría judged him to be politically ideal for mediating between the government and the private sector. This presidential judgment ultimately proved problematic because Margáin sided entirely with private investors and resigned his post as Treasury secretary in 1973.

Margáin's 1972 motivations in proposing a fiscal reform that would eliminate anonymous forms of wealth holding must be deduced from his previous performance on the National Profit-Sharing Commission. His chief preoccupation on the commission was to negotiate a profit-sharing agreement that would not alienate or burden large-scale private investors.[93] At the most fundamental level, then, Margáin's fiscal reformism was essentially consistent with the old *desarrollo estabilizador* strategy. Historical evidence of Margáin's rapport with large-scale private investors abounds. Perhaps most telling is the fact that the largest private industrialists and investors in Mexico *celebrated* the outcome of Margáin's profit-sharing arrangements.[94] Eventually, Margáin's submission to the wishes of large-scale private financiers on tax reform issues precipitated his departure from the post of secretary of Hacienda in 1973. His resignation came squarely in the middle of Echeverría's presidential term.

Initially, however, Margáin's dual reputation as a moderate "reformer" and as a defender of private sector interests won him the trust of both President Echeverría *and* Mexico's largest-scale industrialists in

COPARMEX, the union of major employers.[95] Margáin's willingness to effect a tax reform quickly disintegrated in the middle of the Echeverría government's tax-related negotiations with the private sector. Figures 4.2 and 4.3 show a breakdown of the various segments of the private sector. In one particular meeting between Margáin and representatives of various private sector groups, the Mexican Council of Businessmen (Consejo Mexicano de Hombres de Negocios, or CMHN),[96] the group of the thirty most prominent businessmen in Mexico, vehemently opposed the fiscal reform.[97] The CMHN representatives unexpectedly appeared at the meeting at the last moment.[98] When the meeting concluded, President Echeverría abandoned the fiscal reform, allegedly for fear of massive capital flight initiated by the businessmen who controlled the largest segments of finance capital and dominated the CMHN.[99]

Figure 4.2   Principal Members of Fractions of the Private Sector

Fraction	Operative Organization	Representative Arm	Line of Leadership
Industrialists	Monterrey Industrial Group	Coordinative Council of Businessmen	The Alfa Group (of Monterrey)
	Televisa	(or CCE—Formed in 1975)	Mexican Council of Businessmen (CMHN)
Foreign investors	Transnational Corporations	American Chamber of Commerce in Mexico (CAMCO)	Main Offices in Mexico City (Foreign Govts.)
Financiers	BANCOMER BANAMEX SERFIN COMERMEX	Coordinative Council of Businessmen (CCE)	Mexican Council of Businessmen

Source: Miguel Basáñez, *La lucha por la hegemonia en México, 1968–1980,* 2nd. ed. (Mexico City: Siglo XXI, 1982), p. 87.

Although many details of this formerly secret meeting are still unknown, a number of scholars[100] generally agree that in the meeting, Margáin abandoned the government's proposal for tax reform as soon as he encountered CMHN opposition. Margáin went into the meeting with support from the president of the COPARMEX and partial support from the CANACINTRA, the National Chamber of Transformation Industries.[101]

Figure 4.3   The Political Apparatus of the Private Sector

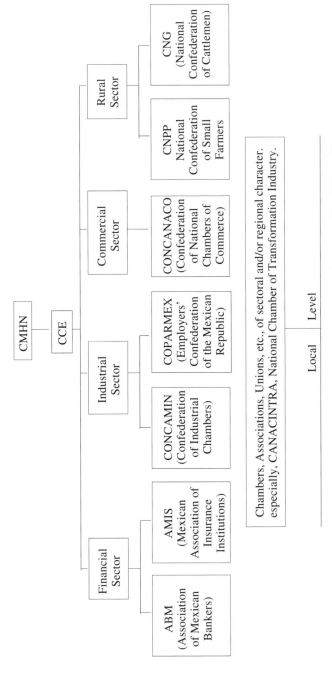

Source: Miguel Basáñez, *La lucha por la hegemonia en México, 1968–1980*, 2nd ed. (Mexico City: Siglo XXI, 1982), p. 99.

However, opposition from CMHN businessmen at the highest decision-making level[102] apparently prevailed because neither Margáin nor the head of the Banco de México proved willing to confront CMHN officials by pushing the administration's fiscal reform any further. Margáin's submissiveness toward large-scale investors in the CMHN was increasingly evident throughout the early Echeverría years as the relationship between Margáin and the president deteriorated. As soon as the administration began to implement economic reform in 1972, relations began to sour. After the CMHN meeting described above, Margáin resigned in May 1973 and was replaced by the president's personal friend, José López Portillo, the head of the moderate group of administrative reformers in Presidencia.

The PRI President Wears No Clothes: Luis Echeverría's Failed Economic Reforms and Contradictory Economic Policies

Luis Echeverría's 1970 appointment of Hugo Margáin as secretary of the Treasury and the Echeverría government's maintenance of stabilizing growth policies until 1972 reflect the private sector's lingering grip on the president and on public spending decisions during the first two years of the Echeverría administration. The fact that Echeverría ever appointed Margáin in the first place reflects the lack of autonomy of the PRI president-elect vis-à-vis large-scale, private investors in 1969 and 1970. As president-elect, Echeverría was able to appoint reformist technocrats as secretaries of Patrimonio Nacional and Presidencia, where reformism was already rampant but stymied. However, Echeverría's key appointment to Hacienda was obviously influenced by large-scale private business preferences. But the fact that Ortiz Mena, author of *desarrollo estabilizador* and secretary of the Treasury for twelve consecutive years, was replaced at all in 1970 signified that the 1968 student massacre[103] had prompted the president-elect to attempt, in some limited fashion, to mend the political damage from the massacre.

In 1969, however, after years of presidential acquiescence to the Treasury's financial dominance, the PRI's presidential candidate was in no position vis-à-vis large-scale investors to appoint a major economic reformer as secretary of Hacienda. The appointment of the moderate Hugo Margáin as a Treasury secretary reflected reduced presidential autonomy in relation both to large-scale private investors and to social movements pressuring the PRI presidency to prove its commitment to social justice. In short, the particular personnel that Echeverría chose to serve in key secretariats during his administration reflected, and in turn contributed to, an emerging deadlock between the forces of change and the strength of the status quo within the state.

The Echeverría administration presided over a rather uncomfortable clash between presidential weakness and temporarily activated state organizational strength, which converged upon governance structures in the late 1960s and early 1970s. As PRI presidential candidate, Echeverría announced a new economic strategy called shared development (*desarrollo compartido*). This new strategy of combining rapid economic growth with increasing social justice and welfare measures formed the core of the presidential candidate's "campaign" promises. Yet as president, Echeverría lacked the reformist drive and autonomous financial leverage vis-à-vis large-scale, private investors to defy the governmental edifice and socioeconomic forces perpetuating stabilizing growth policies. Instead, he opted to continue restrictive monetary policies and to adhere to reduced public expenditure policies until dire economic stagnation in 1972 literally forced him to change.[104]

Actually, much evidence suggests that Echeverría was often not motivated by economic reformism at all.[105] Carlos Arriola describes at length how President Echeverría established a secret personal working relationship with Eugenio Garza Sada, head of the powerful Monterrey Group of industrialists, in order to assure the entire private sector that government reforms would not "go too far" in seriously undermining private interests.[106] As a consequence of the secret Echeverría–Garza Sada relationship and the PRI president's continued adherence to orthodox economic policies until 1972, the Echeverría government and the private sector experienced only two major policy disagreements during the first two years of the *sexenio*.[107]

The first conflict, which occurred from January 1970 to August 1971, concerned the administration's proposal to decentralize industrial activity. The proposed reform sought to prohibit new installation of industry in the Valle de México metropolitan area and thereby encourage industrial relocation in underdeveloped areas of the country. The employers' union (COPARMEX) and the Confederation of Industrialists (CONCAMIN) opposed the reform, and the proposal was eventually dropped.[108] The only other major public-private conflict concerned a proposed 10 percent tax on luxury consumption items and occurred during the first year of the *sexenio*, from December 1970 to December 1971. Every major financial, commercial, and industrial group in Mexico (COPARMEX, CONCAMIN, CONCANACO, AMIS, CANACINTRA, and CAMCO) except the ABM opposed the tax.[109] A luxury tax was eventually imposed, but luxury goods with the largest markets in Mexico were *exempted* from taxation. Clearly, the president did not attempt full-scale redistributive reforms in line with the shared development idea, and the two reform proposals that elicited major private opposition were dropped or altered to accommodate private sector objections. State–private sector relations remained generally amiable through approximately the first two years of the *sexenio*.

By late 1972 and early 1973, however, the Treasury's control of economic decisionmaking began to unravel. At the same time, the relationship between the government and the private sector began to sour.[110] After the government announced its liberation of public expenditures on June 14, 1972, Treasury's dominance of economic decisionmaking began to collapse as public expenditure rose, in spite of the reluctance of Hacienda and the largest segments of the private sector to agree on ways to finance such expenditures domestically. After the Echeverría government retracted its proposed fiscal reform in December 1972, public expenditures continued to increase, as did the public sector deficit.[111] This deficit spending helped precipitate the May 1973 resignation of Hugo Margáin from the Treasury. Margáin's resignation led Echeverría to exclaim, rather prematurely of course, that from this time forward, "finances would be determined from Los Pinos." This overstatement implied that the president rather than Treasury technocrats would assume total control of public revenues and spending.

Contrary to the president's assertion, however, Margáin's resignation did not empower the president to control revenues and spending and conduct a coherent economic program. Echeverría could not and did not consolidate full control of public economic decisionmaking simply because he replaced the previous secretary of the Treasury with his personal envoy and friend, José López Portillo. Margáin's departure and López Portillo's arrival gave the subdirector general of credit, Carlos Tello, freer hand to distribute credit from within the Treasury, but it did not eliminate the private sector's influence over public economic decisions. In fact, under threats of capital flight and investment strikes by private investors, the PRI president failed to empower Patrimonio Nacional to assume full authority for public economic decisionmaking. Instead, with the president's approval, Treasury Secretary López Portillo revived restrictive monetary policy in consonance with the wishes of major private investors. This was entirely contrary to existing policies of expansionary public spending.

In spite of the revival of restrictive monetary policy, after Margáin left the Treasury, relations between the government and the largest-scale industrialists and financiers rapidly deteriorated.[112] Margáin's May 1973 departure was the symptom of an emerging upheaval in economic governance provoked by reformist technocrats. On September 17, 1973, the private sector trust that Echeverría cultivated with the head of the Monterrey Group of industrialists was irreparably shattered when Eugenio Garza Sada himself was assassinated. After Garza Sada's murder, the private sector's economic obstructionism and newspaper attacks on the government escalated, and the state's economic decisionmaking apparatus was gripped by a virtual deadlock between change-oriented spending policies and status quo monetary policy. From this time forward, the neutralization of Treasury influence, which was first set into motion by the liberation of public expenditures in June 1972, proceeded not only at the expense of private influence over the state, but also at the expense of the PRI presidency's image and myth of perpetual power.

From 1973 forward, the president's pursuit of reformist policies in the face of intense private sector opposition reflected a confused mixture of economic reformism and status quo sensitivity to private investors' interests. In every major case of proposed economic reform for which private opposition was aroused, the administration retreated from or bargained away nearly all the important features of its proposals.[113] Appendix 4 is a summarized version of Rosario Green's study of major proposed reforms and presidential retraction or watering down of each proposal. Her study clearly shows that early conflicts between the state and the private sector originated with large foreign investors represented by CAMCO, the American Chamber of Commerce in Mexico, rather than with Mexican investors. The state and domestic capital did not enter into serious conflict until early 1974.

The Echeverría government's troubles with foreign capital were first triggered by the administration's proposal to regulate technology transfers. Two months after the constraints on public expenditures were dropped, the conflict over proposed government regulation of technology transfers began in August 1972 and ended in December 1972, when the government abandoned the most important provisions regarding restrictive marketing practices. Echeverría's proposal to regulate foreign investment as introduced in November 1972 aroused little conflict, since the government largely dropped the proposal's most important regulatory aspects. State–private sector conflicts in 1972 were mostly confined to foreign capital.

However, during 1973 and 1974, CAMCO helped organize the Mexican private sector, thus increasing private business opposition to reform proposals by 1974. The September 1973 assassination of industrialist Eugenio Garza Sada opened the door to the conflict that spanned the years 1974 to 1976. In March and April 1974, for instance, the administration proposed the creation of a fund called FONACOT to subsidize workers' consumption. Furthermore, the government claimed to be in favor of initiating an adjustable salary scale that would tie increases in salaries proportionally to increases in prices. The employers' union (COPARMEX), the Confederation of National Chambers of Commerce (CONCANACO), and the Chamber of Commerce of the Federal District all opposed the measures. In the end, the consumer subsidy fund, FONACOT, was in fact created, but the government abandoned the proposed adjustable salary scale, which was bitterly proposed by the private sector.[114] The administration apparently used the salary scale as a bargaining tool to obtain private agreement to the consumer subsidy fund.[115]

In late 1974, public-private sector conflict intensified further when the administration proposed a price control system. From September to October, a battle arose over the composition of a list of goods whose prices would be allowed to increase only when the real costs of production increased. Every principal industrial and commercial chamber, except CANACINTRA, opposed the price control system. By the end of the conflict, price controls were adopted for only twenty-nine items; 138 other general consumption articles were left uncontrolled.

In confrontation after confrontation, the administration either abandoned or forfeited significant aspects of proposed reforms to accommodate particular private sector objections. For instance, a confrontation with foreign capital took place from July to August 1975 when the administration proposed the imposition of protectionist trade barriers on selected imports and simultaneously proposed subsidies to Mexican export industries. CAMCO and the National Chambers of Commerce (CANACO) both opposed the import restrictions. The measures finally adopted consisted of a selective imposition of import controls. Private exporters received a larger devolution of taxes on exported production, and in consolation to private importers, the government agreed to subsidize capital goods imports used in the production of exported goods. Domestic, Mexican capitalists did not generally agree with foreign capitalists on the issue of import controls, of course, but did form with foreign corporations a united front opposed to the government's late 1975 proposals to regulate human land settlements.

More specifically, between December 1975 and May 1976, a conflict occurred concerning the government proposal to regulate urban real estate and to support collective *ejido* lands.[116] Because the Mexican private sector was investing heavily in real estate speculation instead of riskier productive investment,[117] government regulation of urban real estate was a particularly sensitive issue. In fact, every major industrial and commercial chamber opposed the proposal, with the exception of CANACINTRA. The newly formed Coordinating Council of Businessmen, or CCE, the political group representing Mexican industrialists, helped organize private sector political opposition to real estate regulation.[118] As with other reforms, the government abandoned the most significant provisions of urban real estate reforms in the law's final draft.

Perhaps the single most sensitive economic issue was the exchange rate of the peso. Rosario Green has argued that the administration should have devalued the peso earlier in the presidential term to reduce the public sector's need to contract ever increasing foreign borrowed funds from foreign commercial banks. The overvalued peso, Green asserts, was symptomatic of an administration that caved in to private sector demands that the government maintain a high, stable value for the peso.[119] Like other government attempts at economic reform, the administration abided by private

sector wishes and resisted currency devaluation until economic crisis virtually forced a devaluation in late 1976. Thus, Green is correct: Just as the
PRI president forfeited every other major economic reform proposal,
Echeverría postponed devaluation of the peso in large measure because the
private sector staunchly opposed devaluation.

As Figure 4.4 suggests, the stalemate between the Echeverría government and the private sector reflected the precarious position of a PRI presidency caught midway between a reformist attempt to abandon stabilizing

**Figure 4.4   The Neutralization of Hacienda and Presidential Incapacitation:
The Deadlock Between Expansionism and Orthodoxy, 1973–1976**

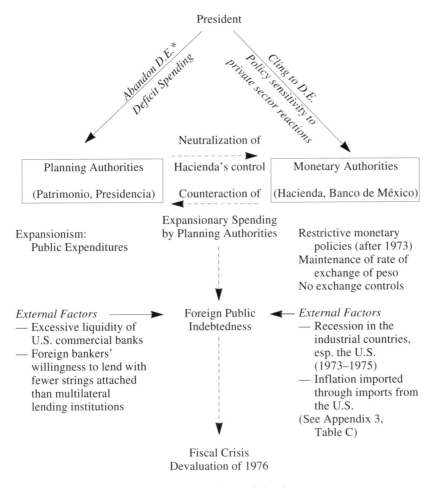

D.E.: Desarrollo estabilizador

growth policies and private sector pressures pushing the president to adhere
to the economic status quo. On the one hand, economic reformers within
the cabinet succeeded in persuading the president to increase public expenditures after economic stagnation hit in 1970 and 1971. On the other hand,
the very reformism that prompted him to abandon restrictive public spending rules elicited intense reactions from private sector actors who successfully pressured the president into a revival of restrictive monetary policies
in July 1973. Margáin's resignation fueled private sector animosity and distrust. In response, López Portillo, the president's personal envoy in
Hacienda, found it advisable to reintroduce restrictive monetary policies
and reaffirm Mexico's pledge to maintain the existing currency value of
12.50 pesos per dollar as well as resist imposing exchange controls of any
kind.[120] Monetary orthodoxy was necessary, in the president's view, to
avoid massive capital flight that would paralyze economic growth.

Unfortunately, the Treasury's restrictive monetary policies directly
contradicted the policy of expansionist public spending pursued by the economic reformers in Patrimonio Nacional. By 1976, the net effect of the two
opposing policies was to cancel each other out, to the detriment of
Mexicans' economic well-being.[121] As a result of this stalemate between
reformist expansion of public spending and private sector interests obligat-
ing the president to preserve restrictive monetary policies, the administration's ability to pursue a coherent strategy of economic development virtually collapsed. The PRI presidency proved incapable of coherent economic
decisionmaking during this period of disarray and upheaval in economic
governance. The president was unable to make coherent economic decisions because he was torn in two opposing directions. He was drawn to
encourage expansion of public spending in order to overcome the political
crisis of 1968 and to avoid the economic stagnation of 1970–1971. On
the other hand, he felt increasingly compelled to reduce private investment strikes and capital flight through maintenance of orthodox monetary
policy.

The Treasury, the state's economic decisionmaking center for some
twenty years, lost strict control over public spending after the government
began to engage in deficit spending and foreign borrowing in and after
1972.[122] The 1960s understanding between private banks and state monetary authorities (Hacienda, Banco de México) whereby the private banking
system helped determine the level of the state fiscal deficit and, with the
aid of the Treasury, the level of public expenditures[123] dissolved by 1973,
when Patrimonio economists accelerated public spending in spite of the
private sector's defeat of tax reform in December 1972. In other words,
deficit spending meant that Hacienda no longer had the public sector financial clout that permitted the Treasury to control economic decisionmaking
for the entire state.

The State's Temporary Organizational Strength
and Persisting Weakness: The Myth of State
Sovereignty as State Strength Shattered

Deficit spending in Mexico from 1972 to 1976 was *not* evidence of a newly found presidential autonomy[124] nor of permanent state strength vis-à-vis private investors. Furthermore, deficit spending did *not* empower Patrimonio Nacional to replace the Treasury at the apex of economic decisionmaking. As suggested in Figure 4.5, deficit spending curtailed the Treasury's financial control over public spending but did *not* empower Patrimonio reformers to reconstitute coherent public economic decisionmaking. Instead, when the government's deficit spending program interrupted the Treasury's monopoly of economic decisionmaking, the PRI presidency showed itself to be incapable of empowering and consistently backing Patrimonio technocrats to pursue consistent economic reform. Thus, for the PRI presidency, deficit spending became a double-edged sword politically speaking: It curtailed Treasury and private sector limitations on public spending but crippled the president with private sector protests, unproductive speculation, capital flight, and overall private refusal to continue to invest in productive enterprise.[125]

The combination of economically damaging private sector protests[126] and contradictory government spending and monetary policies culminated in economic crisis. Political paralysis and demystification of presidential authority resulted as well. While private sector threats of capital flight compelled the president to continue Treasury's restrictive monetary policies, reformist technocrats and economic stagnation persuaded him to increase public spending. In this way, the Echeverría years demonstrated to all that, in spite of years of party rhetoric to the contrary, neither the PRI presidency nor the Mexican state possessed any special gifts for sovereign control over the economy.

A number of scholars, such as Rosario Green,[127] have characterized this period of disarray in which neither the president, Hacienda, Patrimonio, nor Presidencia could effect coherent state action as a period of state weakness. Green, for instance, argues that the years after 1972 reflect a deterioration in the ability of the governing elite to negotiate with the private sector over alternative ways of capturing and mobilizing necessary capital resources to maintain economic growth.[128] She argues that the Echeverría government was unwilling to force the private sector to accept tax reforms in order to mobilize sufficient internal revenue resources to finance increased public expenditures. Therefore, she claims, the Echeverría government chose to engage in deficit spending, most of which the government financed through loans from foreign commercial banks.[129]

Figure 4.5   Policy Contradictions Within the State, 1973–1976

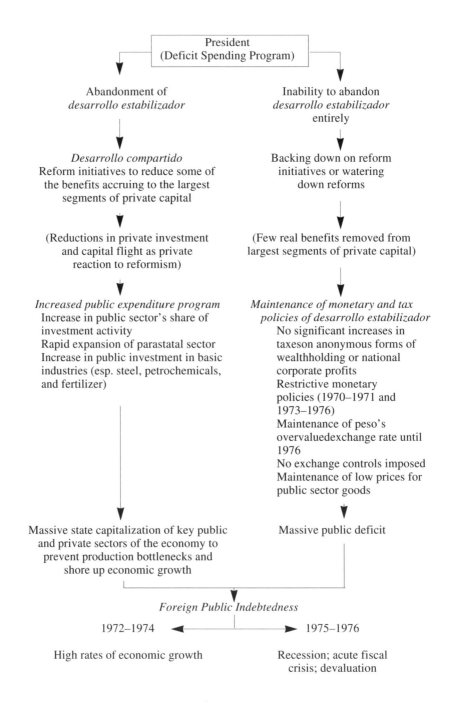

Green implies, however, that the president *chose* to conform to a weak public sector posture vis-à-vis the largest segments of private capital by substituting monies borrowed from foreign sources for revenues the government failed to obtain through tax reform. This argument is historically rather naive. It ignores the fact that the PRI presidency forfeited the state's minimal financial autonomy in relation to private investors many years earlier by relying upon the Treasury to control public sector investment and spending in the interest of private profitability.

Sixteen years of state reliance on the private banking system to finance public spending, and as many years of the Treasury's decapitalization of state enterprise to promote corporate profitability, left Echeverría with few revenue alternatives other than foreign public borrowing. Borrowed funds were needed to sustain economic growth in the face of private investment strikes and capital flight. Notwithstanding, Green asserts that President Echeverría "consciously opted for foreign indebted growth as the politically least costly alternative to tax reform"[130] and that this particular *choice* rendered the state weak vis-à-vis the private sector. Her argument naively suggests, however, that the Mexican state's strength or weakness was merely a matter of presidential choice in 1972 and afterward when the decisions to contract foreign loans were actually made.

In fact, key decisions diminishing the state's financial autonomy and strength vis-à-vis the private sector were made many years earlier by an entire series of PRI presidents, ranging from Avila Camacho in 1940 to Díaz Ordaz until 1970. Over these thirty years of rapid industrialization, all PRI presidents consistently contributed to the state's dependence on large private financiers and investors by relying on the Treasury to control public spending and its financing. Furthermore, all of the PRI presidents of this thirty-year period permitted the Treasury to decapitalize and financially cripple public enterprises in the interest of enhancing the profits of large-scale, private investors. Thus, the Mexican state's lack of financial autonomy from the private sector and the resulting financial weakness of state enterprises and agencies were not suddenly "chosen" by the Echeverría administration.

In reality, the Mexican state was less monolithic and more complex than Green's simple "weak-strong state" dichotomy suggests. By setting up this dichotomy and implying that state strength was at Echeverría's command, Green incorporates into her analysis the assumptions of official party rhetoric depicting the PRI president as the personification of the sovereign strength of the state. Her contention that state strength was a matter of the degree to which Echeverría resolved to defy private investors presumes an underlying state strength perpetually available for the president to activate. In other words, Green implies that the Mexican state was sovereign in the sense of being perpetually strong if only the president possessed the political will to employ the state's "power."

This notion of perpetual state strength is the same myth with which PRI elites legitimated the "revolutionary" PRI presidency. Assumptions of perpetual state strength at the president's command are actually quite parallel to the assumptions of PRI rhetoric: The PRI president can personify and actualize the state's sovereignty defined as continuous strength to control the economy for the benefit of all Mexicans. Green's analysis differs from official rhetoric mainly to the extent that she accuses the PRI president of lacking the political will to activate the state's underlying strength. Thus, whereas she uses the logic to argue that President Echeverría could have commanded a strong state if he desired, PRI elites have employed the same logic to argue that if the party's presidential candidates always prevail, then PRI presidents can personify the sovereignty of the Mexican state.

Such analysis lacks a historical frame of reference and conceives of the state as if it were a monolithic, unified organization. Contrary to such assumptions, the Mexican state of the early 1970s was not monolithic. Instead, the state displayed elements of temporary organizational strength even while some state agencies and actors continued to demonstrate a profound, historically grounded weakness vis-à-vis private investors and financiers. The state's temporary organizational strength stemmed from its vast, historically built parastatal apparatus. State organizational capacity for economic and social intervention was employed by the Echeverría administration's economic reformers to maintain economic growth for two or three years, from 1973 to 1975, while large-scale capitalists in Mexico refused to invest productively. Foreign borrowed money financed such state intervention.

Contrary to official PRI rhetoric describing state sovereignty as state strength, the Echeverría years demonstrated in the starkest terms that PRI presidents possess no special ability for perpetuating state strength. Instead, the idea of revolutionary state sovereignty, implicitly touted by official party elites as a form of perpetual state strength guaranteed by PRI presidents, fell into serious disrepute by 1976. President Echeverría demonstrated that he could control neither the economy nor even his own competing central state agencies and technocrats in order to decide upon and implement a logical and coherent set of economic policies. Even though the Treasury had lost its dominance of economic decisionmaking after 1972, neither the president nor Patrimonio Nacional technocrats commanded sufficient control or leverage over the economy to implement a coherent set of reformist economic policies.

Flores de la Peña's liberation of public expenditures from the restrictions of *desarrollo estabilizador* did interrupt the Treasury's financial control over public economic decisionmaking. In this respect, deficit spending constituted an *act of temporary state strength* whereby autonomous reformism from within the state as an organizational expanse introduced an element of upheaval into economic governance structures. This upheaval was sufficiently confounding to disrupt the hyperconcentrated authority of Hacienda. However, President Echeverría's failure to force tax reform on the private sector once such reform was proposed in 1972 is more indicative of the reduced relative autonomy of the Mexican presidency rather than the weakness of the state conceived as if it were a monolithic, unified organization. A handful of reformers applied a new, neo-Keynesian strategy to alter the logic of the economic interventions of the institutional expanse of the state to a sufficient extent to interrupt the pro–private sector policies of the Treasury. In this respect, the state as complex organization was not simply monolithic and weak vis-à-vis Hacienda and the private sector.

By ignoring the effects of the temporary strength of the state apparatus in relation to private investors, one tends to overlook the origins of major changes in the PRI presidency. In the past, there has been an analytical tendency to evaluate the Mexican state's potential for relative state autonomy exclusively in terms of the president's policy options.[131] This leads the analyst to posit the possibility that autonomous state action be initiated by a PRI presidency that had abandoned the popular social impetus to presidential autonomy years earlier. In effect, such analysis posits that real policy choice for controlling the economy could still have resided with the PRI presidency even as late as the 1970s. Studies focusing entirely on the president's inability to force reforms on the private sector are thus insufficient. An exclusive focus on the lack of presidential autonomy tends to overlook the unintended effects on the presidency of the temporary organizational strength of the state from 1972 to 1976. The state's temporary organizational capacity vis-à-vis the private sector was sufficiently strong to interfere with the Treasury's financial dominance of economic decisionmaking. The principal consequences of the collapse of Treasury dominance of economic decisionmaking were then twofold.

First, the presidency's rhetorical claims about sovereign control of the economy were discredited by the economic chaos produced by contradictory policymaking. Second, the ensuing administrative reform in 1976 shifted responsibility for the economy from the president to technocrats in the new secretariat of Programming and Budget (SPP). As a result, Mexico's "political presidency" was eventually replaced after 1976 and 1977 by an emergent "technocratic presidency," which transformed the entire symbolic-rhetorical edifice of the postrevolutionary state.

The collapse of economic governance in the 1970s, then, involved two interrelated phenomena. The first was the collapse of Treasury's dominance over public spending and investment. The second was the collapse of the PRI government's capacity for coherent economic decisionmaking and the PRI political elite's abandonment of the political presidency. A process of technocratization of the presidency began in earnest with the creation of the SPP, which administratively reorganized economic decisionmaking within the state. The Echeverría years encompassed the collapse of Treasury governance of the economy and also the collapse of the government's capacity to make coherent economic policy. However, the actual creation of the SPP did not occur until 1977, under new President López Portillo. With the presidency in political disrepute by the end of the Echeverría term, the actual administrative reform that marked the beginning of the technocratic PRI presidency was completed by Echeverría's successor, President José López Portillo.

As discussed earlier, the technocratic assault on Treasury's control over public expenditures did not lead to a direct transfer of decisionmaking back to the presidency. In fact, the period of economic policy contradiction from 1972 to 1976 was actually a period of standoff or stalemate between Hacienda and the largest segments of the private sector, on one side, and the economic reformers in Patrimonio Nacional on the other. The president was left incapacitated as he attempted to mediate between the contending sides. This stalemate was as much a product of the lingering strength of the private sector and Hacienda as it was of the growing assertiveness of statist economic reformers, the temporary organizational strength of the parastatal apparatus, and the long-accumulated lack of autonomy of the PRI presidency vis-à-vis the private sector. Finally, López Portillo's administrative reformism in Presidencia was important to the reorganization of the state's economic governance structures. In the end, the interruption of Treasury dominance and the ensuing administrative reform eventually led to the formulation of an antistatist, world market–oriented economic growth strategy.

Ironically, the statists in Patrimonio Nacional were the initial catalysts behind these changes. These particular state personnel were the impulse behind the government liberation of public expenditures. Yet due to private sector protest and the president's lack of autonomy vis-à-vis large-scale investors,[132] these technocrats failed to attain complete internal control over economic decisionmaking. In spite of being unable to direct the totality of state economic activities as Hacienda had, the technocrats in Patrimonio Nacional were nevertheless able to disrupt the content of state economic policy long enough after 1972 to disturb Treasury's financial clout, which had positioned it at the apex of economic decisionmaking. When the president gave in to Flores de la Peña's neo-Keynesian recommendations to liberate public expenditures in 1972, Treasury's de facto control of public investment and expenditure dissolved, eventually leaving Hacienda technocrats to compete with Patrimonio technocrats for control over public economic decisionmaking. The incoherent economic policies that ensued culminated in economic crisis in 1976 and shattered the Cardenista myth that the PRI presidency personified a perpetually strong and progressive state.

Conclusion

Luis Echeverría entered office at a particularly inopportune time in the life of the PRI presidency. In fact, he entered the presidency on the eve of a revival of the Cardenista discourse and debate about the "sovereign" responsibilities of PRI governments for protecting the revolution from its enemies "inside" and "outside" Mexico. The *internal* dimension of the original Cardenista discourse of Mexican state sovereignty had been set aside by PRI presidents for thirty years, ever since Cárdenas left office in 1940. That internal discourse was revived during the Echeverría term for three major reasons. First, economic growth began to falter in 1971 during Echeverría's first year in office. A recession in the United States conspired with problems inherent in Mexico's stabilizing growth development strategy to stagnate the Mexican economy. This economic stagnation fueled the flames of an emergent national debate, in and outside government, about the effectiveness and social fairness of Mexico's conservative growth strategy devised in 1954. As the economy deteriorated in 1971, economic reformers in government and critics of stabilizing growth outside government found firmer ground on which to raise questions about the PRI presidency's "revolutionary" credentials and alleged ability to protect Mexico's poor.

A second major reason a debate resurfaced about the ability of PRI governments to deliver revolutionary social justice inside Mexico was the fact that in 1969 and 1970, the incoming president, Luis Echeverría, had promised a shift in development strategy but had hesitated to proceed with reform. The president-elect appointed reformist technocrats to major secretarial posts in 1970 in an attempt to counter the political fallout from the government's involvement in the Tlatelolco massacre of protesting students in 1968. But, in spite of his reformist gestures, as of 1971, Echeverría had still not abandoned the conservative economic policies of stabilizing growth. This hesitation fed the frustration and determination of his reformist technocratic appointees.

When economic stagnation set in, reformist technocrats seized the opportunity to pressure the president to abandon the stabilizing growth program in the interest of reviving the economy and shoring up social welfare. The economic reformers in Patrimonio Nacional, in particular, revived Cardenista arguments for a strong, interventionist state apparatus dedicated to social welfare. Finally, Secretary Flores de la Peña convinced the president to drop stabilizing growth restrictions on government spending and proceed with neo-Keynesian growth strategies. This unleashed a fury of

public debate about appropriate economic policy in and outside government and led to a series of government–private sector confrontations over
the attempted economic reforms.

Third, Cardenista discourse about the presidency's and the state's
"sovereign" control over the economy for protection of the poor inside
Mexico found renewed expression in and outside government because
Echeverría lost control over his own technocrats. Competition and conflict
broke out between Echeverría's reformist and conservative technocratic
appointees, especially those in Patrimonio Nacional and the Treasury.
When reformer Flores de la Peña temporarily won control over public
spending in 1971, the discourse long ignored by the Treasury about the
state's sovereign control of the economy in the cause of social justice
inside Mexico was rekindled. Since 1940, Treasury technocrats and PRI
presidents had emphasized the revolutionary importance of the Mexican
state's strength vis-à-vis outside obstacles to Mexico's industrial development in relation to a competitive world economy. On the other hand,
Patrimonio Nacional technocrats revived notions about the revolutionary
importance of the state's strength vis-à-vis inside obstacles to economic
development and social justice. The public technocratic showdown
between these two rival interpretations of Mexican state sovereignty
peaked in and after 1973 when Treasury Secretary Hugo Margáin resigned
his post over his strong disagreement with the Patrimonio Nacional deficit
spending program.

From this point onward in 1973, the revival of the Cardenista discourse
on revolutionary state sovereignty exercised inside Mexico proved politically devastating not only for the Echeverría government but for the PRI
presidency as well. In its entire history, the Mexican state had never been
more than temporarily and marginally capable of fulfilling Cardenista
promises. Moreover, the PRI presidency was politically ill-equipped in the
early 1970s to attempt to revive Cardenista rhetoric's internal focus on
state control over the domestic economy in defense of Mexico's poor.
Although the state proved to be temporarily strong enough as a complex
organization to substitute public investment for private investment and
revive growth, the president caved in to private sector protest as soon as
Margáin resigned from the Treasury. After the resignation, new Treasury
Secretary López Portillo revived stabilizing growth's restrictive monetary
policy. This was an undeniable demonstration of the presidency's long-
accumulated, historical weakness vis-à-vis private investors. Even though
Echeverría had entrusted Patrimonio Nacional with major decisions on
public spending, Echeverría empowered the Treasury to revive restrictive
monetary policies contradicting and undermining the expansionary economic objectives of Patrimonio spending programs. These contradictory
decisions exposed the president as claiming economic reform but being
incapable of implementing it.

The Cardenista myth about the PRI presidency as the personification of revolutionary state strength was shattered between 1973 and 1976 primarily because the PRI government's technocratic elite were conflicted and divided over economic policy, and that situation was exposed to public view via the president's contradictory policies. The president could not symbolically personify a strong state because he himself was incapable of even deciding which set of economic advisers to rely on. After 1973, in the face of intense private sector protest, investment strikes, and capital flight, Echeverría either watered down or backed down on every major attempted reform he proposed. Because the myth of Mexican state sovereignty as state strength hinged on a PRI presidency that always *appeared* in control, the myth suffered irreparable damage from Echeverría's public display of weakness.

5

Struggling with State Weakness: State Sovereignty Defined as Technocratic Efficiency

Economic Transition and the Secretariat of Programming and Budget, 1977–1982

The SPP:
Its Statist Beginnings and Privatist Ending

This chapter examines the statist impetus behind the emergence of Mexico's national secretariat of Programming and Budget (the SPP) during and after the Echeverría years. It also examines the SPP's administrative creation in 1977 and its consolidation as an increasingly privatist, central state agency in 1981 and 1982.

Part of the initial impetus behind the SPP's 1977 formation was the rapid public sector expansion orchestrated by Echeverría's reformist technocrats in the early and mid-1970s. When economic stagnation occurred in 1970 and 1971, the neo-Keynesian technocrats in Patrimonio Nacional gained a new voice in economic decisionmaking. Their persuasiveness was as much a product of conjunctural economic conditions as of the unwillingness of Treasury technocrats to formulate an alternative to stabilizing growth.

As secretary of Patrimonio Nacional, Horacio Flores de la Peña led the move to activate a temporary state organizational strength by persuading the president to liberate public expenditures from the orthodox spending rules of stabilizing growth. Paradoxically, the private sector's efforts to block economic reform through capital flight and investment strikes actually served to catalyze and accelerate the creation of new public enterprises and the use of state enterprise and public investment as temporary substitutes for private investment. The expansion of public spending, parastatal investment, and public enterprise not only signaled the collapse of Treasury domination of public spending but eventually culminated in a process of reorganization of public sector economic decisionmaking. The SPP was born of this process.

In reaction to the public-private sector confrontations, private capital flight, and general economic chaos of the Echeverría term, López Portillo created the SPP as an administrative reform solution to the political and economic malaise of 1976 and 1977. Whereas the expansion of public sector intervention from 1972 to 1976 temporarily enhanced the role of goal-based economic planners within the state apparatus, the economic crisis of 1976 encouraged the inclusion of orthodox budgeting functions within the new planning secretariat which replaced the Presidencia secretariat in 1977. Carlos Tello, the first SPP secretary and a Cambridge-trained structuralist economist and advocate of economic reform since 1965, resigned his post over policy disagreements with the secretariat of the Treasury and negotiator of Mexico's agreement with the International Monetary Fund (IMF) in 1977, Julio Moctezuma Cid. Moctezuma Cid was a moderate administrative reformer who designed the SPP, including within it both a subsecretariat of planning and one of budgeting, transporting the latter subsecretariat directly from the budgeting apparatus in Treasury. Tello's resignation was indicative of the fact that the new budgeting and planning secretariat was not to champion economic and social reform as Tello envisioned them.

The consolidation of the SPP as the state's leading economic secretariat was not completed until another economic crisis arose in the early 1980s, when the private banking sector was nationalized. The public foreign debt crisis of 1982 was not only a vestige of the Echeverría and López Portillo borrowing and spending years. The debt crisis was also linked to the stabilizing growth strategy, which had fostered an economically powerful private financial sector insistent, by the early 1980s, on siphoning public credit off into dollar accounts rather than employing it in productive investment. The gravity of the crisis as well as the administrative challenge of absorbing private banks galvanized an otherwise internally divided SPP into managing the debt crisis by privatizing and dissolving public sector enterprises.[1] Under the leadership of Secretary Miguel de la Madrid Hurtado, the SPP sought to apply and enforce market criteria of efficiency to public enterprise in order to *redirect* the Mexican economy out of its profound state of financial crisis.[2]

The Costs of the Demise of the State Sovereignty Myth: Public Foreign Debt and the Origins of the SPP

Deficit spending as a product of divisive, reformist impulses within the state apparatus became the impetus to an internal upheaval in the organization of governance of the economy in Mexico during the Echeverría presidency. This internal administrative upheaval eventually culminated in the creation of the secretariat of Programming and Budget, a new, public economic decisionmaking center for the state. While deficit spending was not by itself demonstrative of an autonomous state, it prompted a rapid change in the organizational expanse of the state as well as a debilitation of the myth of a powerful presidency.[3]

As discussed in Chapter 4, the Echeverría years witnessed an accelerated government spending program that neutralized Treasury's fiscal hold over state agencies long enough to permit a rapid expansion of the parastatal sector in both level of investments and number of new agencies created.[4] The number of state-owned enterprises jumped from a total of 175 in 1971 to 458 in 1976. Total current public expenditures increased from 8 percent of GNP in 1966–1972 to 10.7 percent in 1973–1975. Federal government expenditures grew dramatically from 41 billion pesos in 1971 to 145 billion in 1975, a 250 percent increase.[5] Finally, public investment's share of total investment rose from 37 percent in 1970 to 51 percent by the end of the Echeverría *sexenio*.[6] Clearly, the public sector's role in the economy was intensified as the weight of government investments in the total GNP rose from 5.9 percent in 1970 to 9.20 percent in 1975.[7]

This dramatic increase in public spending and in the state's role in total investment was financed, of course, mainly through the Mexican state's contraction of loans from foreign, commercial banks.[8] In the absence of tax reform, increased prices for public sector goods or other measures to increase public revenue, the Echeverría government turned to foreign, private sources to finance its sustained program of public spending. Foreign borrowing from private sources did not begin to accelerate, however, until after the president's attempted tax reform failed to materialize in December 1972. Beginning in 1973, the government's spending of foreign borrowed monies jumped dramatically, as Table 5.1 indicates.

Table 5.1   Mexico's External Public Debt: Net Annual Loan Monies Disbursed (loans with repayment periods exceeding one year)

Year	Thousands of Dollars
1970	782,424
1971	799,214
1972	966,711
1973	2,115,448
1974	3,014,461
1975	4,011,110
1976	5,506,443

Source: IBRD, *World Debt Tables,* EL-167/78 (Washington, D.C., 1978), p. 117.

From 1970 to 1976, Mexico's total external public debt rose from $4,120 million at the beginning of the Echeverría term to $19.6 billion by the end of the term. As Michel Bouchet points out, "At the end of 1976, Mexico was more indebted to U.S. banks than any other nation in the developing world. Over 60% of Mexico's borrowing came from U.S. banks. . . . Furthermore, about 47% of the outstanding debt was due to mature in 1977."[9]

While the federal government was borrowing to cover budget expenditures and to finance external payment obligations, the single greatest percentage of foreign public debt (approximately 33 percent) contracted by the middle of 1975 was contracted by Nacional Financiera (NAFINSA), the major state-owned, industrial development bank.[10] In fact, during this period of accelerated foreign public borrowing from 1973 to 1976, NAFINSA became the "public sector's principal financial agent in terms of contracting and negotiating external debt."[11] After contracting loans from foreign commercial banks, NAFINSA, in turn, loaned out the foreign borrowed monies to both state enterprises and private firms in an effort to stimulate productive investment.[12]

Two-thirds of NAFINSA's financial resources in 1975 were from foreign sources.[13] NAFINSA became the principal state agency for channeling foreign borrowed funds to state enterprises and to the remainder of a rapidly expanding parastatal sector. This meant that, in defiance of the private sector's unwillingness to agree to contribute more tax revenues to cover rising public expenditures and the private sector's reluctance to invest in productive activities,[14] the state borrowed money to finance NAFINSA and other state development banks in order to sustain industrial investment.

As is clear from Table A in Appendix 3, the sectoral allocation of NAFINSA's externally borrowed resources changed fairly dramatically during the Echeverría *sexenio*. Public investments in infrastructure decreased rather precipitously, whereas NAFINSA's investment in industry jumped from 67 percent of total investment in 1973 to 84 percent in 1976. Hence, not only was the public sector lending to itself instead of relying on the level of credit available through the Mexican private banking system, but it was also redefining the purpose of public investment by directing more funds to industrial activities increasingly carried out by state enterprises.[15]

NAFINSA therefore became the main conduit for the distribution of credit to the parastatal sector and to segments of the private sector. Table 5.2 indicates a very substantial increase in the amount of NAFINSA's funds allocated to industrial investment, especially in basic industries. The facts that NAFINSA was the major state borrowing agency by 1975, that two-thirds of NAFINSA's funds by that date were from foreign sources, and that a much greater proportion of its funds from 1970 to 1975 was directed toward investment in basic industries as compared to its allocations for infrastructural investments all suggest that a great deal of the foreign funds borrowed by the public sector were being used to stimulate and/or sustain industrial activity in the Mexican economy from 1973 to 1975. In fact, during the first five years of the Echeverría term, public investment grew at a faster rate than private investment, so that by 1975, 45 percent of all gross capital formation in Mexico was public in origin as compared to 30 percent in 1971.[16]

Table 5.2   Financing Granted by NAFINSA by Economic Sector (millions of pesos)

Economic sectors	1934	1940	1950	1960	1965	1970	1975
Total	16	20	2,237	13,568	25,523	44,864	95,758
Infrastructure	—	3	333	1,305	4,415	13,708	20,396
Industry	7	2	1,460	11,052	18,865	29,432	70,519[a]
Basic	—	2	1,077	8,593	14,520	21,429	54,180
Others of transformation	7	—	383	2,459	4,345	8,003	16,339
Other activities	9	15	444	1,211	2,243	1,724	4,843

Source: Nacional Financiera, S.A. Cited in Rosa Olivia Villa M., Nacional Financiera (Mexico City: Nacional Financiera, 1976).
Note: a. Large increase from the 1970 level

Table 5.3 compares the public and private sector shares in gross fixed investment as a percentage of GNP for the years 1971 to 1976. The private sector's share of investment declined over the course of the presidential term from a high of 12.8 percent of GNP in 1970 to a low of 11.4 percent of GNP in 1976. The public sector's share of investment, on the other hand, experienced a significant increase over the course of the *sexenio,* especially if one takes into account the low of 5.4 percent in 1971 and the sustained high level of 8.7 percent in the final year of the *sexenio.*

Table 5.3   Gross Fixed Investment (as a percentage of GNP at 1970 prices)

	1971	1972	1973	1974	1975	1976
Total	18.2	18.9	20.4	20.6	21.2	20.1
Public	5.4	7.1	8.8	8.2	9.6	8.7
Private[a]	12.8	11.8	11.6	12.4	11.6	11.4

Sources: Banco de México, S.A. Estadísticas de la Oficina de Cuentas de Producción, 1960–1976, documento CP (E) 77/22, Mexico, 1977; Secretaría de Programación y Presupuesto, *Información económica y social básica,* vol. 1, no. 3, Mexico, October 1977. Elaborated by and cited in Tello, *La política económica en México,* p. 194.
Note: a. Includes national and foreign

As is clear from Table 5.4, 417 new parastatal entities were created between 1972—when public expenditures were liberated—and 1976—the final year of the Echeverría *sexenio*. Between 1973 and 1976, the years of most intense public-private sector conflict, 227 public enterprises with majority state participation were created and another twenty-seven enterprises with minority state participation added. Between 1972 and 1973 alone, a total of 216 more financial trusts were added to the public sector. Even more revealing is the fact that the total of all parastatal entities increased from 227 in 1971 to 845 in 1976.

Table 5.4   Parastatal Entities Registered in the Secretariat of Patrimonio Nacional, 1970–1976

	1970	1971	1972	1973	1974	1975	1976
Decentralized organisms	45	54	61	63	65	117	176
Public enterprises (majority state participation)	39	148	176	229	282	323	403
Public enterprises (minority state participation)	—	27	24	28	36	41	55
Financial trusts (credit institutions)	—	48	167	383	387	325	211
Total	84	277	428	703	770	806	845

Source: Informe Anual, Secretaría del Patrimonio Nacional. Cited by Alejandro Carrillo Castro, *La Reforma Administrativa en México* (Mexico City: Miguel Angel Porrúa, 1980).

In the absence of tax reform and private sector economic cooperation with the government's reform efforts, neo-Keynesian technocrats sought other means to finance the dramatic growth in public expenditure and public intervention. The contraction of public sector loans from large, foreign commercial banks was as much a function of the increase in international liquidity in the 1970s as of technocratic reformers' determination to proceed with an alternative growth strategy in spite of the private sector's refusal to finance budget deficits domestically. Massive foreign public borrowing to finance public spending in combination with private sector investment slowdowns and capital flight eventually led to contradictory economic policies after 1973 and then to dire economic crisis in 1976.[17]

In spite of these substantial increases in the public sector's participation in the economy, however, it would be an exaggeration to claim that public investment was designed to replace private investment. In fact, increasing percentages of NAFINSA's funds were being allocated to medium- and small-scale, private industry. In August 1972, for example, FOGAIN, NAFINSA's Trust for Credit and Development of Medium- and Small-Scale Industry, was substantially reformed to expand its range of credit activities beyond serving as a mere intermediary between private banks and medium- and small-scale business.[18] After August 1972, FOGAIN's dramatic increase in credit operations was financed through its issuance of bonds and through resources transferred to it from the federal government through national credit institutions, especially NAFINSA.[19] Once FOGAIN's credit activities were extended beyond reliance on domestic private banks, the balance of its portfolio increased by 21 percent between 1972 and 1975.[20] Table 5.5 illustrates the extent to which liberalization of credit sources and activities expanded FOGAIN's range of development activities.

Table 5.5   FOGAIN's Operations (cumulative figures)

Type of Operation	August 1972	June 1976	% Increment
Number of authorized credits	12,017	20,617	72
Firms receiving credits	6,163	10,712	74
Total amounts of authorized credits (millions of pesos)	2,943	6,749.1	131
Total amounts of used credits (millions of pesos)	2,811.9	6,373.1	127

Source: Rosa Olivia Villa M., *Nacional Financiera* (Mexico City: Nacional Financiera, 1976), p. 135.

Furthermore, not only were increasing amounts of public sector credits extended to medium- and small-scale private industry, but continued low prices of public sector goods and services themselves continued to represent substantial subsidies to private enterprise. Early on in the term, the government attempted to rationalize and increase the prices of public sector goods and services but abandoned such attempts due to wide-ranging political opposition.[21] The continuation of low prices for public sector goods and services during the Echeverría years eliminated an important potential source of public revenues in a time when public spending was rising rapidly. In short, they represented a very costly public subsidy to private enterprise. Approximately one year after Echeverría left office, the World Bank estimated that public subsidies to the private sector, which were implicit in the prices and rates of public sector goods and services, represented more than 6 percent of GNP in 1977.[22]

The net effect of the rapid expansion of the public sector's role in the economy during the Echeverría *sexenio* was not the economic displacement of the private sector by the state. Instead, public sector expansion manufactured a temporary state organizational capacity for economic interventions in contradiction with the short-term interests of particular segments of private investors, particularly foreign investors enamored of the stabilizing growth strategy.[23] The partial abandonment of the spending rules of *desarrollo estabilizador* allowed reformist technocrats the opportunity to use the parastatal sector as a means of undercutting Treasury's financial and planning hold over public sector activities in general. To expand the parastatal sector's reach into the economy was to undermine Treasury's maintenance of a level of public expenditures that was low enough to permit internal financing of public budget deficits by the local banking system.[24]

Even though restrictive monetary and state revenue-gathering policies were maintained in an attempt to avoid private capital flight and other adverse private sector reactions,[25] revenue restrictions were not sufficient to prevent massive federal government transfers of capital to the parastatal sector to finance its program of expenditures. Carlos Tello estimates that over the six years of the Echeverría administration, federal government current and capital account transfers to the parastatal sector constituted more than 60 percent of the federal government deficit.[26] The price paid for this massive transfer of funds was a burgeoning public, foreign indebtedness. To the president and the reformist technocrats advising him, however, this seemed a less onerous price to pay in 1972 and 1973 than the economic and political consequences of continuing with *desarrollo estabilizador* and Treasury's dominance of public sector spending.

The massive capitalization of the parastatal sector during the Echeverría years was demonstrative of the state's organizational capacity to reorganize, at least temporarily, the nature of public intervention in the economy in spite of private sector disapproval. After sixteen years of restricted public revenues and limited budgets, however, the transfer of large amounts of capital to the parastatal sector constituted an invitation to create huge budget deficits and led to private investment strikes in reaction to increased public expenditures. The private sector's responses to the reformism of the Echeverría administration have been well documented elsewhere.[27] On ten major reformist issues, one or a number of the largest segments of private capital organized in either CONCANACO (large commercial interests), CONCAMIN (large industrialists), COPARMEX (the large employer union), ABM (large banking interests), or CAMCO (foreign investors, mainly transnational corporations) were the principal voices of protest (see Appendix 4).

The tendency toward capital flight (see Table 5.6) as a form of private reaction to the Echeverría government's abandonment of the public spending of *desarrollo estabilizador* contributed to the development of a policy

Table 5.6   **Principal Liabilities of Private and Mixed Banks in Foreign Currency ($ million)**

Balance at the End of:	Total	Checking Accounts	Savings Accounts	Promissory Notes	Certificates of Deposit
1971	400.3	140.3	64.3	195.7	—
1972	357.4	170.0	69.9	117.5	—
1973	587.8	339.8	115.3	132.7	—
1974	540.6	280.6	124.2	131.8	4.0
1975	816.1	319.0	130.0	238.2	128.9
January	508.6	248.8	120.6	127.2	12.0
August	641.9	273.0	118.5	177.7	72.7
September	656.2	257.3	117.4	195.0	86.5
October	675.2	243.3	121.4	206.8	103.7
November	700.3	248.8	121.0	217.0	113.5
1976					
January	828.2	278.1	132.7	264.5	152.9
August	1,681.4	377.5	186.3	335.6	782.0
September	1,574.4	349.3	124.4	313.7	787.0
October	1,798.7	444.7	179.3	307.5	867.2
November	1,911.3	548.7	194.0	96.7	871.9

Source: Secretariat of Programming and Budget, *Información económica y social básica,* vol. 1, no. 3 (October 1977): 312. Cited in Tello, *La política económica,* p. 161.
Note: Excludes loans from foreign banks.

deadlock within the state that essentially paralyzed any remaining presidential abilities to intervene effectively in the economy to promote economic growth. If the president's ability to direct public sector activities had eroded during the previous years of *desarrollo estabilizador,* it fully collapsed during the Echeverría *sexenio* under the weight of the crisis in economic governance structures that began during those years. The policy deadlock between the president's emphasis on abandoning *desarrollo estabilizador* while at the same time continuing to abide by that strategy's monetary and revenue (tax) restrictions to placate the private sector did indeed signal the wholesale collapse of presidential abilities to direct coherent public sector interventionism in the economy. The policy contradictions resulting from presidential ambivalence eventually led to economic recession in 1975 and then acute fiscal crisis and subsequent devaluation of the peso in 1976 (see Figures 4.3 and 4.4).

A number of scholars[28] have characterized this deadlock between presidential pursuit of expansionist policies and the continuation of monetary and revenue restrictions as a period exemplifying severe "limits to reformism" placed on the presidency by the private sector. The policy deadlock did, in fact, reflect the president's inability to push through reforms or to abandon restrictive monetary policies in the face of private sector opposition. Implicit in the deadlock, however, was a temporary invigoration of the state's organizational capacity to promote economic growth by substituting public expansionism for private investment slow-down. In short, the deadlock was a product of presidential sensitivity to private sector paranoia as well as a product of the relatively autonomous impulses of reformist technocrats within the state apparatus, where the real stimulus behind the expansion of public expenditures originated. The president, of course, failed to implement a wholly coherent, noncontradictory set of economic reform policies. One of the most important results of this failure was the transforming effect of the policy deadlock on the structure of economic governance within the state.

The neutralization of Treasury's dominance of public sector spending and revenue policies and therefore of public sector interventionism did indeed reveal the weakness of a presidency unable to formulate and fully implement reformist policies contrary, in the short run, to particular private interests.[29] Of course, the period of *desarrollo estabilizador* had witnessed a gradual erosion of the image of the president as the embodiment of the interests of the popular sectors of society, but presidential weakness vis-à-vis segments of the private sector did not become an acute political liability until 1968 and afterward. Not until *desarrollo estabilizador* and Treasury's hold over public sector activities became problematic in the late 1960s and early 1970s for both the economic and social welfare functions of the state did limited presidential power and autonomy lead to an impasse for public economic governance.

The political crisis of 1968 combined with the economic stagnation of the stabilizing growth strategy in 1970 and 1971 pressured the president to violate the spending and revenue restrictions of stabilizing growth. The impasse in state structures occurred as a result of the presidency having conceded governmental authority over the planning of public sector activities to Hacienda decades earlier. Such concession of authority was as much a function of the financial difficulties of peripheral industrialization as of the peculiar characteristics of Cárdenas-style *presidencialismo*. The Cárdenas presidency was inherently resistant to the transfer of planning authority to state agencies because the ideological keystone of Cardenista presidentialism was premised on one person appearing to wield all the power of the state. Presidential ability to define and implement the national policy agenda for rapid industrialization was not seriously challenged as long as the easy phase of import substitution (begun in 1940) proceeded without the necessity of strict, centralized financial control over the burgeoning parastatal sector. As soon as the financial difficulties of state-led industrialization intensified at the conclusion of the Second World War, the presidency had to tighten executive financial control over the parastatal sector in reaction to the financial difficulties confronting the Mexican industrialization process.

The deadlock between economic expansionism and economic orthodoxy of the Echeverría years reflected a showdown between the long-accumulated power of financial and monetary authorities allied with large, private investors and the attempted assertion of an organizational strength of the state. The outcome of this showdown was not just the president's inability to outmaneuver the largest segments of private capital. In fact, simply to emphasize the importance of reduced presidential autonomy in relation to the private sector is to state an obvious fact that had been true at least since the late 1950s. The Mexican state overcame the impasse in governance structures that occurred from 1973 to 1976 through a reorganization of the structure of public economic governance in the late 1970s and early 1980s. This reorganization redistributed some of the Treasury's vast authority over the economy but was also the result of a profound weakening of the Cárdenas myth of presidential omnipotence. The Echeverría debacle laid the foundation for a new internal organization of economic decisionmaking authority entrusted to the new national Programming and Budget secretariat.

The SPP as an Administrative Reform "Solution" to Technocratic Infighting and Economic Chaos, 1976–1980

Deficit spending per the expansionary plans of Flores de la Peña quickly came to an end by 1976 as a major economic crisis approached, yet the proponents of an equally discredited *desarrollo estabilizador* presented no viable alternative to organizing public economic decisionmaking. By 1976, the obstructionism of the largest segments of the private sector in Mexico had made a return to the stabilizing growth strategy as infeasible as shared development was for restoring some sort of national unity regarding Mexico's developmental strategy. Thus, when López Portillo entered office in 1976 proclaiming the need to organize the government in order to organize the country, his administrative reform solution prevailed even though the proposed Alliance for Production was hardly a well-defined strategy of economic development.

The Organic Law of Federal Public Administration, which formed the core of López Portillo's administrative reform, redistributed planning and budgeting authority over parastatal enterprise to a new secretariat of Programming and Budget whose officially designated tasks were:

I. The collection of data and elaboration—with the participation of interested groups—of national, sectoral, and regional plans of economic and social development; the elaboration of the general plan of public expenditure of the Federal Executive and of special projects designated by the President

II. The planning of public works, . . . and of the use of such works, the planning of regional and local development as directed by the President for the general public good . . .

IV. The planning, authorization, coordination, monitoring, and evaluation of the public investment of the entities [secretariats and departments] of centralized public administration and of the public investments of parastatal entities[30]

Hence, Programming and Budget captured the Treasury's authority over the planning of public expenditures and the budgeting of government spending. It also gained part of Patrimonio Nacional's administrative authority over the parastatals through SPP's new budgeting responsibilities for that sector.

The López Portillo administration portrayed the SPP as an administrative solution to the impasse between statist reformism and private sector obstructionism of the Echeverría years. Clearly, the creation of the SPP did not eliminate private investors' influence on the state. The SPP represented instead a reorganization of economic decisionmaking authority transferring some of the Treasury's long-accumulated budgeting authority and the president's responsibility for overall economic conditions to the SPP. For instance, no longer would the secretary of the Treasury monopolize control over the budget and the subsecretary of Expenditure within the Treasury allocate funds to and audit the central secretariats. The SPP, instead, assumed both actual budgeting tasks as well as a new control over the production of the state's discourse or rhetoric of economic development.

After the 1977 creation of the SPP, official rhetoric claimed that within the SPP, *national economic planning* of mass socioeconomic well-being was to mingle with *budgeting* to establish the central organizing principles of public economic decisionmaking. This rhetoric reflected the López Portillo government's attempted use of the SPP to revive the myth of a strong state dedicated to the provision of popular social welfare rather than simply the promotion of private investment. Until late 1982, this rhetoric appeared plausible for two reasons during most of the López Portillo term.

First, the reorganization of the secretariats of state stripped Hacienda of its monopoly of control over public finance, leaving it with formal authority over monetary policy, the administration of revenue through taxation and credit activities, and the right to administer the use of borrowed funds.[31] The tasks of allocating public funds, auditing public expenditure activities, and evaluating the use of public funds were all transferred to the SPP.

Second, the discovery of large oil reserves in the late 1970s and extensive public sector borrowing on future oil revenues throughout the López Portillo term increased the amount of public revenues available for all sorts of state expenditures. The SPP had more revenues to work with, thus lending credence to its claims of planning for socioeconomic welfare. However, in 1981 and 1982 when world oil prices dropped and interest rates on Mexico's foreign debt soared, public revenues quickly dried up and a much more thoroughly pro–private sector face of SPP technocrats appeared.

Contrary to being anti–private sector in design, the new SPP internalized part of the fiscal orthodoxy of the Treasury. The transfer of Treasury's orthodox, fiscal criteria to the subsecretariat of Budget within the SPP was clear from the moment of the new secretariat's inception. With López Portillo's backing during his campaign for the presidency, Julio Rodolfo Moctezuma Cid designed the new secretariat. Moctezuma Cid had an extended affiliation with the administrative reform movement that arose in the secretariat of the Presidencia in the 1960s.[32] He was clearly *not* associated in a direct manner with the so-called radical reformist technocrats led by Horacio Flores de la Peña in Patrimonio Nacional, but was instead ideologically closer to López Portillo's brand of administrative reformism, which was ambivalent about the particular economic development strategy or economic philosophy espoused.

The full extent of Moctezuma Cid's affinity to Treasury's fiscal orthodoxy came to the foreground in 1976 and 1977 when, as secretary of the Treasury, he presided over Mexico's signing of an agreement with the IMF after the devaluation of the peso in 1976. He clashed rather dramatically with Carlos Tello, the new secretary of Programming and Budget, over the type of economic recovery program Mexico should adopt in 1977.[33] Moctezuma Cid rejected Tello's statist emphasis on expanding the activities of the parastatal sector in order to overcome the structural imbalances and bottlenecks associated with peripheral capitalism.[34] He contended instead that Tello's statist-structuralist approach was too inflationary and advocated that Mexico adopt an economic stabilization policy along the orthodox lines set out in the IMF agreement.[35]

As a result of the policy split, López Portillo asked both Tello and Moctezuma Cid to resign. The fact that the very designer of the SPP was forced into resigning from Treasury as soon as his leanings toward Treasury orthodoxy were opposed by the head of the very agency he had created provides an inside glimpse into the political balancing activity that pervaded the state in 1977 and afterward. The pursuit of a truce between economic orthodoxy and statist reformism was evident in other personnel changes as well as in the very structure of the SPP itself.

The secretariat of Programming and Budget was designed with three principal subsecretariats: Programming, Budget, and Evaluation. The subsecretariat of Programming was charged with the task of formulating a five-year plan and an annual operating program in consultation with Budget on the financing of the plan and in consultation with Evaluation to ensure that the plan could be evaluated.[36] The personnel chosen to staff Programming were drawn principally from Patrimonio Nacional and the extinct secretariat of the Presidencia. The first subsecretary of Programming, Eduardo Pascual, was supportive of Carlos Tello's structuralist critique of monetarist orthodoxy. When López Portillo asked Tello to resign, Pascual also left and was succeeded in 1978 by Alfonso Cebreros as subsecretary of Programming. Cebreros had had an extended career in Patrimonio Nacional and had been a student of Flores de la Peña.[37] In short, the highest personnel in Programming were associated with the statist reformism of the structuralist economists.

The subsecretariat of Budget, on the other hand, which was charged with advising Programming on the financing of public investments, was drawn largely from Treasury. According to John Bailey, when SPP was created, the technical, operating departments of the subsecretary of Expenditure of the Treasury were transplanted "virtually intact" to the subsecretariat of Budget in SPP.[38] The subsecretary of Budget himself, Miguel Rico Ramírez, had formerly served under subsecretary of Expenditure, Enrique Camaño Muñoz, in Treasury. Rico Ramírez was criticized by those in Programming for zealously supervising parastatal budget formulation and implementation, a task that was supposed to have been delegated to the parastatal sector heads.[39] Generally, those in Programming regarded Budget as representative of the fiscal orthodoxy of the Treasury having been transplanted to the SPP, and this did, in fact, appear to be the case.

However, the presence of Treasury orthodoxy was not the only defining feature of the SPP. Instead, the new secretariat was really representative of the institutionalization of a new technocratization of economic decisionmaking to replace the highly visible political infighting between statist reformism and monetarist orthodoxy. The subsecretary of Budget did, in fact, replicate Treasury orthodoxy, but the institutional context of the SPP was such that the old monetarist and statist discourses were increasingly replaced by a new technical rhetoric claiming to replace politics with science.

The establishment of such a technocracy, however, was not without its upheavals in personnel. After Carlos Tello was asked to resign, Ricardo García Sainz became secretary of SPP. García Sainz's earliest public appointment was under Hugo B. Margáin,[40] Echeverría's first Treasury secretary who resigned over policy disagreements regarding the economic expansionism advocated by Patrimonio Nacional (see Chapter 4). García Sainz's preferences for fiscal orthodoxy in general and for the recommendations of the subsecretariat of Budget in SPP became very clear in 1979 when he apparently did not intervene to correct Subsecretary of the Budget Miguel Rico's failure to fund a program given priority by Programming.[41]

In a balancing act, López Portillo removed both García Sainz and Rico several months later in 1979. Tello's removal in 1977 was symptomatic of growing fears that as secretary of SPP, he would allow Programming to dominate policymaking. In a similar respect, García Sainz was removed out of a fear that, as head of SPP, he would allow Budget to gain the upper hand. John Bailey cites evidence of Budget's growing aggressiveness, especially after Tello resigned as secretary of SPP:

> More serious perhaps was the criticism that Budget was doing its own programming. The General Directorate of Investment [in Budget] delved into the details of Investment projects, challenged cost estimates and demanding extensive justification. In at least one case, the Directorate selected certain projects for funding and rejected others, without sufficient regard for the programmatic consequences of its decisions. During the course of budget implementation in 1978, the Subsecretariat of Budget initiated a series of adjustments without consulting officials from Programming or Evaluation.[42]

In an attempt intended, at least in part, to diffuse some of the conflict between the central subsecretariats, the new secretary of the SPP, Miguel de la Madrid Hurtado, who succeeded García Sainz in May 1979, instituted a second phase of López Portillo's administrative reform, which hitherto had been somewhat ignored due to the power struggles and disputes between Programming and Budget. Part of López Portillo's master plan was the reorganization of the entire parastatal sector consisting of approximately 900 agencies; his sectorization plan consisted of organizing all parastatal agencies under eleven "sector heads." According to the plan, sector heads were to take an active part in programming and budgeting by setting goals and allocating funds for their particular sectors.[43] This emphasis on allowing sector heads to take an active part in planning and budgeting introduced an element of contradiction into the entire administrative reform process.

Sectorization as López Portillo envisioned it implied *decentralization* of the planning and budgeting of the parastatal sector through a dispersion of decisionmaking to the sector heads. In contrast, the creation of SPP was itself supposed to entail the centralization of planning and budgeting in the hands of the secretary of the SPP and the SPP's three subsecretariats. De la Madrid's emphasis on sectorization essentially converted the SPP into a *coordinator* of the plans of the various sectors instead of the mechanism of central decisionmaking on planning formally specified in the administrative reform law of 1977.[44] As such, from early 1979 until April 1980, when a global plan was introduced, national planning in Mexico consisted of a collection of sectoral plans rather than a global map for the direction of the entire public sector viewed as a whole.

Sectorization in the absence of global planning resulted in a decentralization that was contrary to the interests of both subsecretariats. Those elements associated with programming naturally preferred that wholehearted emphasis within the secretariat be placed on central planning, with the five-year Global Plan and annual programs taking center stage. Because the details of parastatal agency budgets would be determined by the plan devised primarily by the subsecretariat of Programming, the input of sector heads into the budgeting process would be minimized. This was especially the case since the heads of sectors might not always be entirely sure of the size of their agencies' budget allotments. If the details of parastatal agencies' expenditures were constantly subject to adjustment at the center of the secretariat, then sector heads were allowed only a minimum of information on which to base their plans. Orthodox technocrats within the subsecretariat of Budget, on the other hand, were more interested in minimizing the weight of the central planning function performed by Programming.

The preference in Budget was that the General Directorate of Investment (within Budget) supervise the details of parastatal investment projects and make the decisions as to which projects would or would not be funded. Spending overruns served as Budget's principal rationale for claiming a greater share of Programming's planning authority. When Miguel de la Madrid became the secretary, however, one of his first acts was to meet with sector heads to inform them explicitly what the size of their budget allotments would be.[45] This meant that neither Programming nor Budget retained ultimate control over the planning process.

Approximately one year into de la Madrid's term of office, the SPP presented a Global Plan of Development for the years 1980 through 1982. When López Portillo approved the plan in April 1980, he entrusted the SPP with even greater governmental authority and political responsibility for economic conditions and socioeconomic well-being. The plan included rhetoric related to goals for improving social welfare on the basis of the SPP's and the general public sector's organizational capacity to curve some of the negative effects of market forces on mass socioeconomic welfare. More specifically, the rhetoric of the approved Global Plan for 1980–1982 claimed goals to:

  I. Reaffirm and strengthen Mexico's independence as a democratic, just, and free nation in economic, political, and cultural aspects
 II. Provide the population with employment and a minimum of well-being, attending with priority to the necessities of nutrition, education, health, and housing
III. Promote rapid, sustained, and efficient economic growth
IV. Improve the distribution of income among the populace, the factors of production, and the geographical regions[46]

On approving the SPP's Global Plan, López Portillo established the following formal planning authority for the secretariat vis-à-vis the various sectors, directing the SPP to:

  I. Establish norms and aims for the elaboration and completion of sectoral and regional plans and programs in a way congruent with the Global Development Plan, 1980–82

II. Promote, with sector coordinators, the permanent compatibilization of sectoral and regional plans . . . with the Global Plan . . .

III. Compose the Medium-Term Program of Action of the Public Sector, beginning with the programs of action elaborated by the dependencies and entities (secretariats and departments) of the Federal Public Administration, in accord with the norms, aims, and forecasts of resources established by the SPP in the Global Plan . . .

IV. Promote, with sector coordinators, formulas of persuasion and approval of actions with the popular and private sectors[47]

The SPP's institutionalized juxtaposition of planning and budgeting functions within the framework of a single secretariat eventually enabled the SPP to manage both rapid expansion and contraction of the public sector. Treasury's previous, all-encompassing control of public expenditure was transferred to a secretariat that essentially forced revenue-based planners in the subsecretariat of Budget to interact with goal-based planners in the subsecretariat of Programming, although not necessarily for achieving objectives of enhanced social welfare. Furthermore, the creation of an Evaluation subsecretariat equipped the SPP with an important statistics-gathering capability. In effect, the SPP became a governmental nerve center for collecting and evaluating economic and social data on both the public and private sectors.

All these new technical capabilities related to evaluation, programming, and budgeting meant that the SPP was equipped to manage both the rapid public absorption of previously private economic operations and the rapid privatization of public enterprise. After the SPP gained formal authority over *global* planning and budgeting in the early 1980s, it was legally equipped to play a key managerial role in the 1982 statization of the Mexican private banking system and in the post–September 1982 sweeping program of privatization and dissolution of public enterprise.

Debt Crisis, Bank Statization, and Rapid Privatization: The SPP's Dual Role in Public Sector Expansion and Contraction, 1981–1982

By mid-1981, approximately one year after the Global Plan was approved, Mexico began to enter into a severe economic crisis, which greatly enhanced and consolidated the SPP's scope of authority over the public sector. By mid-1981, a number of economic problems converged to produce a crisis by 1982. In the first place, Mexico's production of exportable goods was declining with respect to total production.[48] Furthermore, foreign indebtedness had continued to grow such that between 1977 and 1981, four-fifths of the deficit in the current account of the balance of payments was due to the growing deficit in debt servicing.

External factors also deeply affected the Mexican economy and balance of payments during this period—in particular, the drop in world petroleum prices in June 1981. The increasing number of imports demanded by Mexican industry since 1977, the increasing imports demanded by the accelerated expansion of the petroleum industry, and increases in food imports had all encouraged greater and greater reliance on petroleum exports for foreign exchange earnings during the López Portillo term.[49] Hence, the drop in petroleum prices soon placed severe strains on Mexico's balance of payments. A second external shock was the rise in interest rates, which affected Mexico's debt servicing. LIBOR-denominated interest rates increased from an average of 6.5 percent in 1977 to 12.7 percent in 1980 and 16.7 percent in 1981.[50] Finally, with regard to Mexico's imbalance of payments disequilibrium, private capital flight reached unprecedented proportions. A total of $2,958 million exited Mexico in 1980 and another $10,914 million was withdrawn in 1981.[51]

Because the public sector had played a principal role in contracting the foreign debt that helped precipitate the economic crisis of 1981–1982, the Mexican executive's reliance on SPP's technical management of public expenditures and investment increased dramatically as the economic crisis deepened. Because of the international economic pressures noted above—in particular, the decline in world petroleum prices and rise in international interest rates—a crisis in public finances crystalized in 1981. In the previous year, 1980, the public sector had obtained foreign exchange (through petroleum exports and contraction of external debt) that exceeded the amounts required by the level of imports and debt service. This foreign exchange was largely proportioned to the Mexican private sector[52] to finance private imports and capital flight.[53] Carlos Tello describes the crisis of public finance, which soon provoked an even more centralized role for SPP as follows:

> In 1981 when the drop in demand and prices of petroleum combined with the rise in interest rates and with increased public expenditures above budgeted levels, the public sector deficit as a percentage of GDP increased substantially: from nearly 7.5% in 1980 it reached 15% in 1981. . . . The public deficit in 1981 was financed in considerable proportion with external public debt, contracted largely under short-run terms, which aggravated the problem of public finance and balance of payments even more. Of the increment of nearly $20 million in the balance of foreign public debt between 1980 and 1981, more than half was contracted under short-run terms (maturity within a year or less). The net foreign indebtedness of the public sector as a percentage of GDP, which was maintained at around 2.5% from 1979–1980, rose to 8% in 1981.[54]

This crisis in Mexican public finance and balance of payments prompted a series of governmental measures that left the SPP as the locus of economic decisionmaking within the state. The fact that foreign public borrowing was financing private capital flight, which was occurring in large measure via the Mexican private banking system itself, led López Portillo to consult privately with several reformist economists to nationalize the Mexican private banking system. Much of the private capital flight that was aggravating Mexico's already acute balance-of-payments problem was occurring on the basis of private savings accounts held in dollars within the Mexican private banking system. The gross profits accruing to private banks as a function of their exchange operations were substantial, especially during the period from January to August 1982.[55] As of August 31, 1982, from a total of 18,400 million pesos of gross profits, more than 8,900 million pesos were derived from exchange operations.[56] In other words, nearly 50 percent of all gross profits of the banking system were derived from exchange operations. By the end of August 1982, there were 11,330 million "Mex-dollars" deposited in private savings accounts within the Mexican banking system,[57] at a time when the Bank of Mexico lacked sufficient foreign exchange reserves to meet foreign obligations.

The role of the SPP in making possible the nationalization of private banks and the conversion of bank assets and liabilities into national currency became clearer early in 1982. In light of the symptoms of economic crisis that had appeared in the second half of 1981, as well as the public sector deficit that emerged in January 1982, the administrative reform law of 1977 was amended to make the SPP's global planning role and central authority over public investment as instituted for the Global Plan 1980–1982 *permanent* attributes of the secretariat. Among other things, the January 4 reform specified that SPP should do the following:

I. Engage in national planning of a global character and elaborate, with the participation of interested social groups, the corresponding national plan . . .

III. Coordinate the planning activities of the integral development of the country, and promote congruence between the Federal Public Administration [secretariats and departments] and the objectives, strategies, policies and goals of the national plan . . .

VII. Authorize the public investment programs of the parastatals, secretariats, and departments of Federal Public Administration.[58]

Precisely two months after this formal declaration of SPP's new permanent authority as a self-contained, centralized secretariat for the negotiation and determination of public spending and investment, the president secretly requested that Carlos Tello and José Andrés de Oteyza prepare a study[59] of alternative strategies to remedy problems related to the value of the peso against the dollar and the capital flight and acute balance-of-payments problems of the second half of 1981.

A devaluation in July 1982 failed to produce the desired foreign exchange results. Capital flight continued; foreign commercial banks suspended credits to Mexico in the same months, and by the beginning of August 1982 the Bank of Mexico lacked sufficient international reserves to meet foreign exchange obligations.[60] In this climate of dire economic crisis in mid-August 1982, the secret Tello–de Oteyza plans for nationalizing private banks and converting the Bank of Mexico into a parastatal ("decentralized") entity were accepted by President López Portillo. The fact that Carlos Tello, the first secretary of Programming and Budget, a Cambridge-trained structuralist economist and proponent of planning since the 1960s, was called upon to devise a solution to the devastating flight of capital siphoned out into dollar accounts in Mexican banks was indicative of the state's recurrent resort to the reformist economists of the early 1970s. From Tello's perspective, the nationalization of private banks represented, "above all [that] the State could once and for all put an end to the principal adversary which . . . had limited the State's capacity to maneuver."[61] His motives were to break the internationalized private sector's hold over the state's financial position.

In private conversations and in his book, *La nacionalización de la banca en México,* Tello insisted that internationalized *private* financial authority continued to constrict the public sector's ability to shape market forces for the achievement of planned social and economic goals in spite of the creation of the SPP as a central planning and budgeting agency. In fact, the infringement of private financial orthodoxy on planning that motivated his departure from SPP in 1977 also motivated his goal to nationalize the Mexican banking system, as he suggests in the following passage from the book:

> During the first half of the decade [of the 1970s], the permanent contradiction between monetary policy on the one hand, and public expenditure on the other, not only limited public sector action and [the public sector's] maneuvering room but also resulted in a process of growth characterized by a combination of slowdown and acceleration of economic activity. In this process, the questions . . . of a financial character compete with those of a productive and social character in the daily tasks of economic policy; the opinions and actions of the financial sphere tended to predominate over the rest, principally because of:
>
> 1. The character of the financial sphere itself where the action of the public sector is planned and, in the last instance, where the economy is planned (how much is to be spent; on which regions; in which activities; how expenditure is to be financed; taxes, subsidies . . . ; the tariffs and controls placed on foreign commerce; wage policy; the price and rates of public sector goods and services . . .). At the same time, the financial sector is where the results of planned projects are evaluated and the results for subsequent plans and decisions are evaluated. The financial sphere . . . is the beginning and the end of economic processes. . . .
> 4. Within the private sector of the economy itself, the banking-financial sphere predominates, basing its power on cohesion; . . . a great deal of the

development policy of the public sector passes through the banking and financial system before reaching industry and agriculture. *In reality, governmental policies to promote private sector activity are designed and in considerable proportion administered by the financial sphere.*[62] (Emphasis added)

Tello's pessimistic analysis of national planning capabilities in Mexico in the early 1980s were accurate. However, the existence of the state's new technocratic programming and budgeting infrastructure in SPP helped make nationalization of the banking system administratively feasible. In fact, given his appreciation for the problems associated with planning in SPP, it is likely that Tello's wish was that nationalizing the banks would shift power within SPP away from the subsecretariat of Budget toward a preponderance of power for Programming. He was well aware of the state's organizational capacity based on its administrative infrastructure for goal-based planning. The SPP was, after all, the administrative nerve center of control for the public sector into which the nationalized banking sector would be incorporated.

In fact, under Tello's scheme, Treasury's previous sister agency, the Bank of Mexico (with private bankers on its board of directors), was transformed into a parastatal entity. Tello's vision was clearly that of establishing the SPP as a premier national planning secretariat with the administrative and financial strength to control Mexico's internationalized market forces in order to achieve improved economic *and* social conditions in Mexico. Implicit in his thinking was the idea that if finance capital were absorbed by the public sector, the Mexican state could shape market forces so as to promote economic and social development in conjunction with the non-oligopolistic elements in the Mexican private sector:

> In the medium term, the nationalization of the banks, with the indirect control over foreign exchange that nationalization implied, would permit the independence of domestic financial policy from the tyranny of the international money and capital markets. With such independence, secular problems in the Mexican economy could be attacked at their roots; problems, such as those of anonymous ownership of stocks, bonds, and other securities, that had impeded . . . an authentic fiscal reform. On another plane, the nationalization implied the elimination of what constituted the true centers of integrated economic and political power, whose oligopolistic strength transcended the strictly financial sphere to include the productive and distributive apparatus, and whose international connections were very dangerous. . . . It was necessary to do everything possible to avoid the country's return to such a situation as was lived [in 1982], a situation so irrational as to be very damaging to the *national interest.*[63] (Emphasis added)

The outcome of the nationalization of the banks on September 1, 1982, did not of course live up to Tello's expectations for eliminating the influence of internationalized financial forces on Mexican economic policymaking. The very depth of the economic crisis, however, and the nationalization of the financial sphere did consolidate the economic decisionmaking authority of the secretariat of Programming and Budget. The early conflict between the two subsecretariats within SPP was subdued by the gravity of the economic crisis and the administrative challenge of absorbing the entire Mexican private financial sector. Budget's potential negative reaction to public sector's absorption of the private banking system was avoided in part through the sectorization law of September 3, 1982, which divided the entire parastatal sector into groups ascribed to each secretariat: Treasury was allotted the Bank of Mexico, now a parastatal organism. Of course, the SPP retained ultimate planning and budgeting authority vis-à-vis the sectors and secretariats, and therefore the scope of the centralized authority of both the subsecretariat of Programming and Budget was enhanced by the nationalization.

As the term of López Portillo drew to a close, the clearest indicator of the SPP's new technical and allegedly apolitical mode of economic decisionmaking was its initiation of a process of liquidation (sale) and dissolu-

Table 5.7   Register of the Parastatal Federal Public Administration (1976–1982)

	1976[a]	1977	1978	1979	1980	1981	1982
Decentralized organisms	124	145	117	110	77	78	75 3 in liquidation
Public enterprises (majority state participation)	387	422	420	420	450	305	486 49 in liquidation
Public enterprises (minority state participation)[b]	52	54	51	53	54	51	40 8 in liquidation
Trusts	197	197	201	178	199	206	142 46 in dissolution
TOTAL	760	818	789	761	780	640	743 106 in liquidation

Source: Secretaría de Programación y Presupuesto.
Notes: a. This column is the number of entities that were under the responsibility of Patrimonio Nacional in 1976 before being transferred to SPP by the reform in 1977.
b. Numbers in this second row are entities in liquidation in 1982.

tion of selected parastatal entities in November 1982. Table 5.7 traces the numbers of parastatals registered between 1976 and 1982, when the privatization process was initiated. The de la Madrid government's new logic of rationalizing the public sector in order to achieve parastatal efficiency was spelled out in the February 1985 resolution, which continued with the process of sale and dissolution:

> Recently the federal government has adopted a series of measures intended to confront the latest economic conditions, correct deviations and maintain the correct direction in economic policy; the measures contemplated being, of fundamental importance, those of proceeding with the dissolution of parastatal entities whose existence is unjustified either because they have ceased to function or because they function ineffectively . . . [in modes] that are contrary to the goals of rationalization, budgetary discipline, and administrative modernization that are the objectives of the Program of Economic Reordering that this administration has been executing.[64]

Parastatal rationalization therefore implied that the public sector itself had to absorb the efficiency criteria imposed by market forces. The SPP came to represent and implement the public sector's new accommodation to internationalized market forces.

Conclusion

Unlike Luis Echeverría, President José López Portillo conceived of Mexican state sovereignty as a matter of public administrative structure and design rather than the power to make difficult economic policy choices. Clearly, the Echeverría administration had failed to sustain an ethos of a progressive state with sovereign control over the economy. Technocratic infighting over economic policy and the Echeverría administration's vacillation between economic reform and the economic status quo had seriously damaged the prestige of the PRI presidency. As Echeverría's successor in 1976, López Portillo did not set forth a bold domestic political-economic strategy for rebuilding the PRI presidency's prestige as the personification of a strong and progressive state. Instead, he opted for an administrative reform solution to the political debacle and economic chaos of 1976.

By reorganizing the secretarial structure of public economic decisionmaking in the executive branch, López Portillo set out to restore internal governmental order to the process of decisionmaking on public spending, investment, and monetary policy. The theme of his administration was "to organize the government in order to organize the country." Implicit in this theme was the idea that if there were administrative "order" within the Mexican government, then the state could exercise sovereign control over the country just as PRI rhetoric had always claimed. Seemingly, the major lesson López Portillo took from the Echeverría years was that an internally conflicted and "disorganized" government doomed a presidential administration to criticism, failure, and crisis. Accordingly, the essence of López Portillo's administrative reformism was to depoliticize the presidency by administratively removing the president from domestically centered political controversies regarding economic policy and social justice. For this purpose, he created the SPP.

In 1977, the SPP was created and entrusted with the planning and budgeting of parastatal investments, the very object of so much disagreement and infighting between the Treasury and Patrimonio Nacional during the Echeverría years. In the year the SPP was formed, the Mexican public sector was truly vast, having expanded so rapidly under the accelerated spending program of the Echeverría years. By removing parastatal budgeting authority from these rival secretariats, the administrative reform removed the vast numbers of public enterprises and agencies from the realm of intrasecretarial infighting and thus founded a new decisionmaking "order" designed to immunize the president from controversy.

López Portillo's new administrative order, which centered on the SPP, did not break free of political infighting until after 1979. In the first two years of the SPP's existence, the old Treasury–Patrimonio Nacional rivalry played itself out again on a smaller scale in squabbles between the SPP's own subsecretariats of Programming and of Budget. However, following several dismissals of subsecretaries and even of the founding SPP secretary, Carlos Tello, the new administrative order so desired by López ´ Portillo began to crystalize soon after the new secretary, Miguel de la Madrid, assumed his post. In effect, when Tello left the SPP, his vision of that body as a premier, goal-based planning authority dedicated to economic reform and social welfare left with him.

The fact that the SPP included both goal-based planning and revenue-based budgeting expertise proved important to the SPP's consolidation as the leading economic secretariat by the early 1980s. In López Portillo's search for the reestablishment of governmental order, he insisted that the SPP include both programmers and budgeters forced to interact and cooperate within a single secretariat. When debt crisis and capital flight in late 1982 made private bank statization financially unavoidable, the SPP's organizational capacity became important for public absorption of the private banking sector. Furthermore, the financial crisis enhanced the SPP's global planning authority over the budgets of all central secretariats as established in April 1980. SPP's forecasts of scarce resources and the parameters this placed on all other secretariats confirmed the SPP's emergent privatist role. Finally, the November 1982 initiation of a program of privatization and dissolution of parastatal enterprises to generate scarce public revenues further entrusted the SPP with what soon became a massive contraction of the public sector under the succeeding president and former SPP secretary, Miguel de la Madrid.

SPP Secretary de la Madrid's selection as PRI presidential candidate was not only a manifestation of the new secretariat's weight within the cabinet, but also indicated that López Portillo's technocratization of PRI governments was to be perpetuated into another term. However, during the next two SPP-derived presidencies, López Portillo's conception of Mexican state sovereignty as perpetual internal administrative order proved to be primarily a transitional discourse. It was soon replaced by the notion that Mexican sovereignty was a matter of the Mexican economy's world market competitiveness rather than of an administratively efficient and strong state.

6

(Dis)Integrating Mexico:
A Return to Legal
and Political Limbo

Neoliberal Economics and NAFTA:
The Quest for "Economic Sovereignty"
Without a "Powerful" State, 1982–1994

"Mexico will be able to strengthen its sovereignty through a stronger economy."
—Carlos Salinas de Gortari, interview with Robert Pastor, Mexico City, July 1990

The creation and consolidation of the secretariat of Planning and Budget (SPP) in the late 1970s and 1980s initiated a political and economic transition that led to a dismantling of much of the state apparatus of economic intervention in Mexico. It also led to an overall reversal of Cardenista rhetoric about Mexican state sovereignty. Out of the policy deadlock and technocratic competition of the Echeverría years, the group that prevailed politically was the pocket of administrative reformers originally associated with the Council for Administrative Reform in Presidencia, in the mid-1960s.

In fact, the early leader and intellectual forerunner of these administrative reformers and planning *técnicos* replaced Luis Echeverría in the presidency in December 1976. When President José López Portillo assumed office, he proclaimed three principal goals: (1) to establish an Alliance for Production to revive social harmony, especially in terms of renewing private sector trust in the state; (2) to effect a political reform to reactivate the legislature, in part by allowing 100 out of 400 deputies in the Congress of Deputies to be elected through proportional representation instead of majority rule; and (3) to carry out an administrative reform with the stated purpose of "organizing the government in order to organize the country." The administrative reform was significant because it initiated a major reor-

ganization of economic governance structures and later of economic policies and governmental rhetoric about sovereignty.

In exploring the transition, this concluding chapter addresses three
principal issues. Reviewed first are the roots of the economic governance
crisis that erupted in the late 1960s and early 1970s. In particular, the chapter focuses on the history of the Cárdenas-constructed presidency, beginning with its political consolidation in the late 1930s and its growing policy
ambivalence regarding how to promote industrialization. In this respect, the
chapter reviews how the Mexican presidency eventually arrived at a position of economic policy deadlock from 1973 to 1976, having been caught
between two political legacies: one of popular nationalism and mass social
welfare and another of authoritarian government promoting a form of
industrialization benefiting only the few. Presidential commitment to rapid
industrialization and continuing reliance on the popular symbolism of
Cardenismo over the years of rapid industrialization eventually resulted in
a profound split within the state apparatus—a split that constituted an
impasse in economic governance during the presidency of Luis Echeverría.

Second, the chapter explores why the deadlock in economic policy and
associated impasse in presidentialist governance occurred when it did during the second half of Echeverría's *sexenio*. In this respect, the focus is on
several distinct yet interrelated sets of factors. The first set of explanatory
factors are conjunctural in nature; that is, they constitute a set of internal
economic and political factors as well as certain external factors that converged in the late 1960s and early 1970s to present Mexican policymakers,
particularly President Echeverría, with extremely difficult and in many
cases crisis-induced policy choices. These conjunctural factors include the
political legitimation crisis provoked by the government's involvement in
the Tlatelolco incident in 1968; the shock effects produced within the
Mexican economy in response to the United States' abandonment of fixed
exchange rates and imposition of a 10 percent surcharge on imports in 1971
and 1972;[1] and, finally, the high liquidity of transnational banks, especially
large commercial banks based in the United States, and bankers' willingness to lend large quantities of funds with few conditions attached.[2] All of
these conjunctural factors converged between 1968 and 1973 to contribute
to a deadlock between proplanning, statist technocrats and promarket monetarists beginning in 1973.

The other major factor accounting for the impasse in economic governance during the Echeverría term is that state-promoted, import-substitution industrialization began to enter a difficult phase by the late 1960s and
early 1970s.[3] By the late 1960s, the phase of vertical import-substitution
industrialization,[4] which had replaced horizontal import substitution[5] in
1954 and 1956,[6] had resulted in an extensive transnational corporate presence in the fastest growing sectors of the economy.[7] It also resulted in the

concentration of domestic, private capital in the hands of a relatively small number of "industrial groups" within Mexico.[8]

Furthermore, by the late 1960s, vertical ISI had shown itself incapable of resolving Mexico's balance-of-payments deficits, which were growing larger in the 1960s.[9] Vertical ISI proved incapable of sustaining high economic growth rates. Even in the presence of orthodox policies carried out through the strategy of stabilizing growth, vertical ISI did not sustain high growth rates by the early 1970s. The fact that vertical ISI stopped producing rapid growth by 1970 and that Mexicanization of production and export diversification became economically more attractive had a profound impact on the Mexican executive. Presidentialist governance arrangements played such an integral role in promoting vertical ISI for more than fifteen years and were subject to rather dramatic change when economic circumstances shifted.

Third, this concluding chapter explores the implications of the transition in economic governance structures initiated during the term of Luis Echeverría for conceptions of state sovereignty. The chapter considers first how the period of internal state disarray during the Echeverría period provided the backdrop for an internal reorganization of economic decision-making authority during the succeeding López Portillo term. President Echeverría proved unable to resolve the deadlock in economic policy between neo-Keynesian expansionism and monetarist orthodoxy. Thus, presidentialism itself as a viable governance structure fell victim to its own long-accumulated ambivalence between authoritarian promotion of industrialization benefiting the few and popular nationalist concerns for mass social welfare. The Echeverría policy deadlock was rooted in a struggle over what type of economic development strategy Mexico should pursue and originated in a policy battle between the structuralist/reformist economists in Patrimonio National and the monetarists in Hacienda and the Banco de México. However, the reconsolidation of economic governance within the state was implemented by administrative reformers originally associated with the secretariat of the Presidencia.

To understand why the administrative reformers finally prevailed in 1977 rather than the prostatist technocrats advocating a wholesale shift in development strategy, it is necessary to examine how the presidency had changed in the face of state-promoted industrialization over the years since 1938, when the Cárdenas administration consolidated the "revolutionary" state. *Presidencialismo* in its Cardenista construction created a myth of an all-powerful presidency. For a time, these arrangements laid to rest the tension between authoritarian centralism and popular nationalist demands for social welfare. State-promoted industrialization, however, gradually aggravated the ambivalent nature of the presidency until intense intrastatal, technocratic conflict over development policy paralyzed economic governance.

What had once been a governance solution in the 1930s became, by the 1970s, an internal obstacle to national presidentialist governance. As an internal organization of state authority that united revolutionary factions in support of a governmentally preeminent executive, the Cardenista presidency represented the consolidation of governability in postrevolutionary Mexico. However, as the expression of an ambivalent executive torn between two developmental paths in the 1970s, Cárdenas-style *presidencialismo* reflected a collapse of a single chain of command for public economic decisionmaking. As economic policy deadlock threatened total economic collapse in 1976, the group of state personnel that promised to reorganize the internal administrative structure of economic governance prevailed over other contending groups.

Without being as ideologically identified with the reformist-statist developmental strategy of Patrimonio Nacional technocrats,[10] José López Portillo and other administrative reformers associated with Presidencia promised "to organize the government in order to organize the country."[11] They implemented an administrative reform that redistributed some of Treasury's past influence over public sector investment and spending and created a new national secretariat of Programming and Budget.[12] In light of this change, the final sections of the chapter explore the implications of the new secretariat's technocrats and their economic discourse, ideologies, and policies for the rhetoric, myths, and legalities of Mexican state sovereignty.

The Roots of the Crisis of Economic Governance in the 1970s: Why Economic Policy Deadlock Occurred During the Echeverría Years

The Cárdenas innovation in governance structures set the president up as the leader of the masses; at the same time, through the official party's corporatist structure, the executive was insulated from organized worker and peasant demands. So during the Cárdenas years, the Mexican presidency was born with a dual character rooted in (1) its mass base of support and (2) the centralist insulation of executive decisionmaking. The contradictions inherent in such an arrangement were not obvious during the Cárdenas presidency itself. This was mainly because state developmental efforts remained concentrated on agrarian reform and social welfare. The government's efforts to increase the efficiency of agricultural production on the *ejido* constituted the core of Cárdenas's developmental efforts. Other governmental initiatives were aimed at augmenting national control over key industries, such as petroleum and electricity, and the parastatal sector expanded in an attempt to fulfill such nationalist, developmental goals. In short, the state's expenditures and intervention to develop Mexico's economic potential generally reinforced the political conception of the presidency as an all-powerful protector of the masses.

Presidential ambivalence grew problematic, however, after the process of import-substitution industrialization accelerated at the conclusion of the Cárdenas *sexenio.* In response to the increased demand for Mexican exports spurred by the outbreak of war in Europe, President Avila Camacho shifted state developmental efforts away from agrarian reform toward state promotion of an economic nationalist project of rapid industrialization. The state invested deeply in infrastructure and heavy industry in order to supplement private investment, while state distribution of land to peasants and state support for striking workers dwindled and gave way to corporatist arrangements for official party manipulation of organized workers and peasants.

The contradictions between the presidency's political roots in popular nationalism versus its propensity for authoritarian promotion of industrialization benefiting the few increased when President Avila Camacho decided to support industrial investor interests over labor demands. This abrupt shift in policy orientation did not undermine the popular political conception of the presidency partly because of the nature of the process of horizontal ISI itself. State encouragement of the local production of nondurable, consumer goods constituted a nationalist response to past import dependency.

Second, Mexico's increased export revenues from wartime markets allowed the Avila Camacho government to invest in heavy industry and other industrial development activities without resorting to austerity measures that might stimulate popular opposition to governmental promotion of industrialization.

Finally, horizontal ISI was in a nascent stage in which the introduction of locally produced consumer goods to the domestic market corroborated the president's rhetoric that industrialization would benefit all Mexicans. The maldistributive effects of industrialization were yet to be experienced. Hence, the Avila Camacho administration benefited from favorable economic circumstances that enabled him to equate the exercise of insulated presidential power to promote rapid industrialization with the political concept of the presidency as the protector of mass well-being.

The contradictions inherent in the PRI presidency's ambivalence continued to increase as financial strains on industrialization intensified at the conclusion of World War II. Avila Camacho's successor, Miguel Alemán, entered office in 1946 confronted with the problem of how to sustain rapid industrialization in the face of (1) decreased postwar demand for Mexican exports; (2) increasing imports of capital goods for industrialization; and (3) a deteriorating balance-of-payments position. The Alemán government responded by continuing to expand state investment in infrastructure and heavy industry and by turning to internal and external credit to finance growing budget deficits.

The problem of financing public expenditures encouraged presidential reliance on the monetary and fiscal authorities in Hacienda and the Banco de México. In no arena was presidential reliance on Hacienda clearer than that of control and direction of the parastatal sector. The first Law of Control of Decentralized Agencies and State Enterprises, passed early in the Alemán period in 1947, placed substantial financial and planning control over the parastatal sector with Hacienda. The Treasury's financial veto over parastatal activities meant that presidential concerns for rapid industrialization shaped parastatal activity much more than the popular sector origins of the PRI presidency. Hence, the Treasury's dominance of the parastatal sector contradicted presidential claims of protection for popular sector interests as industrialization proceeded and presidential reliance on Hacienda increased.

Presidential resort to the Treasury's financial expertise increased further during the presidency of Ruíz Cortines, Miguel Alemán's successor. The inflationary spiral generated during the Alemán years as a result of the government's resort to internal and external credit to finance public deficits reached crisis proportions in 1954. Large reductions in monetary reserves precipitated a major devaluation of the peso that year, and in response the Treasury formulated a new development strategy. The new strategy of stabilizing growth was premised on orthodox monetary and fiscal policies and was designed to encourage private savings and investment. The main intellectual author of the strategy was Antonio Ortiz Mena, who became President López Mateos's secretary of Hacienda in the succeeding presidential term.

The López Mateos term from 1958 to 1964 was a turning point in the evolution of presidential ambivalence for several reasons. First, even through the industrial policies associated with vertical import substitution were formally announced in 1954, ISI phase two first came to fruition during the López Mateos administration. Second, López Mateos entered office in the same year that President Ruíz Cortines violently repressed the Independent Railroad Workers' strike, a major political embarrassment for the PRI presidency. Both of these phenomena contributed to deepening presidential ambivalence. Vertical ISI required more capital-intensive and technologically sophisticated investments than horizontal ISI[13] and resulted in greater reliance on foreign investment by transnational corporations. Therefore, not only did vertical ISI require more state investment and public subsidy for industrialization as opposed to satisfaction of popular welfare demands, but it also implied less national control over productive activities. Both of these factors tended to undermine the presidency's symbolic identification with popular nationalism.

As a result of the political crisis associated with the suppression of the railroad workers' strike and the need for larger government outlays to promote vertical industrialization,[14] the contradictions inherent in PRI presidential ambivalence multiplied by the late 1950s and early 1960s during the López Mateos presidency. On one hand, President López Mateos felt compelled to reward organized workers with a national profit-sharing scheme.

On the other hand, the profit-sharing scheme finally approved was more symbolic than redistributive in nature and was designed to protect the interests of Mexico's largest-scale private investors.

The depth of PRI presidential ambivalence became apparent in the second major wave of central administrative changes of 1958. López Mateos created two new central administrative agencies in 1958: the secretariat of the Presidency (Presidencia) and the secretariat of National Patrimony (Patrimonio Nacional). Patrimonio was ostensibly charged with administrative control of the parastatal sector, whereas Presidencia supposedly assumed primary control over parastatal investment planning with the assistance of Hacienda. The so-called triangle of efficiency consisting of Presidencia, Hacienda, and Patrimonio Nacional was officially designated as the new core of central administrative control of the parastatal sector.

In reality, the triangle reflected a presidency torn between the popular-nationalist face of presidential power and the increasing spending limitations and domestic and international constraints[15] placed upon the president by the financial difficulties of vertical import-substitution industrialization. In spite of official rhetoric, Presidencia never attained primary planning control over parastatal activities. As long as the president adhered to the stabilizing growth strategy, the financial limitations of Hacienda exercised over government expenditures[16] meant that any official planning authority designated to Presidencia was undermined by the financial vetoes that Hacienda retained over parastatal activities.[17]

In the interest of ensuring that the entire public sector remain within the spending constraints of the overall development strategy of stabilizing growth, the planning function López Mateos assigned to Presidencia remained more symbolic than real. Similarly, any efficiency-enhancing administrative changes Patrimonio Nacional might have formulated for state enterprises or decentralized state agencies were ultimately reversed by the Treasury through its network of spending checks. Treasury officials had no interest in permitting the parastatal sector to become anything other than a means of subsidizing private investors. Furthermore, Treasury technocrats opposed the idea that their symbolic rivals in Patrimonio Nacional might develop operative administrative clout over the public sector.

But within ten years after the creation of Patrimonio in 1958, Treasury officials' fear of the potential threat Patrimonio posed to Treasury influence proved well founded. The secretary of Patrimonio Nacional, Flores de la Peña, led a reformist assault against Treasury financial clout in the early 1970s. Flores de la Peña had in fact been a student of Eduardo Bustamante, the first secretary of the newly created Patrimonio Nacional. The creation of Patrimonio and Presidencia by president Adolfo López Mateos in 1958 constituted a formal administrative manifestation of the PRI presidency's increasing ambivalence about how to manage the economy. Even though Presidencia and Patrimonio never exercised authentic control over parastatal activities during the *desarrollo estabilizador* years, they nevertheless generated demands for popular welfare and nationalist policies within the state's economic decisionmaking apparatus. They also eventually helped revive statist-reformist economic policies, in the mid-1970s.

A deadlock in economic policy occurred during the Echeverría *sexenio* partly because conjunctural factors *and* problems associated with vertical ISI allowed technocrats in Patrimonio Nacional and Presidencia to expand, at least for approximately four years, their control over parastatal investment activities. This temporary shift in technocratic control led to the Echeverría government's decision to spend without regard to the restrictive rules of stabilizing growth. However, the Echeverría government's concerns for maintaining the investor confidence of the largest segments of the private sector persisted. Testimony to the strong hold that private investor concerns had over the presidency was the policy aftermath of Hugo Margáin's resignation from the Treasury. When the one cabinet member most attuned to the wishes of the largest segments of private capital resigned his post as secretary of Hacienda, Echeverría's personal friend and envoy to that post, José López Portillo, reintroduced restrictive monetary policies as soon as he became secretary.

Nevertheless, the president also continued to approve of Flores de la Peña's expansionary public spending program. Of course, such spending was premised on external credits through foreign public sector borrowing rather than on revenues obtained through fiscal reform. Furthermore, deficit spending's potentially positive effects on economic growth were eventually blocked by the reintroduction of orthodox monetary policies and private capital flight.[18] However, the expansion of parastatal credit and investment though deficit spending placed Presidencia and Patrimonio Nacional on nearly equal administrative footing with Hacienda for approximately four years. The result of such temporary equalizing conditions was an economic policy deadlock between expansionism and orthodoxy with two rival strains of developmental policy being implemented at the same time and essentially canceling each other out.

SPP Technocrats and
"Sovereignty" Without a "Powerful" State

The new administration of President José López Portillo created the SPP in 1977 in order to reorganize an executive branch intensely divided between technocrats favoring fiscal conservatism and technocrats favoring increased public spending.[19] The newly created SPP was endowed with the Treasury's former thirty-year-old control over public spending and contained both monetarist and statist technocrats housed in two separate subsecretariats, Budgeting and Programming. Budgeting was largely composed of monetarists from the Treasury and statists predominated in Programming. Interaction between these two subsecretariats in final public expenditure decisions led to intense infighting within the SPP during the secretariat's first years of existence, from 1977 to 1981. By 1982, however, the gravity of the country's debt crisis overshadowed intra-SPP squabbles. President López Portillo's statization of Mexico's private banking system called on the SPP to coordinate the public sector's absorption of all private banks. Under the financial strain of debt crisis and with the new SPP in place, the president made the unprecedented decision to appropriate private banks, a major component of the Mexican private sector that PRI presidents had nurtured for decades.

While acute shortages of foreign exchange were the economic catalysts behind the bank expropriation, the administrative foundations of bank statization were grounded in the Mexican state's organizational capacity to absorb and manage private banking operations. This organizational capacity was rejuvenated by the 1977 administrative reform that replaced the triangle of efficiency, consisting of the Treasury, Presidencia, and Patrimonio Nacional with a new programming and budget secretariat, the SPP. Unlike the SPP's main predecessor, the Treasury, the SPP incorporated rival technical experts by including both statist planners and monetarist budgeters.[20] The incorporation of rival economic ideologies and expertise tended to dilute structuralist *and* monetarist rivalry. In fact, after the SPP was created, most vestiges of technocratic competition among economists within the state eventually subsided. The SPP's incorporation of competing technocrats into a new structure of economic governance diffused the rivalry that paralyzed economic governance during the Echeverría presidency and equipped the SPP with a dual administrative capacity for managing rapid public sector expansion as well as contraction.

The SPP's dual administrative capacity essentially steered the Miguel de la Madrid government through the financial crisis of the early 1980s. During the years from 1981 to 1988, debt crisis precipitated the state's rapid appropriation of banks and then rapid unloading of revenue-draining public enterprises. The SPP was equipped to supervise both statization and privatization. Furthermore, technocratic rivalry was diluted by the fact that the SPP engaged in both enterprises. SPP's statist reformers were "rewarded" with private bank acquisition and state control of previously private credit and foreign exchange operations. On the other hand, in the aftermath of the bank expropriation, the SPP's fiscally conservative budgeters were soon rewarded with the task of dissolving or selling off many of Mexico's state-owned enterprises. In fact, as soon as López Portillo's presidency ended in December 1982, the former SPP secretary for the López Portillo government, Miguel de la Madrid, who was the new PRI president, immediately undertook a major privatization project and an economic austerity program favoring private investors.[21] In short, the fact that bank statization was quickly followed by rapid public sector privatization soothed rather than aggravated technocratic rivalry and also permitted the López Portillo and de la Madrid governments to cope with the acute financial crisis of 1982–1983.

The SPP directed the privatization and liquidation of inefficient, costly, or task-duplicating state enterprises in an attempt to generate new public revenues as the debt crisis spilled over into early 1983.[22] This privatization process even included the resale of some of the recently statized bank assets. Such privatization and dissolution were intended not only to generate badly needed public revenues but also formed part of the de la Madrid government's larger strategy of promoting international market criteria of efficiency for both public and private enterprise. As a result of these efficiency criteria, the SPP, led by Carlos Salinas de Gortari, was charged with the job of dismantling much of the public sector side of Mexico's mixed economy. This was because SPP technocrats, such as SPP secretaries Miguel de la Madrid and then Carlos Salinas, denounced much state enterprise as incapable of reaching market standards of competitiveness. In effect, the SPP's predominant role in the post–miracle growth era of the 1980s and early 1990s was to shift Mexico's development strategy toward an export-oriented industrial policy promoting the global market competitiveness of Mexican firms.[23]

SPP technocrats' neoliberal economic policies of the 1980s and 1990s convey a message quite distinct from the PRI regime's national rhetoric of the past fifty years. The policies of sweeping privatization, GATT membership, trade liberalization, advocacy of the North American Free Trade Agreement, and constitutional allowances for the sale of collective *ejido* lands to commercial agriculture all convey the neoliberal message that Mexican "sovereignty" is dependent on a private economy made strong through exposure to world market standards of competition. In other words, a "perpetually strong state" is no longer defined to be the essential ingredient of Mexican national sovereignty. Instead, SPP secretaries-turned-PRI-presidents have redefined sovereignty as "perpetual economic competitiveness" in world markets. Sovereignty defined as perpetual world market competitiveness is said to be best pursued *without* a "powerful" state intervening extensively in the economy. Whereas the regime's rhetoric used to claim that "sovereignty" relied on the PRI presidency's construction and maintenance of a "permanently strong state," the SPP secretaries who became the presidents of the eighties and nineties argue that a "permanently strong state" that is economically interventionist undermines full realization of national "sovereignty" defined as "permanent economic competitiveness."

In portraying Mexicans' socioeconomic well-being as best safeguarded by international market forces, SPP-derived presidents claiming to pursue "sovereignty without a powerful state" reverse PRI governmental orientations of the past five decades. President and former SPP Secretary Miguel de la Madrid and his SPP secretary, Carlos Salinas, initiated this reversal in December 1982 when they launched a privatization program that has continued ever since.[24] The idea behind privatization and liquidation of public enterprise has been twofold: to rid the state of "inefficient" and "revenue-draining" public sector economic intervention and to return to the private sector enterprises that presumably could become competitive if left to private initiative.

This privatization message directly contradicts the claims of PRI governments that for forty years voiced the revolutionary discourse of Lázaro Cárdenas. Cárdenas and the progressive alliance argued that a strong state capable of ownership and intervention in the economy was the only way to ensure social justice and protect national economic interests. Thus, Cardenismo advocated public sector employment, state subsidy of basic human needs, and public ownership of strategic industries, such as petroleum, steel, electricity, communications, and transportation.

Contrary to the Cárdenas-inspired state interventionism of the previous four decades, Presidents de la Madrid and Salinas de Gortari privatized everything from government-subsidized food distribution to copper mining, production of automotives, textiles, cement, and pharmaceuticals, and ownership of telephones and airlines.[25] In December 1982, when de la Madrid assumed the presidency, there were 1,115 parastatals; when he left office in December 1988, parastatals numbered only 449.[26] The sale of state enterprises dearest to the heart of Cardenismo commenced during the first year of the Salinas de Gortari administration. For instance, by March 1990 the Salinas government had already marked for sale Teléfonos de México (the Mexican national telephone company), CONASUPO (subsidized staple products company), DINA (diesel automotive production), Mexicana de Aviación (Mexican national airline), and the Cananea copper mine.[27] In May 1990, Salinas even ordered the reprivatization of all the banks statized by López Portillo in the midst of the debt crisis of late 1982.[28] More than any other single act of privatization, the return of the banks to private hands exemplified SPP technocrat-presidents' abandonment of the Cárdenas concept of an economically interventionist, strong state as the basis for national sovereignty.

Apart from privatizing domestic enterprise in the name of spurring competition and efficiency, the pursuit of "sovereignty without a powerful state" in the 1980s and 1990s has entailed opening the Mexican economy to world standards of market competition. In July 1986, President Miguel de la Madrid reversed forty years of Mexican governments' refusal to adhere to U.S.-dominated international free trade arrangements by presiding over Mexico's accession to the General Agreement on Tariffs and Trade (GATT). The technocratic message conveyed through trade liberalization is that the reduction of tariff and other barriers to foreign imports is the linch-

pin to securing Mexico's "perpetual economic competitiveness." Exposure
of Mexican firms to world market competition is said to be the only route
to ensuring Mexico's long-term economic competitiveness.[29]

This pursuit of sovereignty via perpetual economic competitiveness
reached a fevered pitch in early 1990 when President Carlos Salinas
announced interest in negotiating a Free Trade Agreement (FTA) with the
United States. The message he conveyed with the FTA proposal was
twofold. First, Salinas argued that the key to resolving Mexico's debt crisis
was increased Mexican access to U.S. markets: "trade, not aid."[30] Free
trade would relieve the Mexican government of responsibility for achieving
better repayment terms on foreign debt from commercial banks, terms that
Salinas labeled "foreign aid." Second, the Salinas FTA proposal, in conjunction with the broader concept of a North American free trade area
including Mexico, the United States, and Canada, conveyed the message
that the opening of the Mexican economy to U.S. and Canadian imports
would encourage the Mexican economy to modernize and gain a long-term
competitive edge in world trade. To use Salinas's own words, it would
mean that "Mexico will be able to strengthen its sovereignty through a
stronger economy."[31]

In dismantling Mexican trade protectionism and other interventionist
roles of the state in the economy, SPP secretary-turned-president Salinas de
Gortari distanced himself from many PRI *políticos* and old party bosses as
well as from the party's traditional rank-and-file members within the PRI's
popular sector organizations.[32] The National Confederation of Popular
Organizations, which is dominated by civil service employees, has been
alienated and weakened by widespread civil service dismissals resulting
from privatization. The Confederation of Mexican Workers (CTM), led by
Fidel Velázquez, has clashed more often with the government over the negative effects of neoliberal economic policies on workers' living standards,
which declined throughout the 1980s. These clashes have plagued the CTM
with constant rebellions from independent unions.[33]

Finally, members of the National Confederation of Peasants (CNC),
which was the fundamental rural bedrock of the official party since the
1930s, increasingly abandoned the PRI to follow opposition leader
Cuauhtémoc Cárdenas, the son of Lázaro Cárdenas, who was the CNC's
original political architect and distributor of the most land peasants ever
received after the revolution.[34] President Salinas's distancing from peasant
farmers was exemplified by the Salinas government's constitutional
amendment to permit the sale and individual and commercial ownership of
ejido parcels. Such lands were nontransferable and exclusively reserved for
collective peasant farmers for the past fifty years.[35]

The Salinas government's abolition of the Mexican state's responsibility for guaranteeing land to landless peasants reversed Zapatista revolutionary discourse of the previous eighty years. Contrary to Emiliano Zapata's

legacy to the Mexican constitution requiring the state to provide land to peasants, the Salinista contention has been that Mexico's agriculture will become efficient only if the state ceases to regulate land tenure in the countryside. Unlike Zapatista and Cardenista insistence that the state champion land reform to prevent large rural estates from monopolizing land ownership, Salinas insisted that land be controlled by those who work it most efficiently. In this way, it was claimed that Mexican agriculture will become competitive with the rest of the world, particularly the United States and Canada. The competitiveness of Mexican agriculture presumably depends on increased private investment achieved through the state's withdrawal from the business of making rules prohibiting companies and multinational corporations from owning land.

In reversing the land reforms and state-interventionist legacies of Lázaro Cárdenas in the late 1930s, Salinas did not just reverse the revolutionary discourse of Zapatismo and Cardenismo. He also helped undermine the PRI's political power base. Historically, ever since Cárdenas left office in 1940, the PRI's rural political bosses commandeered the peasant vote by trading state agricultural subsidies and other federal patronage for the votes of *ejidatarios*. The Salinas government's constitutional amendment permitting the sale of *ejidos* is likely to encourage the sale of much *ejido* land to commercial agriculture, thus undermining not only peasant farming but also the vote-gathering clout of the PRI's rural political bosses. Consequently, in championing the idea of perpetual economic competitiveness, SPP technocrat-turned-PRI-president Salinas placed himself in the peculiar position of weakening the very party that guaranteed his own highly disputed election to the presidency in 1988. As mentioned earlier, Salinista policies tended to undermine the party's traditional peasant membership as well as the PRI's support among urban workers and government civil servants.[36] As long as technocratic presidents such as Carlos Salinas remain more concerned about pursuing "perpetual economic competitiveness" than about protecting party bosses' political clout and PRI voters' loyalty, tensions between the party and the party's technocratic presidents are likely to continue.

SPP-Derived Presidents and the Reversal of Revolutionary Rhetoric: Implications for the Politics of Presidential Succession

Traditional PRI *políticos* seemingly lost influence over the presidential succession process to SPP technocrats soon after the political and economic debacle of the Echeverría presidency. The exposure of PRI president Echeverría as a personification of state weakness led to the selection of SPP-derived "economic presidents" claiming that a "strong state" was no

longer an asset but a liability. This "economic presidency," which claimed
to pursue sovereignty through private sector economic competitiveness,
replaced the "political presidency" dominated by PRI political concerns
during the course of the López Portillo administration. In fact, the sequence
of events by which the SPP presidency began to replace the demystified
PRI presidency began as early as 1979, when President López Portillo
appointed Miguel de la Madrid as secretary of Programming and Budget.
At this point it became clear that the newly created SPP would not become
an overwhelmingly prostatist social welfare–oriented planning secretariat
bent on defying private financial interests as Carlos Tello, the SPP's first
secretary, had hoped. Tello believed that the SPP could become an institutional expression of permanent state strength vis-à-vis the financial power
of private bankers and investors, both foreign and domestic. In this respect,
he believed in the old PRI rhetoric of "permanent state strength" activated
by the executive. Tello envisioned that the SPP's dual governmental
responsibility for programming and budgeting would empower the SPP to
make public expenditure recommendations contrary to the wishes of private bankers and investors.

This reformist-statist vision within the SPP died when Tello was
forced to resign as SPP secretary and Miguel de la Madrid was appointed to
that post. Likewise, when SPP Secretary Miguel de la Madrid was selected
as the PRI presidential candidate in 1981, PRI political bosses' influence
on presidential succession seemingly dropped. Although party bosses were
still essential to de la Madrid's "election," his government marked the birth
of a technocratic presidency whose political connections to the party were
minimal. Unlike the PRI political presidency whose candidates were char-
acteristically drawn from the Government secretariat, the economic presidency, whose candidates were derived from the SPP, largely ignored the
political considerations of party bosses, opposed an interventionist, "strong
state" and instead pursued a "strong economy" founded on the world market competitiveness of the Mexican economy.

Until the end of the Echeverría term in 1976, many PRI presidents had
been selected from the secretariat of Gobernación (Interior or
Government), the one cabinet department most intimately associated with
PRI political control.[37] As Echeverría's successor, López Portillo broke this
trend when he was selected PRI presidential candidate while serving in the
Treasury. As President Echeverría's Treasury secretary, however, López
Portillo was never portrayed as a typical Treasury technocrat. He was
depicted instead as "Echeverría's personal envoy" sent to the Treasury presumably to "reclaim" presidential control over a secretariat that had
become dominated by private investor interests.

The political considerations of PRI bosses apparently lost influence
over the process of presidential succession once the SPP emerged as the
cabinet department most suitable for the selection of López Portillo's suc-

cessor. During López Portillo's presidency and de la Madrid's SPP secretaryship, the SPP emerged as both a defender of business interests, per the Alliance for Production, and a statist distributor of public funds borrowed on future oil revenues. With these dual statist-privatist credentials, the SPP apparently became, in López Portillo's eyes, a more suitable cabinet source for the next PRI presidential candidate than either the Treasury or Government secretariat. Echeverría had come to the presidency from the Government secretariat, which had begun to symbolize the debasement of the PRI presidency. Furthermore, because Treasury's image was too intimately associated with large-scale private investors, that secretariat was not a suitable cabinet from which to select the PRI presidential candidate.

On the other hand, the SPP symbolized a new rapprochement between public and private sectors and between statism and private business interests. This public-private rapprochement and the reestablishment of administrative order and peace among economic technocrats had been López Portillo's own primary presidential goals ever since he took office. Thus, as intellectual father of the SPP, López Portillo must have played a central role in deciding that SPP Secretary de la Madrid was the most qualified person to perpetuate such goals as Mexico's next president.

In the following presidential succession in 1988, the SPP was once again the cabinet department from which the PRI presidential candidate was selected. Like Miguel de la Madrid, Carlos Salinas de Gortari was apparently selected on the basis of his technical economic and financial credentials as SPP secretary rather than on the basis of his political standing within the PRI. In this respect, the SPP became a maker of "SPP presidents" who would perpetuate neoliberal economic policies in the post-1982 era of debt crisis.

As soon as possible after the SPP was created in 1977, it supplied Mexico with its very next president, in 1982. In effect, the presidential successions of 1982 and 1988 in Mexico are indicative of a technocratization of the PRI candidate selection process, which traditionally involved intense party politics—albeit secretive, behind-the-scenes politics—of PRI candidate selection. The neoliberal economic policy orientations and cabinet standing of the SPP, perpetuated by the outgoing president, appear to have been the main criteria for the selection of de la Madrid and Salinas rather than the two candidates' political popularity or party credentials.

The technocratization of PRI presidential candidate selection is important in considering the future of Mexico's national political order. First, the new technocratic presidents have reversed the official party's entire rhetoric and policy orientations of the past fifty years. In proclaiming the pursuit of "sovereignty" without a "powerful" state, they have attacked the entire rhetorical-symbolic edifice justifying the PRI's single-party rule. The party's ironclad control of presidential succession has been justified rhetorically in the past by PRI claims of perpetuating a "powerful," "revolution-ary" state dedicated to social justice. The logic has been that PRI presidents should always govern because they perpetuate a progressive, strong state. However, SPP-derived presidents have argued that a strong state under-mines sovereignty, which they define as the Mexican economy's world economic competitiveness. By implication, if a "powerful" state is not essential to national sovereignty, then continuous PRI control of the presi-dency is unnecessary.

Moreover, traditional PRI *políticos'* preference for an economically interventionist state is now deemed destructive of Mexican sovereignty, defined as private sector economic competitiveness. Rhetorically, at least, SPP-derived President Salinas defined himself out of his own party by denouncing the Cardenista state as a hindrance rather than a fundamental building block of national sovereignty. Rather than renaming and attempt-ing to reconstitute the fundamental identity of the party, Salinas promoted only cosmetic party reforms,[38] which left the PRI's historical identity with revolutionary state sovereignty intact. Paradoxically, the PRI now has two contradictory tasks: its historical mission to perpetuate "revolutionary con-stitutionalism" and its new task of politically supporting and helping "elect" presidents who revise, reject, and dismantle basic principles of rev-olutionary constitutionalism.

These contradictions in the late-twentieth-century roles of the PRI were clearly evident in Salinas de Gortari's choice of a presidential succes-sor in late November 1993. Less than two weeks after NAFTA was approved by the U.S. Congress, the PRI's Executive Council announced that Luis Donaldo Colosio Murrieta had been selected as the PRI's candi-date for the presidential elections in August 1994. Predictably, Colosio's cabinet-level ties to Salinas dated back to the SPP in the mid-1980s when Salinas was SSP secretary during the Miguel de la Madrid administration.[39] As a close aid to Salinas in the SPP, Colosio assisted in devising and imple-menting Mexico's neoliberal economic policy shift during the presidency of Miguel de la Madrid.

In spite of the SPP's role in forging ties between Salinas and Colosio, the SPP was not Colosio's cabinet-level stepping stone to the PRI presiden-tial candidacy as it had been for both Salinas and Miguel de la Madrid. This was partly because the SPP's fleeting image in the late 1970s and early 1980s as an agency dedicated to democratic and progressive state planning of the economy did not last much beyond the presidential succession of 1981, when SPP Secretary Miguel de la Madrid was designated to succeed José López Portillo. Under the ensuing SPP secretaryship of Salinas de Gortari from 1982 to 1987, the SPP's already failing reputation for democratic planning vanished completely. In fact, President de la Madrid's selection of the SPP's neoliberal secretary, Carlos Salinas, as the official party's presidential candidate in 1987 prompted a split in the PRI and the partial loss of the party's left wing with the exodus of Cuauhtémoc Cárdenas.

Although as president, Carlos Salinas added the highly visible antipoverty program Solidarity to the SPP, Solidarity's distribution of federal funds to poor Mexican communities was hardly proof that the SPP was exercising the global economic planning authority ascribed to the state in Articles 25 and 26 of the constitution. Instead, the SPP had become overwhelmingly identified with neoliberal economic policies, privatization, and free trade and thus was no longer a politically suitable secretariat from which to recruit a "revolutionary" PRI president. In fact, the Salinas government dissolved the SPP in January 1992, fifteen years after its initial creation by José López Portillo.[40] In anticipation of NAFTA's transfer of economic planning authority to a transcontinental private sector, the SPP was absorbed by the secretariat of Finance (Hacienda), the very cabinet department whose excess and private sector–oriented financial clout the SPP was presumably created to curb.[41]

With the SPP gone, Salinas chose the PRI's (first) presidential candidate for 1994 from the newly created secretariat of Social Development (SEDESOL), the cabinet department that inherited the extinct SPP's control over Solidarity. As head of Social Development, Luis Donaldo Colosio personified the PRI's increasingly contradictory roles in the 1990s. Having evolved from a neoliberal economic aid to Salinas in SPP in the mid-1980s to head distributor of Solidarity's antipoverty funds in the 1990s, Colosio embodied the contradictions between the regime's statist, revolutionary origins and its late-twentieth-century neoliberal shift. Unlike the singular technocratic credentials of Salinas, who split the PRI in 1987, Colosio's extensive political and "electoral" experience kept the party together.[42] He was seen as more than just a technocrat because he had been "elected" to both chambers of the Mexican legislature, first as a PRI deputy and then as a PRI senator. Moreover, as president of the PRI from 1988 to 1992, Colosio claimed to be a reformer and modernizer of the official party, which recognized its first electoral defeat ever for a state governorship in 1989.[43] These sorts of political and electoral credentials were important to Salinas de Gortari's post-1988 attempt to portray the PRI as a bona fide political party willing and able to compete in a competitive electoral arena.

Moreover, Colosio's official "social vocation" credentials as secretary of Social Development, head of Solidarity, and chief of the state environmental agency, SEDUE,[44] made him the government's premier distributor of government welfare funds. Thus, in addition to his official reputation for modernizing and preparing the PRI for electoral competition,[45] Colosio was also paradoxically identified with the regime's oldest, most venerable practice of patronage distribution and influence peddling, albeit via the new, highly innovative, and presidentially controlled Solidarity program.[46] Thus, while symbolizing the reformed PRI's new capacity and willingness to compete electorally, Colosio also reflected the continued urge of regime elites to manipulate voters with government funds and thus the continued unwillingness of PRI elites to risk electoral defeat.

As both a defender and a dismantler of "revolutionary constitutionalism," Colosio had neoliberal SPP origins and new pro–social welfare credentials as head of SEDESOL. These dual credentials helped prevent another split in the PRI over the succession announcement of November 1993.[47] Unlike the unveiling of Salinas as PRI presidential candidate in 1987, the candidacy of Colosio did not generate another split within the official party. While investors, financiers, and other business interests reportedly preferred the selection of Finance Secretary Pedro Aspe, popular elements within the PRI opposed Aspe as too technocratic and distant from popular welfare concerns.[48] Some popular elements within the party favored the well-known mayor of Mexico City, Manuel Camacho Solís, whom business circles opposed as too populist and free-spending.[49]

The designation of Colosio represented a compromise between business interests and populist-leaning PRI members.[50] This was because Colosio simultaneously embodied an unquestionable neoliberal commitment to implementing NAFTA as well as a demonstrated populist penchant for distributing government welfare funds. Undoubtedly, Colosio's projected neoliberal implementation of NAFTA would have further undermined the state's constitutionally prescribed duties and interventionist roles vis-à-vis the economy. Nevertheless, the CTM and the Permanent Agrarian Congress announced their official support for Colosio as the PRI's candidate for the presidency.[51] In doing so, popular sectors within the PRI won the battle against Aspe only to lose the war against Colosio's certain neoliberal dismantlement of the "revolutionary constitutional" authority of the state over the economy, commerce, and economic planning.

But tensions within the PRI regarding the presidential succession of 1994 did not end with the selection of Colosio in November 1993. On the first day NAFTA went into effect, succession debates and tensions were rekindled by an antigovernment rebellion that broke out in Chiapas state on January 1, 1994. Intraparty tensions regarding Salinas's choice of Colosio resurfaced as Manuel Camacho Solís gained increasing political notoriety as the government's chief negotiator with the rebels.[52] Tensions within the party mounted further in February and March 1994 as rumors circulated about the possibility of Camacho running against Colosio as an independent candidate.[53] And Colosio's campaign manager, Ernesto Zedillo, further aggravated internal PRI tensions by sidestepping party traditionalists and their back-room political manipulations, emphasizing instead "modern" focus groups, opinion polls, and televised advertising.[54]

While Colosio himself had worked to weaken traditional peasant and labor interests within the PRI, his campaign manager, Ernesto Zedillo

Ponce de León, further alienated and undermined party *políticos* as the campaign proceeded. Zedillo ultimately prevailed over party *políticos* in a sweeping, albeit rather unpredictable way. Many of the PRI's various labor, peasant, and populist members were dealt a major succession blow when Luis Donaldo Colosio was assassinated during a presidential campaign stop in Tijuana on March 23, 1994. After the assassination, Camacho's popularity and position as a rumored presidential hopeful were virtually destroyed.[55] Moreover, against the public demands of many PRI members, Salinas quickly chose Ernesto Zedillo to replace Colosio as the PRI's presidential candidate.[56] As an archetypical economic technocrat and ex-SPP secretary with absolutely no previous electoral credentials, Zedillo's selection reconfirmed the overwhelming authoritarian dominance of Salinas and the party's neoliberal, technocratic elite over PRI *políticos* and rank-and-file party members.

The Quest for "Economic Sovereignty" Without a "Powerful" State: Contradictions Between Old and New Legends About Sovereignty

Increasing contradictions between neoliberal governmental elites and PRI *políticos* are reflections of even more fundamental inconsistencies between old and new legends about national sovereignty. Although as of late 1994 the PRI still enjoys the status of being virtually a single party of the government, there are increasing pressures for PRI elites to democratize the party's image, internal selection procedures, and electoral practices. The emergence of contradictory roles for the PRI stems from basic incongruities between old and new myths about how to achieve national sovereignty. Lingering notions about sovereignty as the product of a powerful state are inconsistent with new, neoliberal rhetoric about Mexico's achievement of economic sovereignty through a powerful private sector. New, neoliberal rhetoric claims that Mexico's "sovereignty" will be strengthened through an economy made strong by a world-competitive private sector.

Salinas's basic contention was that through NAFTA's strengthening of the private sector, Mexico will be able to enter the First World of wealthy, advanced industrial countries. Politically, however, Salinista rhetoric's insistence that national sovereignty depends on a powerful private sector rather than a powerful state undermines the PRI as a ruling party. In subverting the PRI's historical, revolutionary mission, such rhetoric undercuts the PRI's reasons for existence as a perpetual ruling party. As an official party historically created to institutionalize the revolution, the PRI's official mission was to perpetuate a revolutionary state powerful enough to achieve the social justice goals specified in the constitution of 1917. The

constitution envisioned a powerful state with the legal authority to intervene in the economy to promote economic development and socioeconomic
progress for all Mexicans.[57]

Indeed, the postrevolutionary state's vast legal authority and duties vis-
à-vis the economy symbolically legitimated the PRI's existence as a virtual
single party. In other words, the constitution's ascription of broad legal
authority to the state became a justification for the PRI's monopoly of
political control over the Mexican presidency: Only a "revolutionary" party
and its presidents should be entrusted with such vast duties. Now, however,
Salinas has redefined national sovereignty as being contingent on a strong,
world-competitive private economy whose vitality is *undermined* by a
strong state.

This neoliberal pursuit of "economic sovereignty" without a "powerful" state implies that the PRI's historical mission of perpetuating an economically interventionist state was wrong. Neoliberalism assumes that the
interventionist state envisioned in the Mexican constitution actually
destroys national sovereignty by crippling the private sector. In short,
neoliberal rhetoric rejects the 1917 constitution's emphasis on the national
state's vast legal duties to ensure social justice through economic interventionism. In declaring the Mexican state's vast legal authority over the economy as a hindrance to national sovereignty, neoliberal rhetoric essentially
refutes past rationales for the PRI's perpetual control of the presidency.

It is increasingly difficult to justify the PRI's singular control over the
presidency as neoliberalism discredits the national state as the key to the
fulfillment of revolutionary goals. Since a "powerful" state and a "powerful" presidency are no longer portrayed as the engines of economic development and social justice, PRI presidents need not even attempt to personify the state's sovereign power over the economy. One implication of this
logic is that powerful presidents of a traditional, PRI character should no
longer govern Mexico. Consequently, many of the party's past reasons for
existence as a ruling party are undermined. In fact, one of the Mexican
regime's few remaining rationales for the PRI's continued status as a ruling
party appears to be the PRI's recent role in preventing the election of economically interventionist presidents reminiscent of the regime's past.

However ironic, one key political role left for the PRI is that of helping
prevent the election of an economically interventionist president who
would reactivate the national state's constitutional authority over the economy and renegotiate NAFTA. Thus, rather than perpetuate the rhetoric and
legalities of the revolutionary constitutionalism of the past, the PRI, aided
by the National Action Party (PAN),[58] has become a party whose main
function is to prevent revolutionary constitutionalist figures, such as
Cuauhtémoc Cárdenas, from prevailing in presidential elections. Cárdenas,
of the Democratic Revolution Party (PRD), was the only major opposition
candidate likely to reactivate state interventionism and renegotiate parts of

NAFTA if elected to the Mexican presidency in 1994. Salinista neoliberalism reduced the PRI's mission as a ruling party to ensuring that state interventionist candidates like Cárdenas do not prevail in presidential elections. Indeed, the need of the ruling elite to prevent any interruption in the implementation of NAFTA is a key motivation behind continued PRI presidential victories.

As the focus of Mexico's third major myth about national sovereignty, neoliberal rhetoric about NAFTA as Mexico's ticket to the First World undermines rather than builds upon previous legends about national sovereignty. Mexico's early national legends about political independence in the 1820s claimed that the new Mexican state's legal equality to European states freed Mexicans from foreign domination. Later on, a second major legend about the revolution of 1910 built upon and reinforced Mexico's earlier 1820s myths about national independence. The second myth about revolution claimed that the Mexican state was not just legally equal to other states but was also powerful. The "revolutionary" state's sovereign "power" was said to enable the new regime to deliver social justice to all Mexicans. This second myth gave nineteenth-century political independence a new meaning and an enhanced significance for average Mexicans. They could now look to the national state as a source of political freedom as well as a guarantor of their socioeconomic well-being.

Mexico's third and newest myth about economic sovereignty and NAFTA contradicts the other two in several important respects. Although Salinas once compared himself to Benito Juárez as a legendary figure associated with Mexico's recovery of national sovereignty, the new NAFTA myth about economic sovereignty does not reinforce nineteenth-century legends about national independence from foreign domination. Salinas implied that just as Juárez was the father of Mexico's restored political freedom from the French, so he, Salinas, was reputedly the father of Mexicans' restored economic freedom. However, for many average Mexicans, NAFTA aims to circumvent and undo the Mexican state's legal authority to intervene in the economy on their behalf. This means that NAFTA promises to undermine rather than reinforce any remaining importance that average Mexicans attach to the constitutional autonomy of the Mexican state.

The constitutional autonomy of the Mexican state is itself of little significance to popular sectors in society if the state loses most of its legal authority to intervene in the economy on behalf of average citizens. Since NAFTA is unlikely to raise most Mexicans' living standards very fast, neoliberal promises of economic sovereignty may eventually sound as hollow as promises of "economic progress" did during the Porfiriato. First, NAFTA lacks a bona fide social charter to standardize minimum wages and working conditions across the continent. Second, it fails to posit the long-term, transcontinental mobility of labor. Finally, it leaves in place the three signatory states' sovereign, legal authority over the movement and socioeconomic situations of people. This surviving legal-political framework of state sovereignty promises to perpetuate the vast socioeconomic inequalities already existing among peoples across the continent, especially within Mexico. Consequently, NAFTA promises to undermine the myth of Mexican independence as the basis of an autonomous constitution that promotes the economic well-being and upward mobility of average Mexicans who are poor.

NAFTA's new rhetoric of economic sovereignty is even more diametrically opposed to Mexico's myth of revolution and state power. The old myth of revolution claimed that the state was powerful enough to defy foreign investors in order to implement social justice. Neoliberalism and NAFTA rhetoric make very different claims. First, neoliberalism claims that the private sector rather than the state should be the foremost planner of the economy. Second, a powerful and economically interventionist state is said to undermine rather than bolster private sector powers to generate wealth and socioeconomic well-being. Finally, neoliberal rhetoric about NAFTA claims that private sector economic competitiveness is best promoted by opening the Mexican economy to unfettered foreign investment and to competition from U.S. and Canadian products and services.

Thus, contrary to the revolutionary myth of sovereign state power to defy foreign investors, NAFTA rhetoric embraces foreign investors as key agents of Mexico's economic entrance to the First World. NAFTA logic makes a transcontinental private sector, rather than the Mexican state, the pivotal component of Mexican economic strength and therefore national sovereignty. This contrasts starkly with the past. In the 1930s, Cardenista legends envisioned a revolutionary nation-state powerful enough to expropriate foreign-owned properties in the Mexican national interest. NAFTA rhetoric, on the other hand, mythologizes the economic magic of a transcontinental invisible hand driven by a private sector powerful enough to reverse the national economic disaster of Mexico's mixed-economy past.

(Dis)Integrating Mexico:
A Return to Legal and Political Limbo

NAFTA challenges not only the myths but also the legalities of Mexican state sovereignty. In doing so, it undermines key aspects of Mexico's legal-political order without proposing an alternative transnational legal-political order. So in many respects, NAFTA represents for Mexico a new invitation to legal and political limbo. When the U.S. Congress approved the agreement in November 1993, Mexico was essentially inducted into a regional trade and investment club under the implicit assumption that Mexico could and would soon be economically equal to the United States and Canada.

NAFTA contained no continental social charter to standardize minimum wages and working conditions, and it contained minimal provisions for continental development assistance to help Mexico catch up to the other two economies. Consequently, it implicitly assumed that the Mexican economy could soon compete with the U.S. and Canadian economies and could do so without undue human costs on Mexican citizens.

This assumption is rather parallel to those in the 1820s about Mexico's presumed political equality to other states when the U.S. and British governments recognized Mexican independence. The U.S. government's legal recognition of Mexican independence was parallei in some respects to its legal ratification of NAFTA: In both cases Mexico was invited to partake in some form of legal equality with the United States even though the practical conditions for Mexican equality did not exist. More specifically, in 1822, Mexico was legally invited to become politically equal to the U.S. state. Similarly, with NAFTA Mexico was legally invited to become economically equal to the United States. Producers in Mexico will presumably become so competitive under NAFTA that, within a brief ten to fifteen years, nearly all trade barriers in North America can and will be eliminated. Presumably, the private sector in Mexico will not need the state to protect it against foreign producers.

This NAFTA logic of economic equality is strikingly parallel to the independence logic of political equality of the 1820s. In the 1820s, Mexico was presumably freed from its political subordination as a colony when legal sovereignty was transferred from the Spanish to the Mexican state. Analogously, Mexico has now been legally freed from its economic subordination as a Third World country via NAFTA's transfer of legal authority over the economy and commerce from the Mexican state to a transcontinental private sector.

Although ultimately contradictory, the legal admittance of Mexico to the economic First World via NAFTA shares certain juridical and ideological parallels to Mexico's legal admission to the club of sovereign states in the 1820s. First, both NAFTA and independence involve ideologies about "freedom" derived from liberal political and economic thought. In the 1820s, independence emphasized political freedom from foreign domination. In the 1990s, NAFTA emphasizes economic freedom from state interference. In both eras, liberal ideologies about political or economic freedom were founded on new legal frameworks that helped consolidate myths about national sovereignty and national self-determination. In the 1820s, the international legal framework of state sovereignty officially extended to the Mexican state the same legal rights of sovereignty enjoyed by all other internationally recognized states. Similarly, in the 1990s, NAFTA officially extends to the Mexican private sector the same legal rights to continental free trade and investment to be enjoyed by all private actors across North America.[59]

It mattered little in either case whether the Mexican nation-state in the 1820s or Mexican workers, producers, and consumers in the 1990s were positioned to thrive from the new legal arrangements of either state sovereignty or continental free trade and investment. In fact, in both the 1820s and 1990s, nominal legal entitlements provided no guarantee that most human beings would benefit from Mexico's new legal status. Moreover, as major legal innovations in Mexico's international relations, both political independence and NAFTA incorporated international assumptions about Mexicans' cultural inferiority in world affairs. One need only recall that as soon as U.S. government officials recognized Mexico's legal sovereignty in 1822, they simultaneously decided that Mexicans did not deserve guaranteed sovereignty over nearly as much territory as claimed. Similarly, while NAFTA officially authorizes Mexicans to enjoy commercial equality with U.S. and Canadian citizens, NAFTA simultaneously implies that Mexicans do not deserve a guaranteed minimum wage equal to that enjoyed by U.S. or Canadian workers.

In short, in spite of the formal rhetoric of equality embedded in the legal frameworks of political independence and NAFTA, the practical implications of independent statehood and NAFTA relegate Mexicans to an inferior cultural and socioeconomic status in international relations. Overwhelming disadvantages and inequalities confronting Mexicans in the world of the 1820s and the 1990s made independence and NAFTA international legal invitations to a nominal status of political or economic equality nonexistent in practice.

As in the 1820s, Mexico in the 1990s has entered a period of increasingly uncertain legal, political, and economic conditions. Beginning in the 1820s, Mexico was caught somewhere in between its former legal status as a colony and Western European–style nation-statehood. Although the Mexican state was legally recognized as sovereign, the state's legal sovereignty was constantly disputed at home and abroad. Indeed, most of the first hundred years of Mexican independence were characterized by battles over the state's legal authority and by intense political and economic instability that often bordered on chaos.

Similarly, in the 1990s, Mexico has entered a new period of legal and political limbo. This uncertainty is due in part to Mexicans' cynicism about the state's past control of the mixed economy in light of the socioeconomic failures of the previous fifty years. It is difficult for average Mexicans to believe the old myth that a "revolutionary," economically interventionist state has the power to deliver social justice. In exchange, Mexico's neoliberal governmental elites seek to substitute a new, mass faith in the economic power of an unfettered, transcontinental private sector. Thus, Mexicans are expected to embrace the economic, trade, and investment policies of First World countries while Mexico itself is still mired in the socioeconomic problems typical of semi-industrial, poor countries.

Given the realities of poverty in the 1980s and 1990s, average

Mexicans have little reason to place all their faith in the economic prosperity promised by neoliberalism and NAFTA. Indeed, average Mexicans of the late twentieth century are caught somewhere between their historical faith in revolutionary constitutionalism and the new religion of continental free trade. Their ideological uncertainty about the economic effects of neoliberalism and NAFTA is compounded by the many legal and now political uncertainties associated with NAFTA.

Legally, NAFTA violates the spirit though not necessarily the letter of the Mexican constitution. It does so by calling into question the state's interventionist roles in the economy and much of the state's regulatory authority over commerce, property rights, and investment. Nevertheless, Mexico's legal tradition regards international law as superior to the norms of the Mexican state.[60] In other words, domestic law generally defers to international law by regarding international treaties as federal statutes as long as such treaties do not technically violate the constitution.[61]

Thus, although the Free Trade Treaty (TLC) is not in technical violation of the constitution, it clashes with the general state-interventionist thrust of the Mexican constitution. For example, Articles 25 and 26 of the constitution envision the state as the primary planner and promoter of the economic development of Mexico. However, the TLC assumes that a transcontinental private sector will be the premier planner of investment and production in Mexico and the main engine of economic competitiveness and growth. The TLC also clashes with Mexico's legal tradition of executive authority over commerce, property rights, and investment. The Mexican constitution has traditionally embodied extensive executive branch authority over foreign commerce and over the production, transport, distribution, and consumption of goods and services. Article 131 of the constitution, for instance, originally authorized the Mexican executive to regulate the import, export, and transport of goods and to regulate foreign commerce and the "stability of national production."[62]

Similarly, the Law of Executive Economic Prerogatives authorized the executive to "participate in industrial and commercial activities related to the production, distribution, and consumption" of "food, clothing, essential materials for national industries and products of fundamental industries."[63] In anticipation of NAFTA, however, the Mexican government under the Salinas administration passed two laws curtailing executive authority to regulate commerce and private property. In 1991, the government enacted a stringent new law, the Industrial Property Act, to protect intellectual property, including that of foreign firms. Moreover, in 1993 the government passed a Foreign Investment Law that, among other things, eliminated government-imposed performance requirements on firms and opened up more sectors of the Mexican economy to foreign investors. Correspondingly, the TLC reinforced these domestic legal constraints on the Mexican government's regulatory authority by incorporating them within an international treaty. In short, the TLC not only eliminates national barriers to trade but, most important, it prohibits many national regulations on private property rights, including foreign investment, and it outlaws state-imposed, national performance requirements on private firms and traders.[64]

Indeed, NAFTA's legal establishment of continentwide private property rights violates the spirit of Mexico's constitution in more fundamental ways than NAFTA's free trade provisions. As Jonathan Schlefer points out, NAFTA's sections discussing investment, services, and intellectual property essentially extend U.S.-style property rights throughout the continent.[65] In other words, the TLC introduces new continentwide rules that protect private property rights and investments in Mexico in much the same way private property is protected in the United States.[66]

These new continental property rights provisions contradict the most fundamental symbolism of Mexico's revolutionary constitution, envisioned as a legal document privileging Mexican citizens over foreign nationals. As a symbol of the Mexican revolution's rejection of Porfirio Díaz's policies favoring foreign investors and foreign nationals over Mexican citizens, the postrevolutionary constitution established Mexico's revolutionary state as the arbiter of property rights in the interests of the nation. Indeed, Article 27 authorized the state to expropriate and redistribute privately owned land to peasants and to expropriate foreign-owned industries to serve the public interest. And the constitution's many provisions for state economic intervention to promote agricultural and industrial development and to regulate production, distribution, and consumption of goods all envisioned the state as a master regulator of private and public property for protecting and privileging national interests over foreign interests.[67]

In spite of constitutional legacies to the contrary, NAFTA opens up to legal dispute the Mexican state's juridical sovereignty over property rights, commerce, and the economy to private sector actors from across the continent. Referring to Parts 5 and 6 of the agreement, Schlefer points out:

> Under NAFTA, if a signatory country confiscates a business, imposes performance requirements or violates property rights in other ways, the owners can appeal to an international tribunal for damages. NAFTA even requires Mexico to adopt an American-style legal system to enforce intellectual-property rights. And if Mexico's state enterprises engage in anti-competitive behavior, the tribunal can order the Government to cease or face hefty trade sanctions.[68]

Contrary to the spirit of the Mexican constitution, NAFTA legally privileges transcontinental private sector interests over Mexican national interests in the areas of property rights, investment, trade, and commerce. On the other hand, NAFTA's side agreements leave intact the Mexican state's legal sovereignty over labor, environmental, health, and human rights issues. In these key human welfare and environmental areas, the side agreements fail to set up continentwide rules and stringent enforcement mechanisms parallel to those governing property rights and commerce across the continent. Instead, the side agreements left the three individual signatory states in sovereign charge of their respective human welfare and environmental issues and conditions.

Moreover, unlike property rights disputes, which private parties can bring against the state, private parties cannot dispute the Mexican government's failures to enforce human welfare, human rights, and environmental laws. Only the U.S. or Canadian governments can bring disputes to a NAFTA panel after a "persistent pattern" of nonenforcement of Mexican laws becomes apparent.[69] And the sanctions on the Mexican government would be modest; it would either have to draft an "action plan" for enforcement of its laws or pay at most a $20 million fine.[70] In short, NAFTA's side agreements ironically leave the Mexican state with extensive sovereign authority over Mexican people's wages, working conditions, welfare, and lives even while the neoliberal, commercial thrust of the agreement implies that state intervention is detrimental to people's socioeconomic well-being.

Paradoxically, NAFTA perpetuates the Mexican state's sovereign legal authority over average Mexican citizens while simultaneously implying that the state need not and should not wield sovereign power to protect such citizens. In other words, the Mexican state is still endowed with extensive legal authority over most people's lives but minimal ability to improve most people's lives. In fact, the state's constitutional authority to intervene in the economy, to regulate commerce, and to arbitrate property rights is now substantially circumscribed and subject to dispute from private investors across the continent. These new legal restrictions on the state increase popular uncertainties about NAFTA's effects on average Mexicans. As a result of such popular uncertainty, it is not clear whether the Mexican state is now politically equipped to consolidate a new popular mythology arguing that a transcontinental private sector will catapult Mexicans into the First World.

Legally, there is uncertainty among average Mexicans about whether NAFTA's new rules privilege Mexicans as much as foreigners. Economically, there is popular uncertainty about whether NAFTA's economic impact on Mexico will protect the economic security of average Mexicans as much as NAFTA protects the economic interests and property of private firms. Politically, since an interventionist state is no longer portrayed as the centerpiece of Mexico's national economic sovereignty, PRI *políticos* are implicitly blamed for their long, historical role in perpetuating state interventionism. In fact, the new NAFTA rhetoric implies that average Mexicans need no longer rely on their traditional popular sector organizations within the PRI to protect popular socioeconomic well-being.

Indeed, Mexico's myths about national sovereignty are in considerable disarray. The PRI regime's post-revolutionary culture of national community previously drawing together the diverse inhabitants of modern Mexico is now openly rejected by some Mexicans while still implicitly embraced by others. In the early postrevolutionary era, the political stability of the Mexican nation-state was culturally grounded in the modern state's symbolic links to Mexico's indigenous populace. In fact, the "revolutionary" state of the 1920s and 1930s came to symbolize the triumph of Mexico's indigenous civilizations over foreign intruders. The sovereignty of Mexico's revolutionary nation-state symbolized indigenous freedom from foreign domination and popular political self-determination. As a key founding father of the postrevolutionary regime, Lázaro Cárdenas was popularly embraced as the crowning architect of the revolutionary state as an edifice of popular sovereignty in the 1930s. Now, however, the regime faces relentless criticism from Cárdenas's son and the opposition party, the PRD, who regard the regime as a total affront to popular sovereignty and democratic practices.[71] Cuauhtémoc Cárdenas and the PRD fundamentally dispute the regime's cultural image and claims as representative of indigenous and poor people.[72] Moreover, they critique the TLC for its lack of attention to the needs of Mexican workers, peasants, and poor people.[73]

As if to confirm PRD positions, indigenous and poor people in Chiapas state launched an armed rebellion against the Salinas government on the first day NAFTA went into effect. The Chiapas rebels identify themselves as Zapatistas fighting for indigenous people's rights and socioeconomic well-being. They and their spokesman-leader, Subcomandante Marcos, reject the notion that NAFTA and the Salinas government are the crowning achievements of Mexicans' sovereign, national self-determination. Instead, the rebels originally demanded that Salinas step down from the presidency and that their vision of popular sovereignty be implemented through clean and fair presidential elections in 1994.[74] Clearly the Chiapas rebellion cast a deep shadow over the mythical image of the PRI regime as the political expression of indigenous and poor people's popular sovereignty.

In sum, NAFTA will help fragment Mexico as a national political community even while it galvanizes neoliberal faith in Mexico's national economic potential. This is partly because the traditional myths as well as the legalities underpinning the sovereignty of the Mexican state are in deep dispute. At the same time, NAFTA's transnational economic arrangements do little to supplement or replace the legal-political authority of the Mexican state over average people, workers, and human welfare in general. Instead, NAFTA leaves the Mexican state in charge of mediating disruptions of people's lives caused by continental economic restructuring at a time when state interventionism has been drastically reduced.

In any case, NAFTA promises to have profound and differing effects on average Mexicans' lives. Indeed, NAFTA promises to have widely varying effects on Mexico's different regions, economic sectors, industries, firms, social classes, and ethnic groups.[75] In this respect, the Salinista vision of NAFTA as a means of reconsolidating Mexicans' shared national

identity and their sense of national community is problematic. Unlike legal
independence in 1821, which at a minimum delineated a new national territory as a homeland shared in common by all Mexicans, NAFTA undermines old notions of the importance of a shared national territory as a necessary, common defense against foreign investors and interests. Moreover,
NAFTA will likely increase rather than reduce Mexico's differences in cultural and economic geography by having widely divergent socioeconomic
effects on Mexico's various regions.

While neoliberal economic ideology celebrates NAFTA as Mexico's
threshold to the First World, the Chiapas rebellion and popular sympathy
for it suggest growing skepticism about NAFTA as average Mexicans' sure
route to economic security.[76] In March 1994, the contradictions between
neoliberal rhetoric about Mexico's admittance to the First World and
Mexico's political turmoil reached increasingly absurd levels following the
Colosio assassination. On the day after the assassination, President Salinas
proudly announced that Mexico had been accepted as a new member of the
Organization for Economic Cooperation and Development, the OECD. In
other words, Salinas proceeded to proclaim Mexico's formal admittance to
the club of stable, democratic, First World countries in spite of the overwhelming political-economic anxieties following the assassination.

OECD membership or not, NAFTA tends to undermine the Mexican
nation-state as a stable legal-political order even while simultaneously relying on it as the fundamental basis for political stability in Mexico. Indeed,
NAFTA leaves the Mexican state legally endowed with substantial sovereign authority over average Mexicans' lives but negligible ability to
improve their lives. In that respect, NAFTA perpetuates Mexico's ongoing
integration and disintegration as a nation-state, albeit with nineteenth century–style fragmentation trends instead of twentieth century–style political
unity and stability. Rather than envisioning continental legal and political
replacements for the nation-state in North America, Salinas and the other
political and corporate elites who designed NAFTA lacked transnational
cultural imagination beyond the nation-state. Salinas's successor, Ernesto
Zedillo, promises to continue to implement neoliberal economic integration
in the absence of a continental social charter. Since the PRI as a ruling
party no longer inspires popular political imagination with a sense of strong
national unity and purpose, the Zedillo government is faced with governing
a nation-state in considerable symbolic and political disarray. By definition, the neoliberalism of NAFTA precludes a Mexican governmental shift
toward social welfare-oriented continentalism. Thus, the Zedillo government will likely attempt to reconsolidate the political and symbolic edifice
of the Mexican nation-state with the rhetoric and images of political opening and democratization.

Nation-building premised on democratization images and rhetoric may
prove difficult due, in part, to continuing cynicism about the rationales

behind PRI electoral victories, such as those of August 1994. Considerable cynicism surrounding the 1994 elections as proof of full-scale democratization in Mexico stems from the fact that a highly discredited ruling party was nevertheless credited once again with electoral success. Some interpretations attribute PRI victories to the notion that people voted for a party that they no longer believe in because they are uncertain or fearful of what to believe as an alternative to the PRI regime. This would partly account for the paradoxical fact that as overt electoral fraud diminishes in Mexico, opposition parties often seem less capable of electorally defeating a ruling party as discredited as the PRI is. Accordingly, although election day in August 1994 involved less overt fraud than in the past, many independent observers were reluctant to proclaim the PRI's victories as indicative of full-scale democratic opening in Mexico.

While national political and corporate elites in Mexico will undoubtedly continue to conjure up images of a new, democratic nation, average Mexicans will continue to attempt to secure socioeconomic survival in their neighborhoods and local communities. As NAFTA and continental economic restructuring disrupt more and more lives, nation-building and "democratization" at the national, elite level will become increasingly irrelevant to people's sense of daily socioeconomic security. Community organization and activism at the local level will increasingly become average people's only line of defense against the economic uncertainties of economic restructuring. As a response and a challenge to the national state and political elites' indifference to the social welfare concerns of average people, local political activism and community organization, such as that along the Mexico-U.S. border[77] and in Chiapas imply an alternative integration process.[78] Spurred by grassroots concerns, locally imagined integration is more concerned with basic human needs and is the offspring of increasingly transnational coalitions of local activists and ordinary people rather than national governmental and corporate elites. Thus, while national elites proceed to build a new, "democratic" nation and national "economic sovereignty" based on NAFTA, ordinary Mexicans will increasingly find that their socioeconomic security lies beyond sovereignty, the nation-state, and national borders.

Appendixes

Appendix 1
Presidents of Mexico Since 1914

Venustiano Carranza	August 20, 1914–May 21, 1920
(Conventionist presidents)	November 3, 1914–January 3, 1916
Eulalio Gutiérrez	
Roque González Garza	
Francisco Lagos Cházaro	
Adolfo de la Huerta	June 1, 1920–November 30, 1920
Alvaro Obregón Salido	December 1, 1920–November 30, 1924
Plutarco Elías Calles	December 1, 1924–November 30, 1928
Emilio Portes Gil	December 1, 1928–November 30, 1930
Pascual Ortiz Rubio	February 5, 1930–September 2, 1932
Abelardo L. Rodríguez	September 3, 1932–November 30, 1934
Lázaro Cárdenas del Río	December 1, 1934–November 30, 1940
Manuel Avila Camacho	December 1, 1940–November 30, 1946
Miguel Alemán Valdés	December 1, 1946–November 30, 1952
Adolfo Ruiz Cortines	December 1, 1952–November 30, 1958
Adolfo López Mateos	December 1, 1958–November 30, 1964
Gustavo Díaz Ordaz	December 1, 1964–November 30, 1970
Luis Echeverría Alvarez	December 1, 1970–November 30, 1976
José López Portillo	December 1, 1976–November 30, 1982
Miguel de la Madrid H.	December 1, 1982–November 30, 1988
Carlos Salinas de Gortari	December 1, 1988–November 30, 1994
Ernesto Zedillo Ponce de León	December 1, 1994–

Appendix 2
Political Biography of Luis Echeverría Alvarez

Date and place of birth: January 17, 1922, in Mexico, D.F.

Education: Primary studies in Mexico City and Ciudad Victoria,
Tamaulipas
Secondary studies in Mexico City at the National
Preparatory School, 1938–1940
Special studies in Chile, Argentina, France, and the United
States, on scholarship, 1941
Law studies from the National School of Law, UNAM,
1940–1944
Law degree awarded August 1945. Thesis title: "The
Balance of Power System and the Society of Nations"
Professor of legal theory, National School of Law, UNAM,
1947–1949

Elective
Positions: President of Mexico, 1970–1976

Party
Positions: Joined PRI, March 1946
Private secretary to Rodolfo Sánchez Taboada, president of
the National Executive Committee of PRI, December
1946
Assistant secretary to Rodolfo Sánchez Taboada, regional
director of PRI for the Federal District, March to
December 1946
Platform adviser to the PRI, 1946
Secretary of press and publicity of the National Executive
Committee (CEN) of PRI, 1946–1952
General delegate of the CEN of PRI, 1948
President of the Regional Committee of the State of
Guanajuato
Representative of the CEN of PRI to Sánchez Colín's cam-
paign for governor of Mexico, 1951
Oficial Mayor of PRI, 1957–58

Governmental
positions:
(Appointive) Director of accounts for the secretariat
of the Navy, 1952–1954

Oficial Mayor of the secretariat of Public Education,
  1954–1957
Subsecretary of Government, 1958–1963
Subsecretary in charge of the Government secretariat, 1964
Secretary of Government, 1964–1970
Ambassador to UNESCO, 1977–1978
Ambassador to Australia, 1978

Interest Group
Activity: Student Delegate to the Free World Youth Association, 1943
            Founder, Students for Revolutionary Action, 1947

Relatives and
Friends: Brother Eduardo was a member of the Advisory Council of
            the Institute of Economic, Political, and Social Studies
            (IEPES) of PRI, and president of the Technical Council of
            the subsecretariat of Public Health, 1974.
            Brother Rodolfo was director general of the National
            Cinema Bank.
            Nephew Rodolfo Echeverría, Jr. was *Oficial Mayor* of the
            PRI and a federal deputy.
            Father-in-law José Zuña Hernández was former governor of
            Jalisco.
            Rodolfo Sánchez Taboada was a political mentor.
            Alfonso Noriega and Luis Garrido Díaz were his teachers at
            the National University.
            Luis M. Farías was a fellow student at UNAM.

Special
activity: Delivered the nomination speech for Adolfo López Mateos
            before PRI, November 17, 1957.

Note: This political biography is extracted from the work of Roderic A. Camp,
Mexican Political Biographies: 1935–1981 (Tucson: University of Arizona Press,
1982), p. 90.

Appendix 3, Table A NAFINSA's Disbursements of External Resources—Sectoral Allocation, 1968–1979 (percentages)

	1968	1969	1970	1971	1972	1973	1974	1975	1976	June 1977–July 1978	1979
Infrastructure	24	25.4	33	28	24	32	16	14	14	17	19
Communications	2.4	1.4	0.4	0.4	0.2	2.8					
Roads, bridges	4.6	6.3	9.0	7.5	6.3	9.1					
Irrigation	9.6	10.3	11.1	10.8	9.0	10.6	4.2	6	5	3.5	3.4
Agriculture	4.1	2.6	10.8	8.2	7.4	7.3					
Industry	74	72	64	70	74	67	82	85	84	82	80
Basic industries	57	49	45	45	35	25	65	36	19	25	30
Electric energy	18.2	25	20	22	15	12	17	4	4	9.5	3.8
Petroleum	0.5	4	—	10.4	—	—					
Steel	5.4	4.1	3.4	1.1	4.2	3.7					
Transportation	33.2	16.3	21.5	9.8	15.5	8.7					
Transportation equipment	7.0	12	8.3	9.1	6.1	7.6					
Manufacturing	16.6	23	19	25	39	43	17	50	65	57	50

Source: Nacional Financiera, S.A.; cited in Bouchet, p. 27.

Appendix 3, Table B External Resources Obtained by NAFINSA (disbursements in $ millions)

	1968	1969	1970	1971	1972	1973	1974	1975	1976	June 1977– July 1978	1979
Total disbursements	357	396	376	410	499	621	1,032	1,447	1,384	1,310	1,438
% Public sector	43	42	45	51	51	31					
Debt service payments	364	318	312	333	394	488	481	565	685		
Net transfer	79	173	170	193	244	294	772	1,156	1,033		

Source: Nacional Financiera, S.A.; cited in Bouchet, p. 285.

Appendix 3, Table C   Increases in Internal Prices (percentages)

	Attributable to:	
	Changes in International Prices	Other Factors
1970	58.0	42.0
1971	48.1	51.9
1972	80.0	20.0
1973	72.7	27.3
1974	43.9	56.1
1975	12.3	87.7

Source: Tello, *La política económica en México,* p. 172.

Appendix 3, Table D   The Depressions in the North American Economy and Their Relation to Mexico's Financial Deficits and Its Foreign Indebtedness, 1971–1979

Years	Deficit (Millions of Pesos)	Foreign Debt (Thousands of Millions of Pesos)
1971	6,166	56.7
1974	34,153	124.6
1975	58,078	180.5
1976	65,635	302.7
1977	63,800	517.3
1978	7,690	597.9
1979	150,113	678.4
1980	106,808	776.9

Source: IV Informe de Gobierno, 1980, Anexo I, Estadístico-histórico, p. 218. Para 1980, *V Informe Presidencial,* Anexo I, p. 201; cited in Padilla Aragón, p. 52.

Appendix 4
Major Public-Private Sector Conflicts
(1970–1976)

1. *First conflict*: Attempts at industrial decentralization
   (January 1970 to August 1971)
   > *Policy objectives*: Dispersion of industrial establishments from highly developed to underdeveloped industrial zones
   > *Proposed measures*: Prohibition of the installation of new industry in the Valle de México and surrounding areas
   > *Private opposition*:[b] COPARMEX; CONCAMIN[c]
   > *Outcome*: Policy proposal dropped

2. *Second conflict*: 10 percent tax on luxury goods
   (December 1970 to December 1971)
   > *Policy objectives*: Taxation of luxury goods
   > *Proposed measures*: Development of a list of articles of luxury to be taxed at the rate of 10 percent
   > *Private opposition*: COPARMEX; CONCAMIN; CONCANACO; AMIS; CANACINTRA; CAMCO
   > *Outcome*: Original list of luxury items to be taxed amended to exclude a series of luxury goods with very large markets in Mexico

3. *Third conflict*: Regulation of technology transfers
   (August to December 1972)
   > *Policy objectives*: Regulation of foreign technology transfers to stimulate Mexican exports and to reduce foreign interference in the administration of domestic firms
   > *Proposed measures*: Elimination of all restrictive marketing practices, especially contracts involving the acquisition of foreign technology allocated on the condition that it be used only in the production of goods for the domestic Mexican market
   > *Private opposition*: CAMCO; ABM
   > *Outcome*: New regulations governing technology transfers imposed, but most important proposed regulations regarding restrictive marketing practices abandoned

4. *Fourth conflict*: Law to regulate foreign investment
   (November 1972 to February 1973)
   > *Policy objectives*: Regulation of foreign investment activities and avoidance of the absorption of Mexican firms by foreign capital
   > *Proposed measures*: State to decide on geographic location of foreign enterprise in designated provinces; no foreign firm allowed to own more than 49 percent of the shares of a firm; property titles and operations of foreign firms subject to registration; foreign par-

ticipation in the administration of firms limited to match foreign firms' percentage of ownership

Private opposition: Avoided through process of watering down legislation

Outcome: Most important regulatory aspects—localization of foreign enterprise to designated provinces; ensured Mexican, participatory ownership in foreign investment activities; and reduction of Mexican firms being sold to foreign capital—watered down in the final legislation

5. *Fifth conflict*: Creation of FONACOT (National Fund for the Guarantee and Promotion of Workers' Consumption) and the Adjustable Salary Scale Initiative
(March and April 1974)

Policy objectives: To subsidize the purchase of durable consumer goods for salaried workers and to ensure that salaries of workers keep pace with inflation (Adjustable Salary Scale Initiative probably used as a bargaining chip by government to obtain private sector's acquiescence to FONACOT)

Proposed measures: Establishment of lines of credit that salaried workers could draw on to purchase durable consumer goods at state subsidized prices; establishment of a scale for salaries that would automatically adjust itself to increases in price levels

Private opposition: COPARMEX; CONCANACO; la Cámara de Comercio del Distrito Federal

Outcome: Idea of an adjustable salary scale completely dropped; FONACOT, the lesser of two evils for private sector, created

6. *Sixth conflict*: Establishment of a system of price controls
(September to October 1974)

Policy objectives: To control prices of goods by allowing price increases only when real costs of production had increased

Proposed measures: Specification of a list of 29 articles of popular consumption (meat, milk, coffee, etc.) whose prices would be frozen; establishment of a price control scheme to allow goods with variable production costs to increase in price if costs of production had increased by at least 5 percent

Private opposition: CONCANACO; COPARMEX; CANACO; CONCAMIN; Asociación de Industriales del Estado de México

Outcome: Price controls adopted for the 29 articles of basic consumption, but 138 articles of generalized consumption excluded from any types of control

7. *Seventh conflict*: Establishment of controls on imports
(July to August 1975)

Policy objectives: Selective control of imports to enhance Mexican industry, especially Mexican export industries

Proposed measures: Establishment of restrictions on imported goods through protectionist measures; state subsidies of export industries

Private opposition: CAMCO; CANACO

Outcome: Selective controls on imports imposed, but devolution of taxes on exported production increased; up to 75 percent of taxes on capital goods imports used in the production of goods for export to be covered by government subsidies

8. *Eighth conflict*: General law of human land settlements
(December 1975 to May 1976)

Policy objectives: To enhance the collective exploitation of *ejido* lands and to regulate urban real estate and congestion

Policy measures: Establishment of basic norms governing foundation, conservation, improvement, and growth of cities; transfer of authority regarding use and destinies of land, water, and wooded areas to state and local governments; transfer to local governments of authority to regulate use of land and growth of cities; regulation of speculation and monopolization of urban real estate

Private opposition: CONCANACO; CONCAMIN; CCE; COPARMEX

Outcome: Law passed, but with important modifications: all local authority over land use, etc., eliminated from the legislation; new legislation to specify that houses of private individuals would not be confiscated and that strangers would not be allowed to invade such private properties

9. *Ninth conflict*: Devaluation and flotation of the peso
(August to October 1976)

Policy objectives: To abandon fixed exchange rates and devalue peso to correct for an imbalance of payments and to enhance Mexico's export position

Proposed measures: Adoption of floating exchange rates as a permanent mechanism for adjusting exchange rate

Private opposition: CCE; CONCANACO; CONCAMIN; COPARMEX; CANACO; CANACINTRA

Outcome: Flotation of peso adopted, but certain steps to placate private sector taken: application of taxes on exported goods to be flexible; peso to be allowed to float only within certain parameters; new subsidies and incentives to export industries adopted

10. *Tenth conflict*: Presidential recommendation of a salary increase of 23 percent
(September 1976)

Policy objectives: To cushion devastating effects of the devaluation and ensuing inflation on workers' consumption

Proposed measures: A 23 percent increase in the salaries of workers on minimum wage (although organized labor had requested a 65 percent increase) and up to a 21 percent increase in salaries above minimum wage

Private opposition: CCE; CONCAMIN

Outcome: Salary increases of 23 percent and 21 percent put into effect, but 10 percent increase in prices also authorized.

Notes: a. Appendix 4 is a summary version of Rosario Green's analysis. See Green, *Estado y banca transnacional en México,* pp. 78–109; 309–327.

b. The major voices of private opposition

c. For an exposition of the various private sector groups in Mexico, see Chapter 4 and Figures 4.2 and 4.3. These acronyms and each group's composition are explained in same chapter. CANACO refers to Cámaras Nacionales de Comercio (National Chambers of Commerce).

Acronyms

ABM	Association of Mexican Bankers
AMIS	Mexican Association of Insurance Institutions
ASU	Arizona State University
BANAMEX	National Bank of Mexico
BANCOMER	Commercial Bank
CAMCO	American Chamber of Commerce in Mexico
CANACINTRA	National Chamber of Transformation Industry
CANACO	National Chambers of Commerce
CAP	Commission of Public Administration
CCE	Coordinative Council of Businessmen
CCM	Confederation of Mexican Peasants
CEIMSA	Mexican Export-Import Company, Inc.
CEN	National Executive Committee
CGOCM	General Confederation of Workers and Peasants of Mexico
CMHN	Mexican Council of Businessmen
CNC	National Confederation of Peasants
CNG	National Confederation of Cattlemen
CNPP	National Confederation of Small Farmers
COMERMEX	Multi-Bank Comermex
CONASUPO	National Staple Products Company
CONCAMIN	National Confederation of Industrial Chambers
CONCANACO	National Confederation of Chambers of Commerce
COPARMEX	Employers' Confederation of the Mexican Republic
CROM	Regional Confederation of Mexican Workers
CTM	Confederation of Mexican Workers
DINA	National Diesel
FOGAIN	Trust for Credit and Development of Medium- and Small-scale Industry (NAFINSA)
FONACOT	National Fund for the Guarantee and Promotion of Workers' Consumption
FTA	Free Trade Agreement
GATT	General Agreement on Tariffs and Trade
IEPES	Institute for Economic, Political, and Social Studies

IMF	International Monetary Fund
ISI	Import Substitution Industrialization
NAFINSA	National Development Bank
NAFTA	North American Free Trade Agreement
OECD	Organization for Economic Cooperation and Development
PAN	National Action Party
PEMEX	Mexican Petroleum Company
PNA	National Agrarianist Party
PNR	National Revolutionary Party
PRD	Democratic Revolutionary Party
PRI	Institutional Revolutionary Party
PRM	Party of the Mexican Revolution
SEDESOL	Secretariat of Social Development
SEDUE	Secretariat of Urban Development and Ecology
SERFIN	Serfin Bank, Inc.
SHCP	Secretariat of the Treasury/Finance
SPP	Secretariat of Programming and Budget
TLC	Free Trade Agreement
UNAM	National Autonomous University of Mexico
UNESCO	United Nations Educational, Scientific, and Cultural Organization

Notes

Chapter 1

1. The Dutch theorist Hugo Grotius first posited the international law of nations. See Hugo Grotius, *De Jure Belli ac Pacis Libri Tres,* trans., Francis W. Kelsey (New York: Oceana, 1964). This seminal work, whose English title is *On the Law of War and Peace,* was published in 1646. Although Grotius's theories of international law were supposedly applicable beyond Europe because of their reliance on presumably universal principles of human reason, his theories of international law were European in cultural origin as well as in most of their applications until the twentieth century.

2. Michael C. Meyer and William L. Sherman, *The Course of Mexican History,* 3d ed. (New York: Oxford University Press, 1987), pp. 294–297.

3. Robert Jackson distinguishes between negative sovereignty ("a formal-legal condition . . . defined as freedom from outside interference") and positive sovereignty (a "substantive condition" and the capabilities and "means which enable states to take advantage of their independence; . . . a positively sovereign government possesses the wherewithal to provide political goods for its citizens"). See Robert H. Jackson, *Quasi-States: Sovereignty, International Relations, and the Third World* (New York: Cambridge University Press, 1990), pp. 27–29.

4. In Robert Jackson's terms, Mexico has negative sovereignty, or formal-legal entitlement to nonintervention from other states, but not much positive sovereignty, defined as the state's wherewithal to provide political goods for its citizens. See Jackson, p. 29.

5. Ibid., pp. 72–73; 54–55.

6. J. Fred Rippy, *Rivalry of the United States and Great Britain over Latin America (1808–1830)* (Baltimore: The Johns Hopkins University Press, 1929; New York: Octagon Books, 1964), pp. 254–256.

7. Ibid., pp. 256–258; 308–309.

8. José Vasconcelos, *La raza cósmica: Misión de la raza iberoamericana* (Madrid: Aguilar, 1961).

9. See Jackson, p. 55, who cites Alfred Cobban, *The Nation-State and National Self-Determination* (New York: Crowell, 1969), chap. 4.

10. Article 10 of the Covenant of the League of Nation stated: "The Members of the League undertake to respect and preserve, as against external aggression, the territorial integrity and existing political independence of all Members of the League. In any case of any such aggression, or in case of any threat or danger of such aggression, the Council shall advise upon the means by which this obligation shall be fulfilled."

11. Jackson, pp. 66; 75–76.

12. Ibid., pp. 75–76.

13. F. P. Walters, *A History of the League of Nations,* vol. 1 (London: Oxford University Press, 1952), pp. 63–64.

14. Jackson, p. 76, and F. S. Northedge, *The League of Nations: Its Life and Times, 1920–1946* (New York: Leicester University Press, 1986), pp. 63–65.

15. Walters, vol. 1, pp. 390–392. Also, Northedge, pp. 63, 86. Article 21 of the Covenant of the League of Nations stated: "Nothing in this Covenant shall be deemed to affect the validity of international engagements, such as Treaties of Arbitration, or regional understandings like the Monroe Doctrine, for securing the maintenance of peace."

16. Walters, vol. 2, pp. 461–462. See also Northedge, pp. 267–268.

17. Walters, vol. 2, pp. 295–310; 412–422.

18. Edwin Lieuwen, *Mexican Militarism: The Political Rise and Fall of the Revolutionary Army* (Albuquerque: University of New Mexico Press, 1968), pp. 113–138.

19. Jackson, pp. 76–77.

20. See, for example, Luis H. Alvarez, "Political and Economic Reform in Mexico: The PAN Perspective," in Riordan Roett, ed., *Political and Economic Liberalization in Mexico: At a Critical Juncture?* (Boulder: Lynne Rienner Publishers, 1993), pp. 143–148.

21. For a compelling analysis of the human costs of Mexico's economic development in the late twentieth century, see Judith Hellman, "The Mexican Road to Development" and "The Human Costs of Mexican Development," in Judith Hellman, *Mexico in Crisis,* 2d ed. (New York: Holmes & Meier Publishers, 1983), pp. 59–102; 103–124.

22. In his inaugural address of 1933, U.S. President Franklin Roosevelt pledged to be a "good neighbor" vis-à-vis Latin American countries.

23. Jackson (p. 64) notes that Mexico did not begin to participate in the European diplomatic system until the turn of the century. According to Jackson, Mexico's participation in the Hague Conferences of 1899 and 1907 "marked the formal extension of the club of sovereign states (the 'Family of Nations') beyond Europe and the United States."

24. Thomas Skidmore and Peter Smith, "The Colonial Foundations, 1492–1880s," in Thomas Skidmore and Peter Smith, *Modern Latin America,* 3d ed. (New York: Oxford University Press, 1992), pp. 31–32.

25. Meyer and Sherman, pp. 294–296.

26. Ibid., pp. 387–392.

27. William R. Manning, "British Influence in Mexico, 1822–26," in H. Morse Stephens and Herbert E. Bolton, eds., *The Pacific Ocean in History* (New York: Macmillan, 1917), pp. 331–348. See also Rippy, pp. 116–120; 247–269.

28. Rippy, pp. 117–124; 256–261.

29. Manning, pp. 342–344.

30. Rippy, pp. 116–121.

31. Ibid.

32. Stuart A. MacCorkle, *American Policy of Recognition Towards Mexico* (New York: AMS Press, 1971), p. 41.

33. Meyer and Sherman, pp. 328–331; 387–391.

34. Ibid., p. 324.

35. Manning, pp. 333–334. See also Rippy, pp. 112–116; 249–250.

36. Rippy, pp. 247–250; 256–259.

37. Ibid., pp. 112–116.

38. Manning, pp. 331–332.

39. Ibid., pp. 340–341.

40. Ibid., p. 334.

41. Rippy, p. 297.

42. Ibid., pp. 91–106.

43. Howard W. V. Temperley, "Later American Policy of George Canning," *American Historical Review,* vol. 11, p. 781, citing British Museum manuscripts. Temperley citation is found in Manning, p. 341.

44. Rippy, pp. 255–260; 286–300.

45. Ibid.

46. Ibid., pp. 286–287.

47. MacCorkle, p. 38.

48. Meyer and Sherman, p. 295.

49. Ibid., pp. 291–292.

50. Rippy, p. 314.

51. Meyer and Sherman, p. 432.

52. Remberto H. Padilla, *Historia de la política mexicana* (Mexico City: Editores Asociados Mexicanos, 1992), p. 23.

53. Meyer and Sherman, p. 337. In fact, the insurgent Texans chose Lorenzo de Zavala as vice-president of the Lone Star Republic.

54. Meyer and Sherman, p. 337.

55. Ibid., pp. 342–344.

56. MacCorkle, pp. 44–45.

57. Meyer and Sherman, pp. 343–344.

58. Ibid. The former Lone Star Republic, newly annexed to the United States in 1845, claimed thousands of square miles of territory between the Nueces River and the Rio Grande. After the annexation of Texas, the U.S. government also claimed this territory.

59. Ibid. This included, among other things, Texas, New Mexico, and California.

60. Ibid., p. 353.

61. MacCorkle, p. 47.

62. Meyer and Sherman, pp. 380–388; 383.

63. MacCorkle, pp. 44, 55.

64. Ibid., p. 53.

65. Ibid., pp. 50–51.

66. Ibid., pp. 51–53.

67. Meyer and Sherman, p. 387.

68. Ibid., pp. 391–392.

69. The First Mexican Empire began on May 18, 1822, and ended a little less than one year later on March 19, 1823. The Second Mexican Empire began on May 28, 1864, and ended almost three years later, on May 15, 1867.

70. Meyer and Sherman, p. 395.

71. Ibid., p. 398.

72. Ibid., p. 399.

73. Francisco Madero, *Plan de San Luis Potosí,* October 5, 1910; text found in Isidro Fabela, ed., *Documentos históricos de la revolución mexicana,* vol. 6 (Mexico City: Fondo de Cultura Económica y Editorial Jus, 1960–1973), pp. 69–76.

74. Meyer and Sherman, p. 442.

75. MacCorkle, pp. 71–72.

76. Ibid., p. 77.

77. MacCorkle, p. 87.

78. Ibid., p. 91.

79. Ibid., p. 90.

80. Ibid.
81. Ibid., pp. 91–93. Also Meyer and Sherman, p. 539.
82. Meyer and Sherman, p. 541.
83. Ibid., pp. 542–545.
84. Ibid., p. 544. See Articles 3 and 27 of *Constitución política de los Estados Unidos Mexicanos,* February 5, 1917 (Mexico City: Editorial Porrúa, 1992), pp. 22–33.
85. Article 27, Section I of the Mexican constitution of 1917 begins: "Sólo los mexicanos por nacimiento o por naturalización y las sociedades mexicanas tienen derecho de adquirir el dominio de las tierras, aguas y sus accesiones, o para obtener concesiones de explotación de minas o aguas. El estado podrá conceder el mismo derecho a los extranjeros, siempre que convengan ante la Secretaría de Relaciones en considerarse como nacionales respecto de dichos bienes y en no invocar por lo mismo la protección de sus gobiernos por lo que se refiere a aquellos." *Constitución,* pp. 25–26.
86. Meyer and Sherman, pp. 489–490.
87. MacCorkle, p. 94.
88. Ibid.
89. Meyer and Sherman, p. 577.
90. MacCorkle, pp. 40–41; 55–57.
91. Meyer and Sherman, p. 578.
92. Ibid.
93. MacCorkle, p. 100.
94. Nora Hamilton, *The Limits of State Autonomy: Post-Revolutionary Mexico* (Princeton: Princeton University Press, 1982), pp. 90–100.

Chapter 2

1. Brian R. Hamnett, *Roots of Insurgency, Mexican Regions, 1750–1824* (Cambridge: Cambridge University Press, 1986), pp. 45–46.
2. See Hamnett, pp. 24–46.
3. Claudio Véliz, *The Centralist Tradition of Latin America* (Princeton: Princeton University Press, 1980), pp. 218–236.
4. Ibid., pp. 70–89.
5. Hamnett, p. 202.
6. Anthony Giddens, *The Nation-State and Violence* (Berkeley: University of California Press, 1985), pp. 116–119.
7. See Hamnett, pp. 60–73.
8. Véliz, pp. 223–236.
9. Giddens, p. 116.
10. Ibid.
11. Véliz argues that nationalism in nineteenth-century Latin America, including Mexico, was outward-looking and was imported from Britain and France via liberal economic and political philosophies and that such nationalism was largely confined to elites. See Véliz, pp. 163–188.
12. Alan Knight, *The Mexican Revolution, Vol. I: Porfirians, Liberals, and Peasants* (Cambridge: Cambridge University Press, 1986), p. 2.
13. Alan Knight, "Peasant and Caudillo in Revolutionary Mexico, 1910–1917" in David Brading, ed., *Caudillo and Peasant in the Mexican Revolution* (Cambridge: Cambridge University Press, 1980), pp. 19–20; 28–29; 31–32.

14. See Arnaldo Córdova, *La ideología de la revolución mexicana: La formación del nuevo régimen* (Mexico City: Ediciones Era, 1973), pp. 262–268. See also Edwin Lieuwen, *Mexican Militarism: The Political Rise and Fall of the Revolutionary Army* (Albuquerque: University of New Mexico Press, 1968), pp. 57–79; 90–104.

15. Hamnett, pp. 13–21; 56–59; 74–101.

16. Ibid., pp. 202–213.

17. Knight, "Peasant and Caudillo," p. 39.

18. Knight, *The Mexican Revolution,* Vol. I, pp. 78–148.

19. Knight, "Peasant and Caudillo," p. 49.

20. The Northern Dynasty of presidents from 1921 to 1933 consolidated a national administrative monopoly over the means of violence after the revolution but failed to fully implement key reforms in the 1917 constitution that would have popularized nationalist sentiments among average Mexicans.

21. Lieuwen, pp. 18–61.

22. Córdova, pp. 287–306.

23. These interim presidents, whom Calles controlled during the Maximato, were Emilio Portes Gil (1928–1930); Pascual Ortiz Rubio (1930–1932); and Abelardo L. Rodríguez (1932–1934).

24. Arnaldo Córdova, *La política de masas del cardenismo* (Mexico City: Ediciones Era, 1974), pp. 41–42.

25. Hamilton, pp. 67–68.

26. Córdova, *La política de masas,* p. 42.

27. Ibid., pp. 43–44.

28. Nora Hamilton, *The Limits of State Autonomy: Post-Revolutionary Mexico* (Princeton: Princeton University Press, 1982), pp. 113–115.

29. Ibid., pp. 67; 125–126.

30. Ibid., p. 125.

31. The supporters of independent labor included the CGOCM, the Mexican Communist Party, and the union of electricians, as well as other progressive groups. See Hamilton, pp. 125–126.

32. Córdova, *La política de masas,* pp. 41–49.

33. Ibid.

34. Luis Javier Garrido, *El partido de la revolución institucionalizada: La formación del nuevo estado en México (1928–1945)* (Mexico City: Siglo XXI, 1982), pp. 192–193.

35. Hamilton, pp. 74–103.

36. Ibid., pp. 115–128.

37. Córdova, *La política de masas,* pp. 41–48.

38. Hamilton, p. 127.

39. Córdova, *La política de masas,* p. 84.

40. Because Cárdenas was most identified as an agrarian leader, the labor movement was not as clearly a natural political ally of his as the peasantry was. See Hamilton, pp. 119, 124.

41. See Arturo Anguiano, *El estado y la política obrera del cardenismo* (Mexico City: Ediciones Era, 1975), pp. 127–139. See also Córdova, *La política de masas,* pp. 177–201.

42. Hamilton, pp. 139–140.

43. Ibid., p. 140.

44. Ibid.

45. See Knight, *The Mexican Revolution,* vols. 1 and 2.

46. Ibid., p. 2.

47. Ibid.
48. Claudio Véliz argues that Latin American nationalisms, including Mexico's, were outward-looking emulations of European and U.S. ideas. See Véliz, pp. 148–149; 163–172.
49. Ibid., pp. 242–243.
50. Córdova, *La política de masas*, pp. 177–201.
51. Hamilton, pp. 104–141.
52. Córdova, *La política de masas*, pp. 44–45.
53. Ibid.
54. See Nathaniel Weyl and Sylvia Weyl, *The Reconquest of Mexico: The Years of Lázaro Cárdenas* (London: Oxford University Press, 1939), p. 124.
55. Córdova, *La política de masas*, p. 71.
56. Weyl and Weyl, p. 240.
57. Córdova, *La política de masas*, pp. 62, p. 70; Córdova, *La clase obrera*, p. 218.
58. Córdova, *La política de masas*, p. 62. Also see Cárdenas's personal statement in Lázaro Cárdenas, *¡Cárdenas habla!* (Mexico: La Impresora, 1940), pp. 15, 48.
59. Córdova, *La política de masas*, pp. 42–47.
60. Ibid., pp. 62, 95.
61. Ibid., pp. 34–36.
62. Ibid., pp. 38–39.
63. Ibid., pp. 70–71.
64. Ibid.
65. Ibid., pp. 103–104; 147–149; 161.
66. Ibid., pp. 147–149.
67. See Córdova's explanation of mass volatility in *La política de masas*, p. 66.
68. Ibid., pp. 67–68. The CGOCM broke off from CROM to become an independent labor union.
69. Ibid., pp. 64, 66. Speeches by Cárdenas are cited in which the president affirms his belief that the postrevolutionary state could not survive without the support of the popular sectors.
70. Hamilton, pp. 113–115.
71. Córdova, *La política de masas*, p. 69.
72. Hamilton, pp. 100–124.
73. Upon becoming governor of Michoacán in 1926, Cárdenas distributed land to 15,373 peasants and then armed women's leagues to guard the fields against landowner attacks on peasant workers. These facts are cited by Hamilton, p. 98.
74. Hamilton, p. 124.
75. See Córdova, *La política de masas*, pp. 35–40, for a discussion of the influence of the depression on Cárdenas's evaluation of the importance of the labor movement to the strength of the state.
76. Hamilton, pp. 104–141.
77. Ibid.
78. Weyl and Weyl, p. 237.
79. Hamilton, pp. 93–94.
80. This was a function of the distrust between peasant and labor leadership.
81. Weyl and Weyl, p. 256.
82. Ibid.
83. Ibid., pp. 258–259.
84. See Hamilton, p. 100, especially for details of Calles's attempts to destroy agrarian reform.

85. Calles's support to CROM damaged the PNA's organizational strength.

86. Obregón's rallying of peasant support for electoral purposes in the 1920s involved very little redistribution of land. See Hamilton, p. 100.

87. Hamilton, pp. 175–176.

88. Ibid., pp. 99–100.

89. Ibid.

90. Anguiano, pp. 63–65; 72–74; 92–93.

91. Weyl and Weyl, pp. 188–190.

92. Córdova, *La política de masas,* pp. 163–164.

93. Ibid., pp. 102–111.

94. Ibid., pp. 112; 121–122.

95. Ibid., pp. 112–122.

96. Ibid., pp. 112–113.

97. Portes Gil demonstrated a basic distrust of organized labor (including Toledano). See Córdova, *La clase obrera,* pp. 24–26. Portes Gil retained this distrust when he served as president of the PNR under the Cárdenas administration. See Hamilton, pp. 152–153.

98. Hamilton, pp. 152–153.

99. Ibid.

100. Ibid.

101. Ibid.

102. Ibid., pp. 151–153.

103. Weyl and Weyl, pp. 255–259.

104. Hamilton, p. 242, drew my attention to these dates.

105. Poder Ejecutivo Federal, Estados Unidos Mexicanos, *Diplomatic Notes Exchanged Between the Mexican and British Governments on Account of the Oil Industry Expropriation* (Mexico City: Talleres Gráficos de la Nación, DAPP, 1938), pp. 13–14.

106. Ibid., p. 7.

107. Ibid., pp. 12–14.

108. Ibid., p. 15.

109. Arnaldo Córdova cites this passage from the notes of Lázaro Cárdenas in Córdova's book, *La política de masas,* p. 202. The original source is Lázaro Cárdenas, *Apuntes 1913–1940,* in *Obras UNAM* (Mexico City: UNAM, 1972), p. 233. (My translation.)

Chapter 3

1. See Nora Hamilton, *The Limits of State Autonomy: Post-Revolutionary Mexico* (Princeton: Princeton University Press, 1982).

2. After Cárdenas transformed national governance, the Mexican nation-state linked state and society culturally and politically via the revolutionary symbolism surrounding the presidency.

3. Some of the fruits of industrialization were located locally but were very unevenly distributed. Hence, wealth was national in terms of its spatial location but not its distribution.

4. See José Luis Reyna and Richard Weinert, *Authoritarianism in Mexico* (Philadelphia: ISHI, 1977).

5. See Claus Offe, *Contradictions of the Welfare State* (Cambridge: MIT Press, 1984), for a theoretical discussion of the state's reliance on the private accumulation process for revenue.

6. This is discussed in Chapters 4 and 5.

7. The secretariat of the Presidencia was given formal planning authority and Patrimonio Nacional was given formal administrative authority over parastatals in 1958.

8. Horacio Flores de la Peña was the leading economist in this group; he was in Patrimonio Nacional.

9. See Clark Reynolds, "¿Por qué el desarrollo estabilizador en la realidad se desestabilizó?" (Washington, D.C.: Subcommittee on Interamerican Economic Relations, 1977).

10. A number of scholars agree on this date as the actual beginning of import-substitution industrialization phase one. See Clark Reynolds, *The Mexican Economy* (New Haven: Yale University Press, 1970); Gary Gereffi and Peter Evans, "Transnational Corporations, Dependent Development, and State Policy in the Semiperiphery: A Comparison of Brazil and Mexico," *Latin American Research Review* 16 (1981); and J. Ricardo Ramírez Brun, *Estado y acumulación de capital en México, 1929–1975* (Mexico City: Universidad Nacional Autónoma de México, 1980).

11. Reynolds, pp. 197–215.

12. José Fernández Santillán, *Política y administración pública en México* (Mexico City: Ediciones INAP, 1980), p. 61. Nora Hamilton, *The Limits of State Autonomy: Post-Revolutionary Mexico* (Princeton: Princeton University Press, 1982), p. 238.

13. Hamilton, p. 238.

14. *Presidencialismo* was deemed popular and national as a governance structure only if the presidency appeared all-powerful. See Chapter 2.

15. López Mateos, for instance, created Presidencia as a planning entity in 1958, but kept it as an ineffective appendage of the chief executive.

16. Hamilton, p. 238.

17. Ibid.

18. See Hamilton, pp. 234–239.

19. Ibid., p. 238.

20. Ibid., pp. 235–236.

21. The mystique surrounding the Cárdenas presidency involved the chief executive's *symbolic* personification of the interests of Mexico's popular sectors. Symbolically, therefore, the popular sectors of society were the state because they, through the presidency, supposedly controlled the state.

22. Fernández Santillán, pp. 47–64.

23. Rosario Green, *Estado y banca transnacional en México* (Mexico City: Nueva Imagen, 1981), p.19.

24. Ibid.

25. Presidencia de la República, *Decreto que crea la Comisión Federal de Planificación Económica como órgano consultivo de la Secretaría de la Economía Nacional, Diario Oficial,* Article 2, July 9, 1942.

26. Presidencia de la República, *Decreto que crea la Junta de Economía de Emergencia,* Articles 1–5, *Diario Oficial,* May 18, 1943.

27. Presidencia de la República, *Decreto que crea la Comisión Nacional de Planeación para la Paz, Diario Oficial,* February 15, 1944.

28. Ibid., Article 1.

29. Ibid., Article 8.

30. Fernández Santillán, p. 57.

31. Ibid.

32. Congreso de Diputados, *Ley para el control por parte del gobierno federal*

de los organismos descentralizados y empresas de participación estatal, December 31, 1947.

33. Fernández Santillán, pp. 30–31.

34. Ibid., pp. 33–34.

35. Alejandro Carrillo Castro, *La reforma administrativa en México: Evolución de la reforma administrativa en México (1971–1979)* (Mexico City: Miguel Angel Porrúa, 1980), p. 53.

36. See Hamilton, pp. 162–181.

37. Carrillo Castro, p. 52.

38. See Table 3.8, this chapter.

39. *México a través de los informes presidenciales (política agraria),* cited in Carrillo Castro, p. 62, footnote 14.

40. Ariel José Contreras, *México 1940: Industrialización y crisis política* (Mexico City: Siglo XXI, 1977), pp. 59–59.

41. Carrillo Castro, p. 51.

42. Ibid.

43. Gereffi and Evans, pp. 38–39.

44. Ibid., p. 38.

45. Due to Mexico's external economic association with the world economy, wealth became increasingly located nationally in spatial terms but did not necessarily become national in cross-class, distributive terms.

46. This does not imply that the presidency was able to defy market forces sufficiently to guarantee an equitable, national distribution of wealth.

47. Green, pp. 19–22.

48. Fernández Santillán, pp. 74–75.

49. Ibid.

50. Ibid., p. 70.

51. The presidency's claims to nationalist promotion of local wealth were premised on the state's ability to promote national industrialization, even though such promotion did not guarantee equitable distribution of national wealth.

52. Fernández Santillán, p. 69.

53. Ibid.

54. Nacional Financiera, S.A., *La economía mexicana en cifras* (Mexico City: NAFINSA, 1981), p. 354.

55. Fernández Santillán, pp. 76–77.

56. Congreso de Diputados, *Ley para el control por parte del gobierno federal de los organismos descentralizados y empresas de participación estatal,* Article 5, December 31, 1947. (My translation.)

57. Ibid.

58. Presidencia de la República, *Decreto que crea la Comisión Nacional de Inversiones, como el organismo encargado del control, vigilancia, y coordinación que menciona la Ley para el Control de los Organismos Descentralizados y Empresas de Participación Estatal,* Article 2, December 31, 1947.

59. Ibid.

60. This technocratic opposition originated in the secretariats of the Presidencia and Patrimonio Nacional.

61. See Congreso de Diputados, *Ley de Secretarías y Departamentos de Estado, Diario Oficial,* December 24, 1958.

62. Carrillo Castro, p. 33.

63. Ibid.

64. Green, pp. 21–23. Most of the loans, as Green notes, were from the Eximbank, IBRD, and the IMF.

65. Gereffi and Evans, p. 39.

66. See Gereffi and Evans.

67. Ibid., p. 39.

68. Ibid.

69. Ibid.

70. They were "limited" in the sense of providing for only a small percentage of the total population that was in need.

71. For discussions of Hacienda as the author of *desarrollo estabilizador,* see E.V.K. FitzGerald, "Stabilization Policy in Mexico: The Fiscal Deficit and Macroeconomic Equilibrium, 1969–1977," in Rosemary Thorpe and Lawrence Whitehead, eds., *Inflation and Stabilization in Latin America* (London: Macmillan, 1979); and Carrillo Castro, p. 35.

72. Presidencia de la República, *Acuerdo que dispone que la Comisión de Inversiones dependa directamente del Presidente de la República,* Third Stipulation, *Diario Oficial,* October 29, 1954. (My translation.)

73. Ibid.

74. See Table 3.12, this chapter, for a comparison of secretarial budget allocations.

75. Miguel S. Wionczek, "Antecedentes e instrumentos de la planeación de México," in Horacio Flores de la Peña, et al., *Bases para la planeación económica y social de México* (Mexico City: Siglo XXI, 1965), pp. 41–42. (My translation.)

76. Ibid., p. 34.

77. López Mateos said this in his presidential acceptance speech.

78. See Juan Manuel Martínez Nava, "El conflicto estado-empresarios en los gobiernos de Cárdenas, López Mateos, y Echeverría," Licenciatura thesis, El Colegio de México, 1982.

79. Ibid.

80. Fernández Santillán, pp. 108–109.

81. Ibid.

82. Alejandro Carrillo Castro, "La reforma administrativa en México," *Revista de Administración Pública,* no. 26 (September–December 1973), in *Revista de Administración Pública, Antología 1–54, 1956–1983* (February 1983), p. 115.

83. Fernández Santillán, p. 96.

84. Congreso de Diputados, *Ley de Secretarías y Departamentos de Estado, Diario Oficial,* December 24, 1958. (My translation.)

85. Wionczek, pp. 43–44.

86. Presidencia de la República, *Acuerdo por el que se constituye una Comisión Intersecretarial integrada por representantes de las Secretarías de la Presidencia y de Hacienda y Crédito Público, con el fin de que se proceda . . . a formular planes nacionales,* Article 1, *Diario Oficial,* March 2, 1962. (My translation.)

87. Ibid., Article 3.

88. Carrillo Castro, "La reforma administrativa," p. 115.

89. Congreso de Diputados, *Ley para el control y vigilancia de los organismos públicos descentralizados y de las empresas de participación estatal, Diario de los Debates,* Article F, December 30, 1963. (My translation.)

90. Ibid.

91. The stabilizing growth development program was still in place.

92. Alvaro Rodríguez Reyes, "Diagnosis administrativa del gobierno federal," *Revista de la Administración Pública,* no. 16 (January–March 1964), p. 83. (My translation.)

93. See Horacio Flores de la Peña, "Problemas de planeación y desarrollo," in

Bases para la planeación económica y social en México (Mexico City: Siglo XXI, 1965); the book also contains a list of participants.
94. Ibid., p. 81.
95. Ibid.
96. Ibid., pp. 83–84.

Chapter 4

1. When the Treasury's singular governance of economic affairs collapsed within the state apparatus, the administration's pursuit of a coherent economic development program collapsed. Once the president could no longer *claim* to have control over the economy or even over his own economic technocrats, the myth of presidential strength was shattered as economic policy became more and more contradictory and economic crisis ensued.
2. The largest segments of the private sector in Mexico were the most potent forces undermining the administration's pursuit of a coherent economic policy. The private sector generally refused to allow the president to switch development strategies as a means of coping with the economic stagnation of 1971–1972.
3. Over the years of "stabilizing growth," the presidency's endorsement of pro–private investor policies had accustomed the private sector to a logic of state intervention entirely geared toward supporting and subsidizing private profitability. The administration's proposed increased emphasis on popular welfare provoked private opposition.
4. Alejandro Carrillo Castro, *La reforma administrativa en México: Evolución de la reforma administrativa en México* (1971–1979) (Mexico City: Miguel Angel Porrúa, 1980), p. 35.
5. E.V.K. FitzGerald, "Stabilization Policy in Mexico: The Fiscal Deficit and Macroeconomic Equilibrium, 1960–1977," in Rosemary Thorpe and Lawrence Whitehead, eds., *Inflation and Stabilization in Latin America* (London: Macmillan, 1979), p. 34.
6. Ibid. One-fourth of new bank funds were captured by the Banco de México during the period of *desarrollo estabilizador.*
7. Ibid.
8. Ibid., pp. 34, 38.
9. Ibid., p. 38.
10. Ibid., p. 39.
11. Ibid.
12. Ibid.
13. Ibid., p. 38.
14. Lawrence Whitehead, "La política económica del sexenio de Echeverría: ¿Qué salió mal y por qué?" *Foro Internacional* 20, no. 3 (1979–1980), p. 491.
15. FitzGerald, p. 31.
16. Ibid.
17. Ibid.; Carrillo Castro, p. 35.
18. FitzGerald, p. 31.
19. Ibid.
20. Later on, the Echeverría administration also attempted to eliminate the *anonimato* and failed.
21. FitzGerald, p. 31.
22. Hugo Margáin became a figure identified with both reformism and private sector interests.

23. Hugo Margáin became President Echeverría's secretary of Hacienda. Margáin had also been head of the National Profit-Sharing Commission for López Mateos. He resigned from Hacienda due to policy disagreements with Echeverría.

24. Susan Kaufman Purcell, *The Mexican Profit-Sharing Decision* (Berkeley: University of California Press, 1975), p. 69. López Mateos's desire to pursue a symbolic gesture toward organized labor came in the wake of the repression of the Independent Railroad Workers' Strike right before López Mateos came into office. See Kaufman Purcell, p. 73.

25. Ibid., p. 102.

26. Ibid., p. 110.

27. Ibid., p. 123.

28. Ibid., p. 124.

29. The state's expenditures on welfare were increasing but were highly selective in nature. In comparison to the state's expenditures on industrial development, however, welfare spending was quite low. See FitzGerald, pp. 30, 38.

30. Miguel S. Wionczek, "Antecedentes e instrumentos de la planeación en México," in Horacio Flores de la Peña, et al., *Bases para la planeación económica y social en México* (Mexico City: Siglo XXI, 1966), pp. 38–39. (My translation)

31. Ibid., p. 39.

32. And, so long as a fixed, convertible currency was sustained, this statement is true.

33. FitzGerald, p. 37.

34. Ibid.

35. "Monopoly capital" refers to the largest owners of capital: the domestic private banking system; large, often foreign associated industrialists; and TNCs.

36. The instrumental Marxist approach as advanced by Ralph Miliband, for example, would likely argue that the period of *desarrollo estabilizador* is illustrative of the state being an instrument of class forces (specifically, of monopoly capital). The argument to be developed here is that the PRI president's relative autonomy was minimal but that the overall state's relative autonomy still existed to a degree. In the 1960s, relative state autonomy was not observable because the interests of PRI governments (and presidents) and monopoly capital generally converged during that time. When the *desarrollo estabilizador* strategy began to fail, the PRI president's interests were no longer as congruent with those of the banking sector, and the president became entangled in a policy deadlock. Reformist technocrats within the state used state enterprises and credit to temporarily sustain economic growth in the face of private investment strikes and capital flight.

37. This will be documented in Chapter 5.

38. FitzGerald, p. 33; Fernández Santillán, p. 97.

39. Douglas Bennett and Kenneth Sharpe, "The State as Banker and Entrepreneur: The Last Resort Character of the Mexican State's Intervention, 1917–1976," *Comparative Politics* (January 1980), pp. 165–189.

40. Ibid.

41. FitzGerald, p. 33.

42. Ibid.

43. Ibid.

44. Fernández Santillán, p. 96.

45. Roderic A. Camp, *Mexican Political Biographies: 1935–1981*, 2d ed. (Tucson: University of Arizona Press, 1982), p. 103.

46. Flores de la Peña's role in advocating the abandonment of the tight public spending rules of the *desarrollo estabilizador* strategy is discussed later in this chapter.

47. Camp, p. 10.

48. Camp, p. 228.

49. Interview with Carlos Tello in Mexico City, April 1983.

50. Carrillo Castro, pp. 116–117.

51. José López Portillo had been a friend of Luis Echeverría since grammar school days. See Camp, p. 177. López Portillo later succeeded Echeverría as president of Mexico (1976–1982).

52. Camp, p. 176.

53. Carrillo Castro, p. 118.

54. According to Vincent Padgett, the fatality figure was high (officially 75–200) due to an error in the government's timing of military action: "When heavy weaponry was brought in, the [Tlatelolco] square and surrounding areas held not only protesting students, but also heavy evening traffic (theater crowds, shoppers, etc.). Unknown numbers of innocent bystanders were fatally injured." Vincent Padgett, *The Mexican Political System* (Boston: Houghton Mifflin, 1976), p. 55. Luis Echeverría, as secretary of Gobernación (Interior) was most likely involved in the decision to repress the protest with force. On Echeverría's role in provoking the violence, see Antonio Jáquez, "En el 68, Echeverría aisló, desinformó y le calentó la cabeza a Díaz Ordaz: Farías," *Proceso* 884 (October 11, 1993), pp. 6–11.

55. Carrillo Castro, p. 119.

56. Camp, p. 177.

57. Camp, p. 65.

58. For discussions of Echeverría's less than radical political past, see Daniel Cosío Villegas, *El estilo personal de gobernar* (Mexico City: Editorial Joaquín Mortiz, 1974); and Padgett, pp. 55–57.

59. It is argued throughout this chapter that it was less Echeverría's own personal commitment to reform than that of the *técnicos* in certain key secretariat positions that propelled him into a new development strategy. These *técnicos* gained influence with him mainly as a consequence of decaying economic conditions in 1970 and 1971. Echeverría did not begin to implement the new growth strategy promised in his campaign until 1972.

60. Carlos Tello, *La política económica en México, 1970–1976* (Mexico City: Siglo XXI, 1979), pp. 11–90. See also Whitehead, pp. 490–493; and Miguel Basáñez, *La lucha por la hegemonía en México, 1968–1980,* 2d ed. (Mexico City: Siglo XXI, 1982), pp. 140–168.

61. Echeverría did not opt to liberate public expenditures from the financial rules of *desarrollo estabilizador* until 1972. See Whitehead's discussion of continued orthodoxy from 1970 to 1971 in Whitehead, p. 494.

62. Whitehead, p. 493; Basáñez, pp. 157–158.

63. FitzGerald, p. 25; Tello, pp. 11–40.

64. FitzGerald, p. 28; Tello, pp. 11–40.

65. FitzGerald, p. 25; Tello, pp. 11–40.

66. FitzGerald p. 28; Tello, pp. 11–40.

67. Gary Gereffi and Peter Evans, "Transnational Corporations, Dependent Development, and State Policy in the Semiperiphery: A Comparison of Brazil and Mexico," *Latin American Research Review* 16 (1981), pp. 39–40.

68. In particular, see Leopoldo Solís, "A Monetary Will-o'-the Wisp: Pursuit of Equity Through Deficit Spending," Discussion Paper No. 77 (Princeton: Woodrow Wilson School, 1977); C. W. Reynolds, "¿Por qué el desarrollo estabilizador en la realidad se desestabilizó?" (Washington, D.C.: Subcommittee on Interamerican Economic Relations, 1977); and Gerardo M. Bueno, "Las estrategias del desarrollo estabilizador y del desarrollo compartido," in Gerardo Bueno, ed.,

Opciones de política económica en México, después de la devaluación (Mexico City: Editorial Tecnos, 1977).

69. FitzGerald, p. 28.

70. Ibid.

71. Ibid.

72. Horacio Flores de la Peña, *Teoría y práctica del desarrollo* (Mexico City: Fondo de Cultura Económica, 1976), pp. 29–104.

73. Whitehead, p. 493; Basáñez, pp. 147–168.

74. Carrillo Castro, p. 119.

75. Ibid.

76. Ibid., p. 126. While he was Secretary of Hacienda, López Portillo reinstated restrictive monetary policies. See Tello, p. 72.

77. Tello, p. 72; FitzGerald, pp. 40, 58.

78. Camp, p. 64.

79. Carlos Tello is only "radical" if compared to the other reformist *técnicos,* such as López Portillo. Whitehead, p. 50, states that even the so-called left within the state did not believe a contradiction existed between the long-run economic interests of the private sector and the long-run plans of the state. See Tello's own statement to this effect in Tello, pp. 80–81.

80. Carlos Tello, a structuralist economist trained at Cambridge University, wrote a book about the effort to change development strategies from 1970 to 1976. See Tello, 1979.

81. The position of subdirector general of credit was an important post for channeling foreign borrowed monies to state enterprises, especially through NAFINSA. Although one can only speculate, perhaps Tello was needed most in Hacienda to ensure that foreign borrowed monies were directed to the "proper" state agencies for the "proper" uses in order to sustain economic growth in the face of private sector investment strikes and capital flight. (See Appendix 3, Tables A and B.)

82. Carrillo Castro, p. 124.

83. Treasury's dominance was not really undermined until after Hugo Margáin resigned his post as secretary of Hacienda in May 1973.

84. Carlos Tello was a longtime friend and assistant to López Portillo. See Camp, p. 296.

85. Julio Moctezuma Cid was the architect of the SPP.

86. Basáñez, pp. 150–168; Whitehead, p. 493.

87. Tello, p. 51.

88. See Basáñez, p. 69. Juan F. Noyola Vázquez and Ricardo Torres Gaytán were also vocal reformist economists with views similar to Tello's.

89. See Tello, p. 55.

90. Rosario Green, *Estado y banca transnacional en México* (Mexico City: Nueva Imagen, 1981), p. 67; Whitehead, p. 499.

91. See the discussion of tax reform proposals during López Mateos's term in Chapter 3.

92. The smallest firms had to share the largest percentages of their profits. See Chapter 3.

93. Susan Kaufman Purcell, *The Mexican Profit-Sharing Decision* (Berkeley: University of California Press, 1975), pp. 122–123; 6.

94. Ibid., pp. 11–115.

95. See Américo Saldívar, *Ideología y política del estado mexicano,* 2d ed. (Mexico City: Siglo XXI, 1981), p. 104. Recall that the benefits of the López Mateos profit-sharing scheme had gone mainly to the largest industrialists, who

ended up sharing the smallest percentages of the profits. For a detailed look at the concentration of industrial enterprises in the fifty largest industrial groups in Mexico, see Salvador Cordero and Rafael Santín, *Los grupos industriales: Una nueva organización económica en México* (Mexico City: Cuadernos del Centro de Estudios Sociológicos del Colegio de México, 1977).

96. The Mexican Council of Businessmen is at the apex of the pyramid of political control over the private sector organizations in Mexico.

97. See Basáñez, pp. 98, 101.

98. Saldívar, pp. 103–105; Whitehead, pp. 499–501; Tello, pp. 60–61.

99. The CMHN was mainly dominated by the heads of finance capital in Mexico.

100. This includes both Lawrence Whitehead and Américo Saldívar.

101. Basáñez, p. 104. CANACINTRA represented a younger group of industrialists who generally favored public sector intervention in the economy. CANACINTRA was not invited to the meeting of business organizations that formed the CCE (Coordinating Council of Businessmen) to coordinate private sector protest of the Echeverría government in 1975. See Carlos Arriola, "Los grupos empresariales frente al Estado (1973–1975)," *Foro Internacional* 16, no. 4. (April–June, 1976), p. 59.

102. Basáñez, pp. 99, 101.

103. See Basáñez for a detailed discussion of the roots of the student protest in 1968, pp. 169–174.

104. Whitehead, pp. 494–495.

105. See Echeverría's political biography in Appendix 2.

106. Arriola, p. 42.

107. Ibid., p. 42.

108. Green, pp. 78–82.

109. Ibid., pp. 82–85.

110. On one hand, pro–private investor policies had led to the state's acceptance and accommodation to private investors to such an extent that certain state secretariats had internalized the private interests that they were nurturing. This was the case with Treasury and the Bank of Mexico. On the other hand, pro–private investor policies involving state interventionism led to an increase in the state's organizational scope and to increases in state personnel opposed to the stabilizing growth strategy itself.

111. Karin L. DeBally, "Política monetaria y financiamiento del sector público: El caso de México (1965–1976)," Licenciatura thesis, El Colegio de México, 1980), pp. 103–105.

112. Green, pp. 67–110; Arriola, p. 42; Guadalupe González González, "Los intereses privados norteamericanos en México: La Cámara Americana de Comercio de México," Licenciatura thesis, El Colegio de México, 1979), pp. 256–298.

113. Green, pp. 78–109.

114. Ibid., pp. 88–91.

115. Ibid.

116. Ibid., pp. 317–318.

117. Tello, pp. 59, 77.

118. The Coordinating Council of Businessmen was born on May 7, 1975, and was composed of business leaders from CONCAMIN, CONCANACO, COPARMEX, ABM, CMHN, and the Asociación Mexicana de Instituciones de Seguros.

119. Green, pp. 67–109.

120. Tello, p. 72.

121. FitzGerald, pp. 40–43; Tello, p. 72.

122. See DeBally, pp. 103–106, for an explanation of how *encaje legal* (the Central Bank's reserve requirements on private banking system) was no longer an instrument of monetary policy after the 1972 liberation of public expenditures.

123. FitzGerald, p. 57.

124. See note 36.

125. FitzGerald, pp. 42–43.

126. See Tello.

127. See Whitehead's explanation of the state's lack of relative autonomy, p. 497. See also Rosario Green's explanation of state weakness from 1970 to 1975 in Green, pp. 67–110.

128. Green, pp. 67–68.

129. Ibid.

130. Ibid., p. 67. (My translation.)

131. Ibid., pp. 509–510.

132. Stabilizing growth had nurtured a private sector with increasingly oligopolistic segments. See Basáñez; Green.

Chapter 5

1. Rationalizing the parastatal sector implied dissolving or selling public enterprises that were unnecessary or inefficient. In essence, it implied the application of market criteria of efficiency to the public sector.

2. At its creation, the SPP touted a new rhetoric of public sector organizational strength. It claimed to protect both statist-reformist interests in mass socioeconomic welfare and private investor interests. When debt crisis hit in 1982, the SPP's overwhelmingly pro–private sector character was revealed.

3. Economic contradiction and collapse during the Echeverría term so incapacitated the presidency that presidential resistance to a new technical economic secretariat was no longer sustainable.

4. José Fernández Santillán, *Política y administración pública en México* (Mexico City: Ediciones INAP, 1980), p. 125.

5. Michel Bouchet, "A Political Economy of External Public Debt: The Mexican Case," Ph.D. diss., University of South Carolina, 1981, p. 252.

6. Ibid.

7. Ibid., p. 248.

8. Rosario Green, *Estado y banca transnacional en México* (Mexico City: Nueva Imagen, 1981), pp. 60; 51–54. See also Bouchet, pp. 252–258.

9. Bouchet, p. 237.

10. Rosa Olivia Villa M., *Nacional Financiera: Banco de Fomento del Desarrollo Económico de México* (Mexico City: Nacional Financiera, S.A., 1976). Villa M. cites the other major public borrowing agents at the end of 1975 as:

1.	Nacional Financiera	33%
2.	Banco Nacional de Obras y Servicios Públicos (BANOBRAS)	11%
3.	Federal government	10%
4.	Petróleos Mexicanos	9%
5.	CFE (Federal Electric Commission)	9%

6.	Banco Nacional de	±9%
	Comercio Exterior	
7.	Teléfonos de México; Banco	4%
	Nacional Agropecuario	
8.	Fifteen other institutions	Negligible %
	and organisms	

11. Villa M., pp. 61–70; Jeffrey A. Frieden, "Third World Indebted Industrialization: International Finance and State Capitalism in Mexico, Brazil, Algeria, and South Korea," *International Organization* 35 no. 3 (Summer 1981), p. 418.

12. Villa M., p. 100.

13. Ibid.

14. Bouchet, p. 255, states that "in 1975, private sector investment at constant 1960 prices declined in absolute terms for the third consecutive year." See also Carlos Tello, *La política económica en México, 1970–1976* (Mexico City: Siglo XXI, 1982), p. 77.

15. E.V.K. FitzGerald, "Stabilization Policy in Mexico: The Fiscal Deficit and Macroeconomic Equilibrium, 1960–1977," in Rosemary Thorpe and Lawrence Whitehead, eds., *Inflation and Stabilization in Latin America* (London: Macmillan, 1979), p. 45, claims that credit expansion to the private sector remained fairly stable in relation to GDP during the period 1971–1975. This was because state development banks, such as NAFINSA, were not only pumping funds into state enterprise but also lending to the private sector. So, private investment activity was being supplemented by public investment in industry, not replaced by state enterprise.

16. Tello, p. 193.

17. Because the public sector (from 1972 to 1976) was engaging in both neo-Keynesian expansionism and restrictive monetary policies, and because the private sector was protesting reformism through investment slowdown and capital flight, the Mexican economy entered a deep crisis in 1975 and 1976.

18. Villa M., p. 134.

19. Ibid., p. 135.

20. Ibid., p. 134.

21. See Lawrence Whitehead, "La política económica del sexenio de Echeverría: ¿Qué salió mal y por qué?" *Foro Internacional* 20, no. 3 (1979–1980), pp. 484–513.

22. IBRD, *Special Study of the Mexican Economy,* p. 46, cited by Tello, p. 188. This estimate of the extent of public sector subsidy to private enterprise via the prices of public sector goods and services is likely to be generally applicable to the Echeverría administration as well, since the prices of such goods were not likely to have been higher in the first year of the López Portillo *sexenio* than during Echeverría's term.

23. Implied here is Nora Hamilton's conception of "instrumental state autonomy," which refers to the state's ability to contradict certain immediate, private sector interests in order to create favorable conditions for capital accumulation in the longer run. See Nora Hamilton, *The Limits of State Autonomy: Post-Revolutionary Mexico* (Princeton: Princeton University Press, 1982), pp. 8–39.

24. See Chapter 3, which discusses the arrangements for financing public deficits under *desarrollo estabilizador.*

25. Examples of such reactions during the Echeverría years were employer lock outs, rumor-spreading to undermine investor confidence, antigovernment publicity in nationally circulated newspapers, and speculative activity.

26. Tello, p. 200.

27. See Appendix 4 for a list of the reform initiatives that elicited state–private sector conflicts during the Echeverría years as detailed in Green. See also Guadalupe González González, "Los intereses privados norteamericanos en México: La Cámara Americana de Comercio de México," Licenciatura thesis, El Colegio de México, 1979; Carlos Arriola, "Los grupos empresariales frente al Estado (1973–1975)," *Foro Internacional* 16, no. 4 (April–June, 1976); Miguel Basáñez, *La lucha por la hegemonía en México, 1968–1980,* 2d ed. (Mexico City: Siglo XXI, 1982); Américo Saldívar, *Ideología y política del estado mexicano,* 2d ed. (Mexico City: Siglo XXI, 1981); Juan Manuel Martínez Nava, "El conflicto estado-empresarios en los gobiernos de Cárdenas, López Mateos, y Echeverría," Licenciatura thesis, El Colegio de México, 1982.

28. Examples: Carlos Pereyra, "México: Los límites del reformismo," *Cuadernos Políticos,* no. 1 (July-September 1974), pp. 52–65. See also Whitehead, Green, Saldívar, and Basáñez.

29. Relative autonomy here refers to what Nora Hamilton terms "instrumental state autonomy." See Hamilton, p. 10.

30. Congreso de Diputados, *Ley Orgánica de la Administración Pública Federal,* Article 32, December 29, 1976. (My translation)

31. Ibid., p. 51. The Treasury's retention of the right to determine the uses of funds derived from borrowing implied a great deal of retained policy leverage, since the amounts of funds borrowed from external sources during the López Portillo *sexenio* were enormous.

32. Roderic A. Camp, *Mexican Political Biographies: 1935–1981,* 2d ed. (Tucson: University of Arizona Press, 1982), p. 204.

33. John J. Bailey, "Presidency, Bureaucracy, and Administrative Reform in Mexico: The Secretariat of Programming and Budget," *Inter-American Economic Affairs* 34, no. 1 (Summer 1980), pp. 47–48.

34. Ibid.

35. Ibid., p. 48.

36. Ibid., p. 49.

37. Camp, pp. 45–46.

38. Bailey, pp. 45–46.

39. Ibid., p. 53.

40. Camp, p. 117.

41. Bailey, p. 54.

42. Ibid., p. 50.

43. Ibid., pp. 37; 52–53.

44. Instituto Latinoamericano de Planeación Económica y Social (ILPES), "El marco para el análisis de la planeación en la región," *Revista de Administración Pública,* no. 55–56 (June-December 1983), pp. 279–281.

45. Bailey, p. 58.

46. Presidencia de la República, *Decreto por el que se aprueba el Plan Global de Desarrollo 1980–1982,* Article 3, *Diario Oficial,* April 17, 1980. (My translation.)

47. Ibid.

48. Carlos Tello, *La nacionalización de la banca en México* (Mexico City: Siglo XXI, 1984), p. 69.

49. Ibid., p. 71.

50. Ibid., p. 74.

51. Ibid.

52. Ibid., p. 75.

53. Ibid., p. 77.
54. Ibid., p. 75. (My translation)
55. Ibid., p. 108.
56. Ibid.
57. Ibid., p. 176.
58. Congreso de Diputados, *Reformas a la Ley Orgánica de la Administración Pública Federal*, Article 32, *Diario Oficial*, January 4, 1982. (My translation)
59. Author's interviews with Carlos Tello in Mexico City, April 1983 and November 1985.
60. Tello, *La nacionalización*, p. 11.
61. Ibid., p. 122.
62. Ibid., p. 123. (My translation)
63. Ibid., pp. 126–127.
64. Secretaría de Programación y Presupuesto, *Resolución para proceder a la disolución, liquidación, extinción y transferencia de las entidades paraestatales que se indican*, February 13, 1985. (My translation)

Chapter 6

1. Gary Gereffi and Peter Evans, "Transnational Corporations, Dependent Development, and State Policy in the Semiperiphery: A Comparison of Brazil and Mexico," *Latin American Research Review* 16 (1981), pp. 39–40.
2. Ibid.
3. Ibid.
4. Vertical import-substitution industrialization refers to a phase of industrialization involving the local production of capital and intermediate goods which were previously imported.
5. Horizontal import substitution refers to a phase of industrialization involving the local production of nondurable consumer goods that were previously imported.
6. Gereffi and Evans, pp. 39–40.
7. Ibid., pp. 40–41.
8. Salvador Cordero and Rafael Santín, *Los grupos industriales: Una nueva organización económica en México* (Mexico City: Cuadernos del Centro de Estudios Sociológicos del Colegio de México, 1977).
9. Gereffi and Evans, p. 42.
10. Recall that López Portillo, as the head of CAP, had never been as adamant about a particular developmental path as Flores de la Peña. Furthermore, as Echeverría's secretary of Hacienda, López Portillo had reintroduced restrictive monetary policies after 1973.
11. This was one of López Portillo's campaign slogans.
12. Alejandro Carrillo Castro, *La reforma administrativa en México: Evolución de la reforma administrativa (1971–1979)* (Mexico City: Miguel Angel Porrúa, S.A., 1980), p. 32.
13. Gereffi and Evans, p. 42.
14. See Chapter 3.
15. These constraints involved the presidents' desires to encourage private savings and investments by keeping government expenditures low. Presidents also wished to assure the private sector that the state's political control over the labor movement was sound, in order to build savers' confidence in the maintenance of low levels of inflation. See Chapter 4.

16. The *desarrollo estabilizador* strategy also involved limitations placed on external borrowing and denied significant increases in government revenues derived from increases in the prices of public sector goods. Finally, it also generally excluded fiscal reform.

17. See the discussion in Chapter 3 of Treasury's financial vetoes over public spending activities.

18. There were other complications as well, including U.S. inflation and recession. See Carlos Tello, *La política económica en México, 1970–1976* (Mexico City: Siglo XXI, 1979), p. 30.

19. On technocratic schism, See Horacio Flores de la Peña et al., *Bases para la planeación económica y social en México* (Mexico City: Siglo XXI, 1966; reprint ed., 1983); Carlos Tello, *La política económica en México, 1970–1976* (Mexico City: Siglo XXI, 1979; reprint ed., 1982).

20. John J. Bailey, "Presidency, Bureaucracy, and Administrative Reform in Mexico: The Secretariat of Programming and Budget," *Inter-American Economic Affairs* 34, no. 1 (Summer 1980), pp. 27–59.

21. For Miguel de la Madrid's political biography, see Robert A. Camp, *Mexican Political Biographies: 1935–1981*, 2d ed. (Tucson: University of Arizona Press, 1982), p. 81.

22. "Reestructuración de la industria paraestatal," *Excélsior*, February 17, 1985, pp. 4–5; "Reestructuración del sector paraestatal," *Excélsior*, March 4, 1985, pp. 12A–13A; (based on data from the resolutions of Carlos Salinas de Gortari, secretary of Programming and Budget) *Diario Oficial*, Secretaría de Gobernación, February 13, 18, 21, 1985.

23. Susan Kaufman Purcell, "Mexico in Transition," in Susan Kaufman Purcell, ed., *Mexico in Transition* (New York: Council on Foreign Relations, 1988), pp. 3–17.

24. Marko Voljc and Joost Draaisma, "Privatization and Economic Stabilization in Mexico," *The Columbia Journal of World Business* 28, no. 1 (Spring 1993), pp. 122–133.

25. Barbara Belejack, "Chipping Away at Government Ownership," *Business Mexico* 7 (March 1990), pp. 32–39.

26. Ibid., p. 32.

27. Ibid., p. 34.

28. "Doing the Impossible Takes a Little Longer," *The Economist* 315 (June 9, 1990), p. 43.

29. For summary statements to this effect, see Carlos Salinas de Gortari, *Ideas y compromisos* (Mexico City: PRI National Executive Committee, 1988), pp. 123–128.

30. Matt Moffett, "Latin Turnaround: Long-Sickly Mexico Has Investment Boom as Trade Hopes Grow," *Wall Street Journal*, May 24, 1991, p. 1.

31. Carlos Salinas de Gortari. Interview with Robert A. Pastor, July 1990, Mexico City. Cited in Robert Pastor, "Post-Revolutionary Mexico: The Salinas Opening," *Journal of Interamerican Studies and World Affairs* 32 (Fall 1990), p. 19.

32. "Doing the Impossible Takes a Little Longer," p. 43.

33. Ibid.

34. Ibid.

35. "Mexico Frees Its Farms, Too," *The Economist* (November 16, 1991), p. 49.

36. Gerardo Albarrán de Alba, "El PRI acaba la era de Salinas derrotado, dividido y empantanado en los vicios que se propuso superar: Lejos de ser un partido

político real, se revuelve en la corrupción, la antidemocracia, el crimen y la ira," *Proceso,* no. 910 (April 11, 1994), pp. 11–17.

37. See Martin Needler, *Mexican Politics: The Containment of Conflict,* 2d ed. (New York: Praeger, 1990), pp. 38–39; 87–97.

38. Albarrán de Alba, pp. 11–17.

39. Eduardo Kragelund, "Mexico: Man in the News—Colosio Seen as Skilled Politician," *Reuters Newswire, Central and South America, Reuters Economic News,* November 28, 1993.

40. "Fusión de Hacienda y SPP, Iniciativa de Carlos Salinas de Gortari al Congreso," *Excélsior,* January 8, 1992, pp. 1A, 10A.

41. Ibid. See also Chapters 4 and 5.

42. Christine Tierney, "Mexico: Mexico PRI Candidate Viewed as Shrewd Compromise," *Reuters Newswire, Central and South America, Reuter General News,* November 28, 1993.

43. This was the race for the state governorship of Baja California in 1989.

44. During the Salinas administration, SEDUE, the Urban Development and Ecology secretariat, was placed within SEDESOL, the newly created Social Development secretariat, which was created in 1992. Luis Donaldo Colosio was named head of SEDESOL, which included SEDUE, in late 1992.

45. See Colosio's chapter proclaiming the PRI's electoral competitiveness: Luis Donaldo Colosio, "Why the PRI Won the 1991 Elections," in Riordan Roett, ed. *Political and Economic Liberalization in Mexico: At a Critical Juncture?* (Boulder: Lynne Rienner Publishers, 1993).

46. Stephen D. Morris, "Political Reformism in Mexico: Past and Present," *Latin American Research Review* 28, no. 2 (Spring 1993), pp. 200–203. See also "Paradox in Mexico (A Survey of Latin America)," *The Economist* 329, no. 7837 (November 13, 1993), p. L21.

47. Tierney.

48. Christine Tierney, "Mexico: Markets Seen at Ease with Mexican Presidential Candidate," *Reuter Newswire, Central and South America, Reuter Economic News,* November 28, 1993. See also Tierney, "Mexico: Mexico PRI Candidate Viewed as Shrewd Compromise."

49. Tierney, "Mexico: Markets Seen at Ease."

50. Ibid.

51. Tierney, "Mexico: Mexico PRI Candidate Viewed as Shrewd Compromise."

52. Jeff Franks, "Colosio Death Shakes Mexico Political System," *Reuter World Service,* March 24, 1994. See also Elías Chávez, "Colosio y Camacho, enredados y enfrentados por Salinas, muestran sus armas y hacen más bolas al priísmo," *Proceso,* no. 906 (March 14, 1994), pp. 6–9.

53. Chávez, pp. 6- 9. See also Pascal Beltrán del Río, "Salinas no ha tomado la decisión de quién será finalmente el candidato del PRI: Cuauhtémoc," *Proceso,* no. 907 (March 21, 1994), pp. 6–13; Elías Chávez, "Su actitud de no combatir públicamente a Camacho le valió a Colosio un abucheo en Monterrey," *Proceso,* no. 907 (March 21, 1994), pp. 14–17; Gerardo Galarza, "Moya y del Mazo le recomiendan disciplinarse, Salinas lo elogió y Camacho vuelve a considerarse factor de presión para lograr elecciones limpias," *Proceso,* no. 907 (March 21, 1994), p. 16; Timothy Golden, "Mexico Mediator Hints at Renegade Bid for President," *New York Times,* March 12, 1994, pp. N2, L2.

54. Timothy Golden, "Mexican Leader Picks Successor to Slain Nominee: Candidate Is Criticized," *New York Times,* March 30, 1994, p. A6.

55. Guillermo Correa, Salvador Corro, and Julio César López, "El asesinato

de Colosio, 'un ajuste de cuentas interno, una provocación para el endurecimiento': Marcos," *Proceso,* no. 908 (March 28, 1994), pp. 32–35. See also Raúl Monge, "El miércoles 16, en una cena íntima, Colosio y Camacho habían puesto fin a sus diferencias," *Proceso,* no. 908 (March 28, 1994), pp. 12–13.

56. Prominent and veteran PRI members sent a letter to Salinas insisting on PRI members' right to participate in deciding who should replace Colosio. Members of Democracia 2000, a prodemocratization faction within the PRI, also published their demands for a democratic selection process within the PRI to choose Colosio's replacement. See the Democracia 2000 advertisement in *Proceso,* no. 908 (March 28, 1994), p. 3. See also Pascal Beltrán del Río, Elías Chávez, and Gerardo Galarza, "Distinguidos priístas piden en el nuevo candidato características que ninguno de los aspirantes tecnócratas reúne," *Proceso,* no. 908 (March 28, 1994), pp. 6–13. See also Elías Chávez, "Ante la incipiente rebelión priísta, Salinas aplacó a Ortiz Arana, mobilizó a Córdoba y designó a Ernesto Zedillo," *Proceso,* no. 909 (April 4, 1994), pp. 6–11.

57. See especially Articles 27 and 123, *Constitución política de los Estados Unidos Mexicanos* (Mexico City: *Diario Oficial,* 1983), pp. 46–58; 127–138.

58. The PAN presidential candidate's relentless personal attacks on Cárdenas in the presidential debate of May 12, 1994, contributed substantially to the PRI's efforts to defeat PRD candidate Cárdenas in the August 21, 1994, presidential election. According to multiple opinion polls, Diego Fernández de Cevallos of the PAN reportedly won the debate. See Rafael Rodríguez Castañeda, "Acicateados por Fernández de Cevallos, Cárdenas y Zedillo le entraron parcialmente al pleito: Noventa minutos que transformaron la campaña por la Presidencia," *Proceso,* no. 915 (May 18, 1994), pp. 6–11. On the poll results after the debates, see Fernando Mayolo López and Sonia Morales, "La mayoría de las encuestas inmediatas dió el triunfo en el debate a Fernández de Cevallos, pero favoreció Zedillo con el voto," *Proceso,* no. 915 (May 18, 1994), pp. 10–11. For a PRD interpretation of the impact of Fernández de Cevallos on the Cárdenas campaign, see Pascal Beltrán del Río, "El fenómeno Diego forma parte del proyecto de Salinas de perpetuarse en el poder: Muñoz Ledo," *Proceso,* no. 916 (May 23, 1994), pp. 8–9.

59. See *North American Free Trade Agreement Between the Government of the United States, the Government of Canada and the Government of the United Mexican States,* vols. 1–2 (Washington, D.C.: Government Printing Office, 1992).

60. See James F. Smith, "Confronting Differences in the United States and Mexican Legal Systems in the Era of NAFTA," *United States–Mexico Law Journal* 1, no. 1 (1993), pp. 97–98, where Smith cites renowned Mexican jurist César Sepúlveda, who argues that "in general International Law is superior to the norms of the Mexican state." (Smith's translation of Sepúlveda)

61. Ibid.

62. Smith, p. 99.

63. Ibid.

64. *North American Free Trade Agreement,* vol. 1, pp. 11-1–11-10.

65. Jonathan Schlefer, "History Counsels 'No' on NAFTA. . .," *New York Times,* November 14, 1993, p. F11.

66. Ibid. See also *North American Free Trade Agreement,* vol. 1, "Part Five: Investment, Services and Related Matters" and "Part Six: Intellectual Property," pp. 11-1–17-31.

67. See, for instance, Articles 25, 26, 27, 28, 32, 73, 123, 131, and 134, *Constitución política de los Estados Unidos Mexicanos* (Mexico City: Ediciones Prisma, 1992).

68. Schlefer, p. F11. In the NAFTA text, see Part Five, Chapter 11,

"Investment," pp. 11-1–11-29; Chapter 15, "Competition Policy, Monopolies and State Enterprises," pp. 15-1–15-5; and Chapter 17, "Intellectual Property," pp. 17-1-7-31.

69. Schlefer, p. F11.

70. Ibid.

71. Cuauhtémoc Cárdenas Solórzano, interview with Carlos B. Gil, in Carlos B. Gil, ed., *Hope and Frustration: Interviews with Leaders of Mexico's Political Opposition* (Wilmington, Del.: Scholarly Resources, 1992), pp. 149–172. See also Roberto Zamarripa, "Vigilado, hostigado, prohibido, Cárdenas apela a la ética de los medios," *Proceso,* no. 883 (October 4, 1993), pp. 7–9. See also, Pascal Beltrán del Río, "Los candidatos del PRD y del PAN opinan sobre el presidencialismo: Es válido y puede ser positivo: Cárdenas; lo que ocurre es que se ejerce en forma corrupta: Cuauhtémoc," *Proceso,* no. 914 (May 9, 1994), pp. 10–12.

72. Sanjuana Martínez, "Chiapas dañó la imagen de México y de Salinas; políticos, los peores efectos," *Proceso,* no. 903 (February 21, 1994), pp. 54–57.

73. Cuauhtémoc Cárdenas, "Mexico: Political Freedom and Economic Development," *Review of Radical Political Economics* 24, no. 2 (Summer 1992), pp. 104–108. See also James M. Cypher, Chris Tilly, Ricardo Grinspun, "Mexico's Road to Nowhere: the PRD's Cuauhtémoc Cárdenas Discusses Corruption, Debt, and Free Trade," *Dollars & Sense,* no. 175 (April 1992), pp. 12–15; and Pascal Beltrán del Río, "Suprimir los efectos de la actual política llevará lo menos quince años: Muñoz Ledo," *Proceso,* no. 872 (July 19, 1993), pp. 6–13.

74. Vicente Leñero, "El Subcomandante se abre: 'Lo aposté todo a la montaña; estoy viviendo de prestado y por eso escribo como loco; si no les gustan mis cartas, me vale madre,'" *Proceso,* no. 903 (February 21, 1994), pp. 7–15.

75. See Teresa Rendón and Carlos Salas, "The Probable Impact of NAFTA on Non-agricultural Employment in Mexico," *The Review of Radical Political Economics* 25, no. 4 (December 1, 1993), pp. 109–119. See also Emilio Pradilla Cobos, "The Limits of the Mexican Maquiladora Industry," *The Review of Radical Political Economics* 25, no. 4 (December 1, 1993), pp. 91–108; and Ricardo Grinspun, "NAFTA and Neoconservative Transformation: The Impact on Canada and Mexico," *The Review of Radical Political Economics* 25, no. 4 (December 1, 1993), pp. 14–29.

76. Guillermo Correa, Salvador Corro, and Julio César López, "Campesinos e indígenas de todo el país apoyan las demandas del EZLN y marchan hacia la capital," *Proceso,* no. 910 (April 11, 1994), pp. 36–40.

77. See Ricardo Hernández and Edith Sánchez, *Cross-Border Links: A Directory of Organizations in Canada, Mexico, and the United States* (Albuquerque, N.M.: Inter-Hemispheric Education Resource Center, 1992).

78. See Julie Erfani, ed. *Beyond Free Trade: Integration, Globalization, and Human Welfare in the Americas* (Philadelphia: Temple University Press, forthcoming).

Bibliography

Aguilar Zinser, Adolfo. "Open to Business, Sí to Dissent, No. Mexico: Salinas, Fearful That His Critics Will Jeopardize a Free-Trade Deal, Puts Democratization on Hold." *Los Angeles Times,* October 5, 1990, B7.

Albarrán de Alba, Gerardo. "El PRI acaba la era de Salinas derrotado, dividido y empantanado en los vicios que se propuso superar: Lejos de ser un partido político real, se revuelve en la corrupción, la antidemocracia, el crimen y la ira." *Proceso,* no. 910 (April 11, 1994): 11–17.

Alford, Robert R., and Roger Friedland. *Powers of Theory: Capitalism, the State, and Democracy.* Cambridge: Cambridge University Press, 1985.

Alonso, Jorge. *La dialéctica clases- élites en México.* Mexico City: Ediciones de La Casa Chata, 1976.

Alvarez, Luis H., "Political and Economic Reform in Mexico: The PAN Perspective," in Riordan Roett, ed., *Political and Economic Liberalization in Mexico: At a Critical Juncture?* (Boulder: Lynne Rienner Publishers, 1993), pp. 143–148.

Anderson, Benedict. *Imagined Communities.* London: New Left Books, 1983.

Anderson, James, ed. *The Rise of the Modern State.* Atlantic Highlands, N.J.: Humanities Press International, 1986.

Anguiano, Arturo. *El estado y la política obrera del cardenismo.* Mexico City: Ediciones Era, 1975.

Arriola, Carlos. "Los grupos empresariales frente al Estado (1973–1975)." *Foro Internacional* 16, no. 4 (April–June 1976): 449–495.

Ashley, Richard K. "The Geopolitics of Geopolitical Space." *Alternatives* (October 1987): 403–434.

———. "Political Realism and Human Interests." *International Studies Quarterly* 25 (1981): 204–236.

———. "The Poverty of Neorealism." *International Organization* (Spring 1984): 225–286.

Auerbach, Stuart. "Closer U.S.-Mexico Trade Ties Urged; Commerce Ministers Go on Tour to Push for Greater Investment." *Washington Post,* October 23, 1990, C3.

———. "Mexico Urges U.S. to Put Free-Trade Talks on Fast Track." *Washington Post,* May 27, 1990, A12.

Bailey, John J. "Presidency, Bureaucracy, and Administrative Reform in Mexico: The Secretariat of Programming and Budget." *Inter-American Economic Affairs* 34, no. 1 (Summer 1980): 27–59.

Barkin, David. *Distorted Development: Mexico in the World Economy.* Boulder: Westview Press, 1990.

Basáñez, Miguel. *La lucha por la hegemonía en México, 1968–1980.* 2d ed. Mexico City: Siglo XXI, 1982.

Béjar Navarro, Raúl. *El mexicano: aspectos culturales y sociales.* Mexico City: Universidad Nacional Autónoma de México, 1981.

Belejack, Barbara. "Chipping Away at Government Ownership." *Business Mexico,* March 7, 1990, 32–39.

Beltrán del Río, Pascal, "El fenómeno Diego forma parte del proyecto de Salinas de perpetuarse en el poder: Muñoz Delo," *Proceso,* no. 916 (May 23, 1994), pp. 8–9.

———. "Los candidatos del PRD y del PAN opinan sobre el presidencialismo: Es válido y puede ser positivo: Cárdenas; lo que ocurre es que se ejerce en forma corrupta: Cuauhtémoc." *Proceso* no. 914 (May 9, 19944: 10–12.

———. "Salinas no ha tomado la decisión de quién será finalmente el candidato del PRI: Cuauhtémoc," *Proceso* (March 21, 1994): 6–13.

———. "Suprimir los efectos de la actual política llevará lo menos quince años: Muñoz Ledo," *Proceso* (July 19, 1993): 6–13.

Beltrán del Río, Pascal, Elías Chávez, and Gerardo Galarza. "Distinguidos priístas piden en el nuevo candidato características que ninguno de los aspirantes tecnócratas reune." *Proceso* (March 28, 1994): 6–13.

Benítez, Fernando. *Lázaro Cárdenas y la revolución mexicana, Vol. II: El caudillismo.* Mexico City: Fondo de Cultura Económica, 1977.

———. *Lázaro Cárdenas y la revolución mexicana, Vol. III: El cardenismo.* Mexico City: Fondo de Cultura Económica, 1978.

Bennett, Douglas, and Kenneth Sharpe. "The State and Dependent Development in Mexico, 1917–1970." Paper prepared for delivery at the annual meeting of the American Political Science Association, Conference Group on Political Economy, Denver, Colorado, September 4, 1982.

———. "The State as Banker and Entrepreneur: The Last Resort Character of the Mexican State's Intervention, 1917–1976." *Comparative Politics* (January 1980): 165–189.

Boggs, Carl. *The Two Revolutions: Antonio Gramsci and the Dilemmas of Western Marxism.* Boston: South End Press, 1984.

Bouchet, Michel. "A Political Economy of External Public Debt: The Mexican Case," Ph.D. diss. University of South Carolina, 1981.

Brading, David. *Caudillo and Peasant in the Mexican Revolution.* Cambridge: Cambridge University Press, 1980.

———. *Los orígenes del nacionalismo mexicano.* 3d ed. Mexico City: Ediciones Era, 1985.

Brandenburg, Frank. *The Making of Modern Mexico.* Englewood Cliffs, N.J.: Prentice-Hall, 1964.

Branigin, William. "Mexico Eyes Pacts with U.S., Canada; President Salinas Rules Out Any European-Style Common Market." *Washington Post,* May 24, 1990, E1.

Brásdefer, Gloria. "La empresa pública y el sector social de la economía," *Revista de la Administración Pública,* no. 59–60 (July–December 1984).

Brunhoff, Suzanne. *The State, Capital and Economic Policy.* London: Pluto Press, 1978.

Bueno, Gerardo. *Opciones de política económica en México, después de la devaluación.* Ed. Gerardo Bueno. Mexico City: Editorial Tecnos, 1977.

Bustamante, Eduardo. *Bases para la planeación económica y social de México.* Mexico City: Siglo XXI, 1965.

Camp, Roderic A. *Intellectuals and the State in Twentieth-Century Mexico.* Austin: University of Texas Press, 1985.

———. *Mexican Political Biographies: 1935–1981.* 2d ed. Tucson: University of Arizona Press, 1982.

————. *Mexico's Leaders*. Tucson: University of Arizona Press, 1980.

Canak, William. "The Peripheral State Debate: State Capitalist and Bureaucratic-Authoritarian Regimes in Latin America." *Latin American Research Review* 2, no. 1 (1984): 3–35.

Cárdenas, Cuauhtémoc. "Mexico: Political Freedom and Economic Development." *Review of Radical Political Economics* 24, no. 2 (Summer 1992): 104–108.

————."Misunderstanding Mexico." *Foreign Policy* 78 (Spring 1990): 113–130.

Cárdenas, Lázaro. *Apuntes 1913–1940 in Obras UNAM*. Mexico City: UNAM, 1972.

————. *¡Cárdenas habla!* Mexico: La Impresora, 1940.

————. *Palabras y Documentos Públicos de Lázaro Cárdenas, 1928–1970: Mensajes, discursos, declaraciones, entrevistas y otros documentos*. Mexico City: Siglo XXI, 1978.

Cardoso, Fernando Henrique, and Enzo Faletto. *Dependency and Development in Latin America*. Berkeley: University of California Press, 1979.

Cardoso, Fernando Henrique, Raúl Prebisch, and Rosario Green, eds. *En torno al estado y el desarrollo*. Mexico City: Editorial Nueva Imagen, 1982.

Carmagnani, Marcello. *Estado y sociedad en América Latina*. Barcelona: Editorial Crítica, 1984.

Carnoy, Martin. *The State and Political Theory*. Princeton: Princeton University Press, 1984.

Carpizo, Jorge. *El presidencialismo mexicano*. Mexico City: Siglo XXI, 1978.

Carr, Barry. *El movimiento obrero y la política en México, 1910–1929*. Mexico City: SepSetentas, 1976.

————. *El movimiento obrero y la política en México, 1910–1929, II*. Mexico City: SepSetentas, 1976.

Carriere, Jean, ed. *Industrialization and the State in Latin America*. Amsterdam: Center for Latin American Research and Documentation, 1979.

Carrillo Castro, Alejandro. "La reforma administrativa en México." *Revista de Administración Pública* 26 (September–December 1973) in *Revista de Administración Pública, Antología 1–54, 1956–1983* (February 1983): 111–130.

————. *La reforma administrativa en México: Evolución de la reforma administrativa en México (1971–1979)*. Mexico City: Miguel Angel Porrúa, 1980.

Castañeda, Jorge. "Mexico's Human-Rights Image Taking a Beating. Reform: President Salinas' Economic Progress Has Not Been Matched by a More Open Political System." *Los Angeles Times,* July 22, 1990, M2.

————. "Salinas' Achievement: Staying Afloat." *Los Angeles Times,* November 6, 1989, 7.

————. "Salinas' International Relations Gamble." *Journal of International Affairs* 43 (Winter 1990): 407–429.

————. "Voter Apathy Has Its Cynical Uses." *Los Angeles Times,* December 12, 1990, B7.

Castañeda, Rafael Rodríguez, "Acicateados por Fernández de Cevallos, Cárdenas y Zedillo le entraron parcialmente al pleito: Noventa minutos que transformaron la campaña por la Presidencia," *Proceso,* no. 915 (May 18, 1994).

Castelazo, José R. *Nuestra clase gobernante*. Mexico City: Futura Editores, 1985.

Chávez, Elías. "Ante la incipiente rebelión priísta, Salinas aplacó a Ortiz Arana, mobilizó a Córdoba y designó a Ernesto Zedillo." *Proceso* (April 4, 1994): 6–11.

————. "Colosio y Camacho, enredados y enfrentados por Salinas, muestran sus armas y hacen más bolas al priísmo," *Proceso,* no. 906 (March 14, 1994): 6–9.

————. "Su actitud de no combatir públicamente a Camacho le valió a Colosio un abucheo en Monterrey." *Proceso* (March 21, 1994): 14–17.

Cloud, David S. "Congress Wary of Bush Plan to Open Doors to Mexico." *Congressional Quarterly Weekly Report* 49, no. 8 (1991): 451–454.

Cobban, Alfred. *The Nation-State and National Self-Determination.* New York: Crowell, 1969.

Congreso de Diputados. *Ley de Secretarías y Departamentos de Estado. Diario Oficial,* December 31, 1935. Congreso de Diputados. *Ley de Secretarías y Departamentos de Estado. Diario Oficial,* December 30, 1939.

Congreso de Diputados. *Ley de Secretarías y Departamentos de Estado. Diario Oficial,* December 21, 1946.

Congreso de Diputados. *Ley de Secretarías y Departamentos de Estado. Diario Oficial,* December 24, 1958.

Congreso de Diputados. *Ley Orgánica de la Administración Pública Federal.* December 29, 1976; January 4, 1982.

Congreso de Diputados. *Ley para el control por parte del gobierno federal de los organismos descentralizados y empresas de participación estatal.* December 31, 1947.

Congreso de Diputados. *Ley para el control, por parte del gobierno federal, de los organismos descentralizados y empresas de participación estatal.* January 4, 1966.

Congreso de Diputados. *Ley que reforma de la Secretarías y Departamentos de Estado. Diario Oficial,* December 31, 1940.

Congreso de Diputados, *Ley para el control y vigilancia de los organismos públicos descentralizados y de las empresas de participatión estatal, Diario de los Debates,* Article F, December 30, 1963.

Constitución política de los Estados Unidos Mexicanos. Mexico City: *Diario Oficial,* 1983.

Constitución política de los Estados Unidos Mexicanos. Mexico City: Editorial Porrua, S.A., 1992.

Contreras, Ariel José. *México 1940: Industrialización y crisis política.* Mexico City: Siglo XXI, 1977.

Cordera, Rolando, and Carlos Tello. *México: La disputa por la nación.* 4th ed. Mexico City: Siglo XXI, 1983.

Cordero, Salvador, and Rafael Santín. *Los grupos industriales: Una nueva organización económica en México.* Mexico City: El Colegio de México, 1977.

Córdova, Arnaldo. *La clase obrera en la historia de México: En una época de crisis 1928–1934.* 2d ed. Mexico City: Siglo XXI, 1981.

————. *La ideología de la revolución mexicana: La formación del nuevo régimen.* Mexico City: Ediciones Era, 1973.

————. *La política de masas del cardenismo.* Mexico City: Serie Popular Era, 1974.

————. *La política de masas y el futuro de la izquierda en México.* Mexico City: Serie Popular Era, 1979.

Cornelius, Wayne A. "After 50 years, the 'Outs' Have an 'In' in Mexico." *Los Angeles Times,* November 7, 1989, 7.

Correa, Guillermo, Salvador Corro, and Julio César López. El asesinato de Colosio, 'un ajuste de cuentas interno, una provocación para el endurecimiento': Marcos." *Proceso* (March 28, 1994): 32–35.

————. "Campesinos e indígenas de todo el país apoyan las demandas del EZLN y marchan hacia la capital." *Proceso* (April 11, 1994): 36–40.

Cosío Villegas, Daniel. *El estilo personal de gobernar.* 9th ed. Mexico City: Cuadernos de Joaquín Mortiz, 1979.

————. *El sistema político mexicano.* 13th ed. Mexico City: Cuadernos de Joaquín Mortiz, 1982.

Cox, Robert W. "Gramsci, Hegemony and International Relations: An Essay in Method." *Millennium: A Journal of International Studies* (Summer 1983): 162–175.

————. *Production, Power and World Order: Social Forces in the Making of History.* New York: Columbia University Press, 1987.

————. "Social Forces, States, and World Orders: Beyond International Relations Theory." *Millennium: A Journal of International Studies* (Summer 1981): 126–155.

Cumberland, Charles C. *Mexican Revolution: The Constitutionalist Years.* Austin: University of Texas Press, 1972.

Cypher, James M. *State and Capital in Mexico: Development Policy Since 1940.* Boulder: Westview Press, 1990.

Cypher, James M., Chris Tilly, and Ricardo Grinspun. "Mexico's Road to Nowhere: The PRD's Cuauhtémoc Cárdenas Discusses Corruption, Debt, and Free Trade." *Dollars & Sense,* no. 175 (April 1992): 12–15.

Deas, Malcolm, ed. *Caudillo and Peasant in the Mexican Revolution.* Cambridge: Cambridge University Press, 1980.

DeBally, Karin L. "Política monetaria y financiamiento del sector público: El caso de México (1965–1976)." Maestría thesis. El Colegio de México, 1980.

Dornbusch, Rudiger. "Mexico's Economy at the Crossroads." *Journal of International Affairs* 43 (Winter 1990): 313–326.

DuBois, Marc. "The Governance of the Third World: A Foucauldian Perspective on Power Relations in Development." *Alternatives* 16, no. 1 (Winter 1991): 1–30.

Duvall, Raymond, and John Freeman. "The State and Dependent Capitalism." *International Studies Quarterly* 25, no. 1 (March 1981): 99–118.

Erfani, Julie, ed. *Beyond Free Trade: Integration, Globalization, and Human Welfare in the Americas* (Philadelphia: Temple University Press, forthcoming).

Evans, Peter. *Dependent Development: The Alliance of Multinational, State, and Local Capital in Brazil.* Princeton: Princeton University Press, 1979.

Evers, Tilman. *El estado en la periferia capitalista.* Mexico City: Siglo XXI, 1979.

Fabela, Isidro, ed. *Documentos históricos de la revolución mexicana.* Vol. 6. Mexico City: Fondo de Cultura Economica y Editorial Jus, 1960–1973.

Felipe Leal, Juan. *Agrupaciones y burocracias sindicales en México, 1906–1938.* Mexico City: Editorial Terra Nova and PINEM, 1985.

————. *La burguesía y el estado mexicano.* Mexico City: El Caballito, 1972.

Fernández Santillán, José. *Política y administración pública en México.* Mexico City: Ediciones del Instituto Nacional de Administración Pública, 1980.

FitzGerald, E. V. K. "Stabilization Policy in Mexico: The Fiscal Deficit and Macroeconomic Equilibrium, 1969–1977." In *Inflation and Stabilization in Latin America.* Ed. Rosemary Thorpe and Lawrence Whitehead. London: Macmillan, 1979.

————. "Patterns of Saving and Investment in Mexico: 1939–76." *Working Papers No. 30.* Cambridge: Centre of Latin American Studies, Cambridge University, 1977.

FitzGerald, E. V. K., E. Floto, and A. D. Lehmann. "Fiscal Crisis of the Latin American State." In *Taxation and Economic Development.* Ed. J. F. J. Toye. London: Frank Cass, 1978.

————. "Fiscal Deficit and Development Finance: A Note on the Accumulation Balance in Mexico." *Working Papers No. 35.* Cambridge: Centre of Latin American Studies, Cambridge University, 1979.

————. *Proceedings of the Cambridge Conference on the State and Economic Development in Latin America*. Cambridge: Cambridge University Press, 1976.

Flores de la Peña, Horacco. *Teoría y práctica del desarrollo*. Mexico City: Fondo de Cultura Económica, 1976.

Flores de la Peña, Horacio, et al. *Bases para la planeación económica y social de México*. Reprint. Mexico City: Siglo XXI, 1983.

————. *Bases para la planeación económica y social de México*. Mexico City: Siglo XXI, 1966.

Foucault, Michel. *The Foucault Reader*. Ed. Paul Rabinov. New York: Pantheon Books, 1984.

Franks, Jeff. "Colosio Death Shakes Mexico Political System," *Reuters World Service,* March 24, 1994.

Frieden, Jeff. "Third World Indebted Industrialization: International Finance and State Capitalism in Mexico, Brazil, Algeria, and South Korea." *International Organization* 35, no. 3 (Summer 1981): 407–431.

"Fusión de Hacienda y SPP, Iniciativa de Carlos Salinas de Gortari al Congreso," *Excélsior,* January 8, 1992, 1A.

Galarza, Gerardo. "Moya y del Mazo le recomiendan disciplinarse, Salinas lo elogió y Camacho vuelve a considerarse factor de presión para lograr elecciones limpias." *Proceso,* March 21, 1994, 16.

Galindo López, Jesús. "A Conversation with Cuauhtémoc Cárdenas." *Journal of International Affairs* 43 (Winter 1990): 395–406.

Garrido, Luis Javier. *El partido de la revolución institucionalizada: La formación del nuevo estado en México (1928–1945)*. Mexico City: Siglo XXI, 1982.

Gereffi, Gary, and Peter Evans. "Transnational Corporations, Dependent Development, and State Policy in the Semiperiphery: A Comparison of Brazil and Mexico." *Latin American Research Review* 16 (1981): 31–64.

Giddens, Anthony. *The Constitution of Society: Outline of the Theory of Structuration*. Berkeley: University of California Press, 1984.

————. *A Contemporary Critique of Historical Materialism: Power, Property and the State*. Vol. 1. Berkeley: University of California Press, 1981.

————. *The Nation-State and Violence: Volume Two of a Contemporary Critique of Historical Materialism*. Berkeley: University of California Press, 1985.

Gil, Carlos B., ed. *Hope and Frustration: Interviews with Leaders of Mexico's Political Opposition*. Wilmington, Del.: Scholarly Resources, 1992.

Gilly, Adolfo. "The Mexican Regime in its Dilemma." *Journal of International Affairs* 43 (Winter 1990): 273–289.

Golden, Timothy. "Mediator Hints at Renegade Bid for President." *New York Times,* March 12, 1994, N2, L2.

————. "Mexican Leader Picks Successor to Slain Nominee: Candidate Is Criticized." *New York Times,* March 30, 1994, A6.

González Casanova, Pablo. *La reforma política y sus perspectivas*. Mexico City: Ediciones de la Gaceta Informativa de la Comisión Federal Electoral, 1979.

González Casanova, Pablo, and Enrique Florescano, eds. *México, hoy*. Mexico City: Siglo XXI, 1979.

González González, Guadalupe. "Los intereses privados norteamericanos en México: La Cámara Americana de Comercio de México." Licenciatura thesis. Mexico City: El Colegio de México, 1979.

Gramsci, Antonio. *Selections from the Prison Notebooks*. New York: International Publishers, 1971.

Green, Rosario. "Endeudamiento externo y debilidad estatal: El caso de México." *Foro Internacional* (July–September 1979): 73–117.

————. *Estado y banca transnacional en México.* Mexico City: Nueva Imagen, 1981.

Griffiths, Brian. *Mexican Monetary Policy and Economic Development.* New York: Praeger, 1972.

Grinspun, Ricardo. "NAFTA and Neoconservative Transformation: The Impact on Canada and Mexico." *The Review of Radical Political Economics* 25, no. 4 (1993): 14–29.

Grotius, Hugo. *De Jure Belli ac Pacis Libri Tres.* Trans. Francis W. Kelsey. New York: Oceana, 1964.

Guerrero, Omar. *La administración pública del estado capitalista.* Barcelona: Editorial Fontamara, 1981.

Hall, Linda B. *Alvaro Obregón: Power and Revolution in Mexico, 1911–1920.* College Station: Texas A&M University Press, 1981.

Hamilton, Nora. *The Limits of State Autonomy: Post-Revolutionary Mexico.* Princeton: Princeton University Press, 1982.

Hamilton, Nora, and Timothy F. Harding, eds. *Modern Mexico: State, Economy and Social Conflict.* Beverly Hills: Sage Publications, 1986.

Hamnett, Brian, R. *Roots of Insurgency, Mexican Regions, 1750–1824.* Cambridge: Cambridge University Press, 1986.

Hellman, Judith. *Mexico in Crisis.* 2d ed. New York: Holmes & Meier Publishers, 1983.

Hernández, Ricardo, and Edith Sánchez, *Cross-border Links: A Directory of Organizations in Canada, Mexico, and the United States.* Albuquerque, N.M.: Inter-Hemispheric Education Resource Center, 1992.

Hoffman, John. *The Gramscian Challenge: Coercion and Consent in Marxist Political Theory.* Oxford: Basil Blackwell, 1984.

Jackson, Robert H. "Quasi-States, Dual Regimes, and Neoclassical Theory: International Jurisprudence and the Third World." *International Organization* 41, no. 4 (Autumn 1987): 519–549.

————. *Quasi-States: Sovereignty, International Relations, and the Third World.* New York: Cambridge University Press, 1990.

Jackson, Robert H., and Carl Rosberg. "Sovereignty and Underdevelopment: Juridical Statehood in the African Crisis." *Journal of Modern African Studies* 24, no. 1 (1986): 1–31.

Jáquez, Antonio, "En el 68, Echeverría aisló, desinformó y le calentó la cabeza a Díaz Ordaz: Farías," *Proceso* 884 (October 11, 1993).

Javier Garrido, Luis. *El partido de la revolución institucionalizada: La formación del nuevo estado en México: 1928–1945.* Mexico City: Siglo XXI, 1982.

Kaplan, Marcos. *Estado y sociedad.* Mexico City: Universidad Nacional Autónoma de México, 1978.

Knight, Alan. *The Mexican Revolution, Vol. 1: Porfirians, Liberals and Peasants.* Cambridge: Cambridge University Press, 1986.

————. *The Mexican Revolution, Vol. 2: Counter-Revolution and Reconstruction.* Cambridge: Cambridge University Press, 1986.

Kondracke, Morton M. "A Gorbo for Mexico. Carlos Salinas, Superman." *The New Republic* (February 20, 1989): 11–14.

Kragelund, Eduardo. "Mexico: Man in the News—Colosio Seen as Skilled Politician." *Reuters Newswire, Central and South America, Reuters Economic News,* November 28, 1993.

Krause, Enrique. "The Historic Dimensions of Free Trade with Mexico." *Wall Street Journal,* May 24, 1991.

Labastida, Julio. *El Perfil de México en 1980.* 3 vols. Mexico City: Siglo XXI, 1972.

Labastida Martín del Campo, Julio, coord. *Hegemonía y alternativas políticas en América Latina.* Mexico City: Siglo XXI, 1985.

Laver, Ross. Interview with Carlos Salinas de Gortari. *Maclean's,* March 26, 1990, 45.

Lechner, Norberto. *La crisis del estado en América Latina.* Caracas: El Cid Editor, 1977.

———, ed. *Estado y política en América Latina.* Mexico City: Siglo XXI, 1981.

Leñero, Vicente. "El subcomandante se abre: 'Lo aposté todo a la montaña; estoy viviendo de prestado y por eso escribo como loco; si no les gustan mis cartas, me vale madre.'" *Proceso* (February 21, 1994): 7–15.

León de Palacios, Ana María. *Plutarco Elías Calles.* Mexico City: Instituto Nacional de Administración Pública, 1975.

Lerner de Sheinbaum, Bertha, and Susana Ralsky de Cimet. *El poder de los presidentes.* Mexico City: Instituto Mexicano de Estudios Políticos, 1976.

Lieuwen, Edwin. *Mexican Militarism: The Political Rise and Fall of the Revolutionary Army.* Albuquerque: University of New Mexico Press, 1968.

López, Fernando Mayolo, and Sonia Morales, "La mayoría de las encuestas inmediatas dió el triunfo en el debate a Fernández de Cevallos, pero favoreció Zedillo con el voto," *Proceso,* no. 915 (May 18, 1994).

MacCorkle, Stuart A. *American Policy of Recognition Toward Mexico.* New York: AMS Press, 1971.

Maier, Charles, ed. *Changing Boundaries of the Political.* Cambridge: Cambridge University Press, 1987.

Manning, William, R. "British Influence in Mexico, 1822–26." In H. Morse Stephens, ed. *The Pacific Ocean in History.* New York: Macmillan, 1917.

Manrique, Irma. *La política monetaria en la estrategia del desarrollo.* Mexico City: Editores Asociados Mexicanos, 1979.

Martínez, Sanjuana, "Chiapas dañó la imagen de México y de Salinas; políticos, los peores efectos," *Proceso,* no. 903 (February 21, 1994).

Martínez Nava, Juan Manuel. "El conflicto estado-empresarios en los gobiernos de Cárdenas, López Mateos, y Echeverría." Licenciatura thesis. Mexico City: El Colegio de México, 1982.

Maxfield, Sylvia. "Bankers' Alliances and Economic Policy Patterns: Evidence from Brazil and Mexico." *Comparative Political Studies* 23, no. 4 (January 1991): 419–458.

Mayall, James. *Nationalism and International Society.* Cambridge: Cambridge University Press, 1990.

Memoria institucional de la Secretaría de Programación y Presupuesto : 1977–1980. Mexico City: Secretaría de Programación y Presupuesto, 1977.

Meyer, Jean, Enrique Krauze, and Caetano Reyes. *Historia de la revolución mexicana, Vol. II: Estado y sociedad con Calles.* Mexico City: El Colegio de México, 1977.

Meyer, Lorenzo. "La etapa formativa del estado mexicano contemporáneo (1938–1940)." *Foro Internacional* 17 (April–June 1977): 453–476.

———. "The United States and Mexico: The Historical Structure of Their Conflict." *Journal of International Affairs* 43 (Winter 1990): 251–271.

Meyer, Michael C., and William L. Sherman. *The Course of Mexican History.* 3d ed. New York: Oxford University Press, 1987.

Miliband, Ralph. *The State in Capitalist Society.* London: Weidenfeld & Nicolson, 1969.

Miller, Marjorie. "Mexico Debt Accord Won't Guarantee Full Recovery." *Los Angeles Times,* July 25, 1989, 1.

————. "Mexico, 5 Nations Plan Free-Trade Zone." *Los Angeles Times,* January 12, 1991, D3.

————. "Mexico Warms U.S. Ties; Is Open to Oil Industry Role." *Los Angeles Times,* November 28, 1990, A1.

————. "Salinas, Amid Jeers, Defends His Economic Program." *Los Angeles Times,* November 12, 1989, 8.

Moffett, Matt. "Latin Turnaround: Long-Sickly Mexico Has Investment Boom as Trade Hopes Grow." *Wall Street Journal,* May 24, 1991.

Monsivais, Carlos. "From '68 to Cardenismo: Toward a Chronicle of Social Movements." *Journal of International Affairs* 43 (Winter 1990): 385–393.

Monje, Raúl. "El miércoles 16 en una cena íntima, Colosio y Camacho habían puesto fin a sus diferencias." *Proceso* (March 28, 1994): 12–14.

Morris, Stephen D. "Political Reformism in Mexico: Past and Present." *Latin American Research Review* 28, no. 2 (Spring 1993): 200–203.

Mosk, Sanford A. *Industrial Revolution in Mexico.* Berkeley: University of California Press, 1950.

Nacional Financiera, S.A. *La economía mexicana en cifras.* Mexico City: Nacional Financiera, 1981.

Needler, Martin, *Mexican Politics: The Containment of Conflict,* 2d ed. New York: Praeger, 1990.

North American Free Trade Agreement Between the Government of the United States, the Government of Canada and the Government of the United Mexican States . Vols. 1–2 (Washington, D.C.: Government Printing Office, 1992).

Northedge, F. S. *The League of Nations: Its Life and Times, 1920–1946.* New York: Leicester University Press, 1986.

Offe, Claus. *Contradictions of the Welfare State.* Cambridge: MIT Press, 1984.

————. *Stress and Contradiction in Modern Capitalism.* Ed. L. Lindberg, et al. Lexington: D. H. Heath, 1975.

Ortiz Mena, Antonio. "Desarrollo estabilizador, una década de estrategia económica en México." *Mercado de Valores* 43 (November 1969): 165–175.

Oszlak, Oscar. "Formación histórica del estado en América Latina: Elementos teórico-metodológicos para su estudio." *Estudios Cedes* 1, no. 3 (1978): 5–45.

Padgett, Vincent. *The Mexican Political System.* Boston: Houghton Mifflin, 1976.

Padilla Aragón, Enrique. *México: Hacia el crecimiento con distribución del ingreso.* Mexico City: Siglo XII, 1981.

Padilla, Remberto H. *Historia de la política mexicana.* Mexico City: Editores Asociados Mexicanos, S.A., 1992.

"Paradox in Mexico (A Survey of Latin America)." *The Economist* 13 (November 1993: L21.

Pastor, Robert A. "Post-Revolutionary Mexico: The Salinas Opening." *Journal of Interamerican Studies and World Affairs* 32 (Fall 1990): 1–22.

Perzabal, Carlos. *Acumulación capitalista dependiente y subordinada: El caso de México (1940–1978).* Mexico City: Siglo XXI, 1979.

Peyrera, Carlos. "México: Los límites del reformismo." *Cuadernos Políticos* 1 (July–September 1974): 52–65.

————. "¿Quién mató al comendador? Notas sobre estado y sociedad en México." *Nexos* 13 (January 1979): 3–9.

Pine, Art. "Mexico Reaches Accord on Restructuring Debt." *Los Angeles Times,* July 24, 1989: 1.

Poder Ejecutivo Federal, Estados Unidos Mexicanos, *Diplomatic Notes Exchanged Between the Mexican and British Governments on Account of the Oil Industry Expropriation.* Mexico City: Talleres Gráficos de la Nación, DAPP, 1938.

Poulantzas, Nicos. *State, Power, Socialism.* London: New Left Books, 1978.

Pradilla Cobos, Emilio. "The Limits of the Mexican Maquiladora Industry." *Review of Radical Political Economics* 25, no. 4 (December 1, 1993): 91–108.

Presidencia de la República. *Acuerdo por el que las entidades de la administración pública paraestatal se agrupan por sectores a efecto de que sus relaciones con el Ejecutivo Federal se relacionan a través de las secretarías de estado o departamento administrativo.* September 3, 1982.

Presidencia de la República. *Acuerdo por el que se constituye una Comisión Intersecretarial Integrada por representantes de las Secretarías de la Presidencia y de Hacienda y Crédito Público, con el fin de que proceda . . . a formular planes nacionales.* *Diario Oficial,* March 2, 1962.

Presidencia de la República. *Acuerdo que dispone que la Comisión de Inversiones dependa directamente del Presidente de la República.* *Diario Oficial,* October 29, 1954.

Presidencia de la República. *Acuerdo que dispone que las Secretarías y Departamentos de Estado, Organismos Descentralizados y Empresas de Participación Estatal, elaboran un programa de inversiones anuales durante los años 1960 a 1964.* *Diario Oficial,* June 30, 1959.

Presidencia de la República. *Decreto por el que se aprueba el Plan Global de Desarrollo 1980–82.* *Diario Oficial,* April 17, 1980.

Presidencia de la República. *Decreto que crea la Comisión Federal de Planificación Económica como órgano consultivo de la Secretaría de la Economía Nacional.* *Diario Oficial,* July 9, 1942.

Presidencia de la República. *Decreto que crea la Comisión Nacional de Inversiones.* *Diario Oficial,* January 31, 1948.

Presidencia de la República. *Decreto que crea la Comisión Nacional de Planeación para la Paz.* *Diario Oficial,* February 15, 1944.

Presidencia de la República. *Decreto que crea la Junta de Economía de Emergencia.* *Diario Oficial,* May 18, 1943.

Puente, Ramón. *Hombres de la revolución. Calles.* Los Angeles, 1933; self-published.

Purcell, Susan Kaufman. *The Mexican Profit-Sharing Decision.* Berkeley: University of California Press, 1975.

———. ed. *Mexico in Transition.* New York: Council on Foreign Relations, 1988.

Quirk, Robert E. *The Mexican Revolution, 1914–1915: The Convention of Aguascalientes.* Bloomington: Indiana University Press, 1960.

Ramírez Brun, J. Ricardo. *Estado y acumulación de capital en México, 1929–1975.* Mexico City: Universidad Nacional Autónoma de México, 1980.

Reding, Andrew. "Mexico Under Salinas: A Facade of Reform." *World Policy Journal* 6, no. 4 (Fall 1989): 685–729.

"Reestructuración de la industria paraestatal." *Excélsior,* February 17, 1985, 4–5.

"Reestructuración del sector paraestatal." *Excélsior,* March 4, 1985, 12A.

Rendón, Teresa and Carlos Salas. "The Probable Impact of NAFTA on Non-Agricultural Employment in Mexico." *Review of Radical Political Economics* 25, no. 4 (December 1993): 109–119.

Reyes, Alvaro Rodríguez, "Diagnosis administrativa del gobierno federal," *Revista de la Administración Pública,* No. 16, January–March 1964.

Reyna, José Luis, and Richard Weinert, *Authoritarianism in Mexico.* Philadelphia: ISHI, 1977.

Reyes Osorio, Sergio, et al., *Estructura agraria y desarrollo en México: Estudio sobre las relaciones entre la tenencia y uso de la tierra y el desarrollo agrícola de México.* Mexico City: Fondo de Cultura Económica, 1974.

Reynolds, Clark. *The Mexican Economy.* New Haven: Yale University Press, 1970.

————. "¿Por qué el desarrollo estabilizador en la realidad se desestabilizó?" Washington, D.C.: Subcommittee on Interamerican Economic Relations, 1977.

Rippy, J. Fred. *Rivalry of the United States and Great Britain over Latin America (1808–1830).* Baltimore: The Johns Hopkins University Press, 1929.

Rivas Sánchez, Roberto. *Elementos para un análisis histórico de la administración pública federal en México: 1821–1940.* Mexico City: Instituto Nacional de Administración Pública, 1984.

Rivera Ríos, Miguel A., and Pedro Gómez Sánchez. "México: Acumulación de capital y crisis en la década del setenta." *Teoría y Política* 1, no. 2 (October–December 1980): 73–120.

Roett, Riordan, ed. *Political and Economic Liberalization in Mexico: At a Critical Juncture?* Boulder: Lynne Rienner Publishers, 1993.

Rohter, Larry. "U.S. and Mexicans Cautiously Back Free-Trade Idea." *New York Times,* June 12, 1990, 1.

Roy, Ramashray, R. B. J. Walker, and Richard K. Ashley. "Dialogue: Towards a Critical Social Theory of International Politics." *Alternatives* 13 (January 1988): 77–102.

Ruiz, Ramón Eduardo. *Labor and the Ambivalent Revolutionaries: Mexico, 1911–1923.* Baltimore and London: The Johns Hopkins University Press, 1976.

Saldívar, Américo. *Ideología y política del estado mexicano.* 2d ed. Mexico City: Siglo XXI, 1981.

Salinas de Gortari, Carlos. *Ideas y compromisos.* Mexico City: Secretaría de Información y Propaganda del Partido Revolucionario Institucional, 1988.

Schlefer, Jonathan. "History Counsels 'No' on NAFTA . . ." *New York Times,* November 14, 1993, F11.

Secretaría de Programación y Presupuesto. *Resolución para proceder a la disolución, liquidación, extinción y transferencia de las entidades paraestatales que se indican.* February 13, 1985.

Secretaría de Programación y Presupuesto. *Resolución para proceder a la disolución, liquidación y extinción de las entidades paraestatales que se indican.* March 6, 1985.

Secretaría del Trabajo y Previsión Social y Secretaría de la Presidencia. *México a través de los informes presidenciales.* Mexico City: Ed. Secretaría del Trabajo y Previsión Social y Secretaría de la Presidencia, 1976.

Shafer, Robert. *Mexican Business Organizations.* Syracuse, N.Y.: Syracuse University Press, 1973.

Skidmore, Thomas, and Peter Smith. *Modern Latin America.* 3d ed. New York: Oxford University Press, 1992.

Skinner, Curtis. "Mexico: The Cardenista Challenge and Prospects for the Left." *New Politics* 2, no. 3 (Summer 1989): 67–74.

Solís, Leopoldo. "A Monetary Will-o'-the-Wisp: Pursuit of Equity Through Deficit Spending." Discussion Paper No. 77. Princeton: Woodrow Wilson School, 1977.

Smith, James F. "Confronting Differences in the United States and Mexican Legal Systems in the Era of NAFTA." *United States–Mexico Law Journal* 1, no. 1 (1993): 97–98.

Szekely, Gabriel. "Recent Findings and Research Suggestions on Oil and Mexico's Development Process." *Latin American Research Review* 20, no. 3 (1985): 235–246.

Tardanico, Richard. "State, Dependency, and Nationalism: Revolutionary Mexico, 1924–1928." *Comparative Studies in Society and History* 24, no. 3 (July 1982): 400–423.

Tello, Carlos. *La nacionalización de la banca en México*. Mexico City: Siglo XXI, 1984.

———. *La política económica en México, 1970–1976*. Mexico City: Siglo XXI, 1979.

Tierney, Christine. "Mexico: Markets Seen at Ease with Mexican Presidential Candidate." *Reuter Newswire, Central and South America, Reuter Economic News*, November 28, 1993.

———. "Mexico: Mexico PRI Candidate Viewed as Shrewd Compromise." *Reuter Newswire, Central and South America, Reuter General News*, November 28, 1993.

Tilly, Charles, ed. *The Formation of National States in Western Europe*. Princeton: Princeton University Press, 1975.

Torres Gaytán, Ricardo. *Un siglo de devaluaciones del peso mexicano*. Mexico City: Siglo XXI, 1980.

Uhlig, Mark A. "Salinas Is Riding High on Political Victories." *New York Times*, May 26, 1991.

Vasconcelos, José. *La raza cósmica: Misión de la raza iberoamericana*. Madrid: Aguilar, 1961.

Véliz, Claudio. *The Centralist Tradition of Latin America*. Princeton: Princeton University Press, 1980.

Villa M., Rosa Olivia. *Nacional Financiera: Banco de fomento del desarrollo económico de México*. Mexico City: Nacional Financiera, 1976.

Vizcaya Canales, Isidro. *Los orígenes de la industrialización de Monterrey*. Monterrey: Instituto Tecnológico de Estudios Superiores de Monterrey, 1971.

Voljc, Marko, and Joost Draaisma. "Privatization and Economic Stabilization in Mexico." *Columbia Journal of World Business* 28, no. 1 (Spring 1993): 122–133.

Walker, R. B. J. *One World, Many Worlds: Struggles for a Just World Peace*. Boulder: Lynne Rienner Publishers, 1988.

———. "State Sovereignty, Global Civilization, and the Rearticulation of Political Space." *World Order Studies Program Occasional Paper No. 18*. Princeton: Center of International Studies, Princeton University, 1988.

Walker, R. B. J., and Saul H. Mendlovitz, eds. *Contending Sovereignties: Redefining Political Community*. Boulder: Lynne Rienner Publishers, 1990.

Walters, F. P. *A History of the League of Nations*. Vols. 1–2. London: Oxford University Press, 1952.

Weinstein, Michael A. *The Polarity of Mexican Thought: Instrumentalism and Finalism*. University Park: Pennsylvania State University Press, 1976.

Weyl, Nathaniel, and Sylvia Weyl. *The Reconquest of Mexico: The Years of Lázaro Cárdenas*. London: Oxford University Press, 1939.

Whitehead, Lawrence. "La política económica del sexenio de Echeverría: ¿Qué salió mal y por qué?" *Foro Internacional* 20, no. 3 (1979–1980): 484–513.

White House, Office of the Press Secretary. "Joint Statement by Mexico and the United States on Negotiation of a Free Trade Agreement." U.S. Government, 1990.

Wionczek, Miguel S. "Antecedentes e instrumentos de la planeación de México." In *Bases para la planeación económica y social de México*. Ed. Horacio Flores de la Peña, et al. Mexico City: Siglo XXI, 1966.

Zamarripa, Roberto. "Vigilado, hostigado, prohibido, Cárdenas apela a la ética de los medios." *Proceso*, October 4, 1993, 7–9.

Zermeño, Sergio. "De Echeverría a de la Madrid: Las clases altas y el estado mexicano en la batalla por la hegemonía." *Working Papers No. 118*. Washington, D. C.: Wilson Center, 1982.

Index

About the Book and the Author

Exploring the contradictory nature of Mexican statehood, Erfani explains how a weak national state became a symbol of great domestic strength and, although failing in its domestic economic endeavors, supported a long and stable political regime.

Erfani focuses on the concept of sovereignty as not only a legal status, but also a political myth. She traces the struggles of Mexico's federal governments from 1940 through the 1970s to sustain a myth equating legal sovereignty with state strength vis-à-vis the world economy. She then addresses the demise of that myth and the ensuing shift in the 1980s toward the symbolism and rhetoric of a strong private economy.

In the 1990s, proponents of NAFTA—seeking to dismantle Mexico's legal basis for state intervention in the domestic economy—claim to be replacing the failed legal-political sovereignty of the state with the economic sovereignty of the private sector. This rhetoric of economic strength, concludes Erfani, holds as much potential for fragmenting, as it does for unifying, the national political-economic order.

JULIE ERFANI is assistant professor of political science at Arizona State University West.